DATE DUE

MAY 2 4 '93		
SEP 2 2 1995		
MAR 2 2 2000		
GAYLORD		PRINTED IN U.S.A.

Complete Fencing

Complete Fencing

ALBERT MANLEY

Photography by Larry Jones

Drawings by Ruth F. Newbury

1979
DOUBLEDAY & COMPANY, INC., GARDEN CITY, NEW YORK

Library of Congress Cataloging in Publication Data

Manley, Albert.
Complete fencing.
Bibliography: p. 287
Includes index.
1. Fencing. I. Title.
GV1147.M36   796.8'6
ISBN: 0-385-12075-3
Library of Congress Catalog Card Number 76–56319

To my students,
who have taught and keep on teaching
me how to teach.

Preface

In this presentation of the three branches of modern sport fencing (foil, épée, and sabre) I have relied on a combination of words, photographs, and drawings.

The text addresses itself to three kinds of readers: beginners, more-advanced students, and coaches. A particular section might not make a lot of sense at the first reading, but you will get more out of it at a later stage in your career.

Remember that a photograph is a frozen instant in the midst of a continuous flow. Some of our pictures are in sets of two or three or more, but you must imagine the actions depicted in them as one continuous process. Also you may double the value of the photographs by looking at them in a mirror: If a right-hander is shown, you can see in the mirror what a left-hander looks like doing the same move.

Some of the drawings represent the flow of movement. Even so, we cannot show every point along the way. You will have to match the word descriptions, photographs, and drawings against your own experience. Work it out, like a lab experiment in a science class, where you have a manual to guide you: Fencing is doing.

Every fencer learns from his teachers, his clubmates, and his opponents. My teachers have been: Alfredo Nazareno, a pupil of Maître Clovis Deladrier, then coach of the U. S. Naval Academy; Susan Quinn, a pupil of Maître Joseph Vince; Maestro Nicholas Toth, later coach of the U. S. Air Force Academy; Alan January; Maestro George Santelli, former U. S. Olympic coach; Maestro Edward Lucia, and Arthur Fregosi. Of clubmates and opponents, I have forgotten names, but still remember faces and, most of all, moves with which they hit me.

The foil method I have tried to present is not my invention, but was originated by a man whom I have never had the good fortune to meet, Alex Hern. It was demonstrated and explained to me by two of his pupils, Dr. Leonard Essman and Albert Axelrod, several times U. S. Foil Champion and the most recent American Olympic medalist. Whatever you find good about it, you can credit to them, and if there are misinterpretations, the fault is entirely mine.

I am very grateful to those of my students who posed for the photographs: Velma Sies, Valerie Young, J. D. Ellis, Eliot Meier, Robert Tripp, and Richard Wayland. I also owe a great deal to friends who have helped in one way or another, and from whose constructive criticism this book has benefited: Lenore Klink, Georgia Noble, Gretchen Starkweather, Patricia Summers, Joan and Harold W. B. Chang, Randy Crockett, Ronald E. Miller, and Don S. Naylor. Finally, I want to thank the administrators of the Multnomah Athletic Club, the Portland Y.W.C.A., and Reed College, where I have worked happily for so many years.

Contents

Part One

BEGINNING AND ONGOING

Chapter 1

GENERALLY SPEAKING

A GREAT DEAL has been said and written about how complicated fencing is and how difficult to learn. Even if that were true, those of us who are in it believe that it's worth the trouble because it's such fun.

Indeed, fencing offers seemingly endless variety. You might spend many years at it without feeling that you had come to the end, without becoming bored. People are infinitely variable, and people are your opponents. In that sense the sport is complicated, and you will never learn it all.

I hope to show, however, that the most important elements are relatively few, and that you don't have to know many moves in order to fence skillfully and intelligently. Although some of the postures and movements will be strange, different from anything you have done before, and therefore relatively difficult at first, you won't have to wait many months to start playing the game.

This book is meant to help you if you are a beginner-to-intermediate student fencer, so you can take part in the sport with good understanding of the essentials, in the shortest possible time. Some of the ideas should be useful at any level.

This book is also meant to help you if you are the teacher of beginners, novices, and intermediates. I have indicated those points that are basic and absolutely necessary, as well as those you may skip in your lesson plan to get your students into intelligent, enjoyable bouting without delay.

THE NATURE OF FENCING

The nature of fencing is simple enough. Fencing is fighting.

Fencing has been called "chess with muscles." The famous grandmaster and world champion, Emanuel Lasker, once wrote: "Chess has been represented, or shall I say misrepresented, as a game . . . By some ardent enthusiasts, chess has been elevated into a science or an art. It is neither; but its principal characteristic seems to be—*what human nature mostly delights in*—a fight (italics mine)."*

Just as chess is based on a rather small number of moves that can be used in

* *Common Sense in Chess* (New York: David McKay Co., 1946).

almost infinite combinations, fencing involves a limited number of movements. You can learn enough in five or six weeks, with two class hours a week, to attain a competent (though rough) level of performance.

The main trouble is that fencing is not like any of our familiar activities. We start catching, kicking, hitting, and throwing balls at a very early age. Examples of professional ballplayers are shown to us daily on television. No wonder we can play these games almost at the first opportunity. We don't have to "learn" them, we only have to practice what we already understand (unthinkingly) how to do.

From another standpoint, you might think of fencing as a special kind of game of tag. Yes, the children's schoolyard game. All you have to do is touch the other person. There are numerous rules about how and when, but that is the most basic idea. The complications develop from the fact that just two people play, and both are "it." You have to tag your opponent while he or she is trying to do the same to you.

The student fencer and the teacher must keep in mind that fencing is—at least in our first concept of it—a competitive combat sport. "Good form" in fencing is not posture and movement that look pretty just for the sake of looking pretty. Good fencing form must be efficient in order for the player to attain his objective, i.e., winning. Bad form is that which interferes with competitive performance. We humans naturally enjoy watching somebody, worker or athlete, who does a neat job. We say, "That was a beautiful move," but what we mean is, "It worked, and there wasn't any wasted effort."

BENEFITS OF FENCING

A question many beginners ask is, "What will fencing do for me?"

My answer is, "Nothing."

It is up to you to make of the sport what you want. The achievements will be yours. This is true of anything you study. The teacher can't give it to you, like pouring milk into an empty glass that just sits there. You must take it. You must look at it from several angles, think about it, tear it apart and put it back together, try, make mistakes, correct yourself, practice, ask questions, try again. The teacher can show you, point out where you went wrong, suggest what you can do to improve.

Happily, there is no time limit and no grading. Stick with it and you soon will become proficient. You will know that you have made progress—not in comparison to anybody else, but from your own personal starting place, according to your own characteristics, and toward your own goals, or for your own purposes.

People *start* to fence for various reasons. Many children (and older people, too, I suspect) get excited by movies about Zorro, Captain Blood, Scaramouche, and the three musketeers—modern fencing isn't like that, but is very exciting in its own quieter way. To some, fencing is a challenge precisely because they have heard it is difficult, and everything else they've tried has been too easy. Others have heard that fencing makes you graceful, improves your posture, improves your co-ordination, etc.

I say it again, it is up to you. You can use fencing for recreation, for simple exercise, for working out the competitive urge, for improving the shape and movement of your body. The job of the teacher is to guide you in getting what you want out of it. When the teacher has too many students and too little time to give you this kind of close individualized guidance, well, you're the one who does the really important things anyway. It may take more time, but what you figure out for yourself is your own valuable possession.

The sport does offer certain opportunities. It can be practiced successfully by almost anyone. Size and strength are of comparatively little importance. Because of its adaptability, its demand for combined mental, physical, and temperamental qualities, fencing is a lifetime sport—people have continued with it into their 80s, pitting experienced skill quite well against the supposedly greater vigor and speed of youth.

We often take for granted the fact that exercise promotes health and well-being. One of the advantages of fencing is that, aside from being an excellent form of exercise, it provides a reason for keeping to a health regime. Ordinarily a program of calisthenics becomes monotonous, especially when you try to do it all alone, without a class of fellow sufferers. Dieting may be distasteful. But once you decide that doing these things will increase your enjoyment of fencing, you may be more willing to discipline yourself.

Through fencing you will meet interesting people—anyway, we fencers think we are interesting. When you travel to the cities of Europe, South America, Japan, etc., you can immediately become acquainted with fellow fencers instead of being restricted to the "tourist circuit."

Fencing has the added advantage of convenience. To enjoy the benefits, you need only one partner, a comparatively small space (indoors or out), and an outfit that is fairly inexpensive. But first you must learn how to fence, and for this you need a teacher. You can't learn to fence alone, or with a partner who is just as ignorant as you are. I expect most readers of this book already have a teacher, but if you've just picked it up and want to find an instructor, try calling the Y's, community centers, athletic clubs, and colleges in your area. You may not find a group in your town, but there might be one within driving distance.

Last but not least, you could use fencing, like the Oriental martial arts, as a way to inner self-development. This attitude contrasts sharply with the common Western desire to win, which always leads to disappointment because you are bound to lose at some time or other. Fencing, according to your own personal standards, makes you a winner no matter what goes on the score sheet, since you will always learn more about the sport/art, about other people, and about yourself.

THE THREE WEAPONS

The foil is the weapon used by the great majority of fencers. Until recently it was the only weapon with which women competed formally (and by the way, women beginners who are timid should know that they will not be expected to compete against men, although they will probably practice with men in classroom or club). Foilists undoubtedly outnumber sabreurs and épéeists by a wide margin.

The foil has traditionally been regarded as the basic training weapon, the one that prepares you for épée and sabre fencing. You may change to sabre or épée and specialize in either of them. Some people learn all three, and do quite well as all-around fencers. In a comparatively few cases, students start with one of the so-called advanced weapons and never fence with any other. Most often a person has the opportunity to try all phases of the sport before settling on the weapon that suits his own physique and temperament. The styles and methods of play have become quite distinct for each weapon, and the player usually develops a clear preference for one of them.

The foil resembles the épée in that both are thrusting weapons. They can score only by forward motion of the point, and many of the movements used with both weapons are similar. But not the *same*, as you will see.

The foil resembles the sabre in that both are "conventional" weapons (i.e., governed by arbitrary conventions), with special rules about "right-of-way." The sabre differs from the foil and épée in that it can score by cutting actions. Consequently, the hand techniques are quite different, and very likely the person who was very thoroughly trained in sabre would get into the habit of moving his hand too widely for foil and épée and would not have the necessary point accuracy. Conversely, those who were better trained in foil and épée might not make adequate blocking actions against sabre cuts.

One way in which épée and sabre resemble each other is that the target is extended for both. That is, the fighting arm and hand, and, in épée, the front leg, are legitimate objects of attack. These parts of the body are usually closer to the opponent than the torso, which is the legal target in foil. You can see that you would want to prevent hits on these more exposed areas—and so would your opponent.

Although the épée and sabre have larger guards than the foil, giving more protection for the hand and arm, fencers of these weapons are usually very careful to play at considerably *longer range* than do foilists. This leads, in turn, to different stance and movement. Sabreurs and épéeists have to cover more ground.

To the spectator it seems there is more running back and forth with the advanced weapons than with the foil. Assuming you are just beginning in this sport, you might as well put a few months into foil training to get some combat experience and build up your legs. Good épée and sabre fencing demand greater mobility and put much more strain on your legs—in some ways—than foil play. But in all three phases of the sport today, footwork is dominant. You must have endurance to be able to keep up this rapid, variable footwork through a tournament day.

SUMMARY OF THE RULES

Although fencing is fighting, a number of rules have been developed over the last century or two to make it a safe and enjoyable sport. The official book† contains about seventy pages of regulations. The book's language is very intricate, in a legalistic fashion, and you will probably bog down shortly on your first—or even third or fifth—attempt to read it through. An outline and an explanation of the rules should help you, first, to begin to fence reasonably as soon as you know a few basic moves, and second, to find your way through the book's tangled verbiage when you want to know the details.

The rules are applied and interpreted on the spot by human officials, whose decisions might not agree with yours. Experienced competitors are better able to connect the wording of the rules with actual cases in tournament play. The main ideas are, however, not very complicated, and the official's review of the action should *make sense* to you, even when you see the facts differently. The outline is as follows:

† *Fencing Rules*, Amateur Fencers League of America, Inc., 1974. Copies may be obtained from the AFLA, Inc., Ms. Eleanor Turney, 601 Curtis Street, Albany, CA 94706, for $3.00.

   A. Safety
      1. Environment
      2. Equipment
      3. Technique
   B. Limitations
      1. Weapon
      2. Target
      3. Ground
      4. Time (allowed for a bout)
   C. Conventions
      1. Time
      2. Right-of-way

SAFETY

Safety should be the foremost concern of every fencer. A great many uninformed people think that fencing is dangerous (and some silly ones are attracted to the sport for that reason), but in truth injuries are very rare, and this is to be credited to the vigilance of fencers themselves in applying the rules—and common sense.

We don't want anyone to be injured, even slightly. We want to correct the public impression, which may be a factor in keeping our sport from being more popular, that fencing is dangerous. We want to avoid any publicity that would be detrimental to the sport. The object of the game is *not* to batter your opponent, cripple him, or even diminish his physical capability in any way except by fatigue.

Environment. You must be constantly on the watch for dangerous conditions. The floor should not be slippery, and anything such as a spot of spilled liquid must be removed. A good margin around the fencing strip must be clear of obstacles: equipment, spectators, and other people not at the moment involved as contestants or officials. Adequate lighting should be provided.

Equipment. The uniform and weapons required by the rules must be as safe as possible. Your uniform includes mask, jacket, glove, trousers, stockings, and shoes, and these must be in good condition.

Weapons should be neither too stiff nor too whippy, and should be inspected to make sure the blade is not broken. The rules require that the weapon be attached to the hand by a thong or strap so it can't be thrown out among bystanders.

You must NEVER face an opponent or partner without both of you wearing wire-mesh masks. Get into the habit of pulling the bib of your mask down every time you put it on. Your glove must overlap the end of your sleeve, on the outside. Your trousers must at least cover your knees (no shorts) in any position, and stockings should cover the rest of your legs.

The rules require women to wear rigid breast shields under their jackets. In official competitions, all fencers are required to wear an extra safety plastron (a pad with a half-sleeve fastened to the body by straps) inside their jackets (Fig. 58.).

In sum, the fencer should be completely covered from head to toe, mostly by clothing made of strong duck material (some of it in several layers), and the extremely important mask.

For practice, many people use half-jackets and perhaps even fence in shorts, but you should be aware of the additional risks. Anyone who indulges in free play or bouting should have all the protection he can get.

Plastrons alone are BAD! Some schools have stocked up on plastrons because they are cheaper than jackets or half-jackets. This is a false economy. Administrators should think what a human life is worth. The plastron, as described, is more dangerous than no covering at all, because it gives an *illusion* of safety and encourages more vigorous play. This plastron does not protect two extremely vulnerable areas—the throat and the armpit. Consequently, you should wear at least a half-jacket, which has a collar and a sleeve on the side toward the opponent, even in practice. Full jackets are, of course, required for competition. For further information on equipment, see Chapter 11.

Technique. The rules actually require you to have fairly good technique. Penalties are imposed for unnecessary roughness, intentional or not, and dangerous play—actions that seem to threaten injury. Even the slightest body contact should be avoided, and may be penalized. The penalties include dismissal from the particular competition. The rules say, in effect, "If you can't fence well enough to keep from bumping into your opponent, or from tripping over your own feet and falling down, or from hard slashing, or from losing your balance and control so that you *might* crash into your opponent or the audience, then LEAVE! Go back to school until you do have a reasonable amount of technique." Officials need not, and should not, wait until you have caused an injury before disqualifying you.

I should mention that injuries are also prevented by conditioning. Any physical education instructor will tell you that the athlete in training will have fewer muscle strains, "Charley horses," joint sprains, and bone fractures than the person who does not exercise regularly and who then tries to play a vigorous sport. If injured, the athlete in good condition will probably recover more quickly, too. Since fencing is not a body-contact sport, any injury worse than a bruise is quite rare.

LIMITATIONS

Now we can consider some of the rules that make fencing a game—those on the limitations of the weapon, the target, the ground, and time allowed for a standard bout. Here I will be brief; more details will be given in the chapters on rules and theory for the particular weapons.

Weapon. For theoretical purposes we are primarily concerned with the limitations on how a weapon scores. This topic has been mentioned above, in the section comparing the three weapons.

The foil and the épée can score only with the point. If they were real weapons, they would not have sharp edges along the blade. No damage could be done by slashing, but only by thrusting. Beginners waste a tremendous amount of energy waving the blade from side to side or around in circles.

The sabre has a point too, but its main features are the cutting edges, one the full length of the blade and the other about one third of the length of the blade, measured from the tip back toward the hilt. The sabre can score by thrusting, fore-edge cutting and back-edge cutting.

It shouldn't be necessary to say (but I will) that no weapon can score by striking with the guard, handle, or butt end. Rather, the worst possible penalties will be imposed on the offender.

The weapons are limited in length, weight, stiffness, size of guard, etc. The exact measurements can be found in the rule book. Manufacturers supply blades and other parts that meet these standards, but you have to keep your equipment from deteriorating, or replace defective (damaged) parts.

Target. The foil target is limited to the neck and torso, or trunk of the body, *front and back.* An invalid or "foul" hit is one made against the head (mask and bib), arm, hand, buttock, leg, or foot. Remember that a slap or slash, whether against a valid or invalid area, is *no hit at all:* it is a MISS. Probably the most common mistake of beginners as judges is to call a flat contact a foul. A foul—a hit with the point, thrusting against an invalid surface—stops the action. The president (referee) halts the fencers, tells them to get back on guard, and orders them to start again.

In épée fencing there are absolutely no target restrictions whatsoever. You can score by poking your opponent anywhere, from head to toe, front or back.

The sabre target consists of every part of the body above a horizontal line around the hips—just where the top of the legs connect with the torso. You can strike with point or either edge on the head, both arms, both hands, and the upper trunk, front or back. A thrust or cut below the hips is invalid; just as in foil, the action would be halted when such a hit occurs.

Ground. The official "strip" is a rectangle, 2 meters (about 6′7″) wide and 14 meters (about 45′6″) long. A smaller area may be used depending on local conditions. This strip is used in a different way for each of the weapons.

A fencer who goes off the side is penalized by the loss of ground, and a fencer who retreats more than a limited distance is penalized by having a touch scored against him. You can't run away forever.

Now you see that there are *two* ways to score against an opponent: Hit him properly on a valid target, or scare him so badly that he retreats past the end line.

Time. A normal bout, in all weapons, is for 5 touches, and the time allowed is limited to 6 minutes of action. In some championship tournaments, bouts are run for 10 touches, and the time is increased accordingly.

Épée time and scoring rules differ somewhat from foil and sabre rules, but we will discuss that later. Quite reasonably, in foil and sabre, if time runs out when you are leading, you win, and if the score is tied when time expires, there is unlimited overtime for a "sudden death" winning touch.

CONVENTIONS

Many beginners are confused by the notion of "right-of-way," which governs foil and sabre play. Often, in a flurry of action, both fencers are hit before the president can yell "Halt!" The rules say that a touch cannot be scored against both (in foil or sabre). Which fencer, if any, won that point?

Time. There is no problem in épée. The only consideration is who hits first, and that is determined by an electric machine that is sensitive to differences of $\frac{1}{25}$th of a second. If one fencer hits $\frac{1}{25}$th of a second ahead, that turns off his opponent's circuit so that no hit will show in the opposite direction. When both fencers are hit inside of $\frac{1}{25}$th of a second, a touch is scored against *both.*

Now for foil and sabre: If the president saw that one hit was made *clearly* before the other, then, quite reasonably, the earlier hit is correct.

Sometimes the first hit is foul: It strikes an invalid surface (with a thrusting point in foil; with point, main edge, or back edge in sabre). There is no score, because even if the opposing hit is good, it is too late. The foul hit stops the action. Indeed, as we often see when using the electrical foil, a fencer might be fast enough to hit twice before his opponent hits once. If he hits foul and then good, no score is allowed.

Right-of-way. Suppose there is no clear difference (let's say, roughly, ⅕th of a second) in time between the actual hits—two good fast fencers come together in sharp play, and both are hit at the same moment. The president must decide who, if either, had right of way.

Again it is a matter of time. If one fencer *starts* an attack ahead of the other, he is said to have the right-of-way.

An attack is a movement of the striking part of the weapon (tip in foil, tip or main edge or back edge in sabre) toward target, and it must have a chance of hitting *very soon.* That is, a similar movement made from twenty feet away can hardly be thought of as a threat—and you can narrow that down until you're talking about a movement made from just barely out of reach. If that genuinely threatening movement continues without hesitating or faltering, it is correct: It has the right-of-way.

When you attack, your opponent might hastily stick his own blade out, and thus both of you would be hit at the same time. For example, supposing you lunge (see Glossary). Your move naturally takes more time, and during that time your opponent is able to bring about a double hit. But he is wrong to do so since his move did not start first, and the score will be against him. An attack that has the right-of-way, or *initiative,* must be avoided or deflected (or blocked, in sabre).

When a fencer does successfully block or deflect an attack, for an instant *nobody* has the right-of-way. Nobody is threatening. The original attacker might quickly make another attack, or his opponent might grab the right-of-way by making an attack of his own. (An immediate return attack made by a fencer who has deflected an attack against him is called a *riposte.* This immediate return has preference over a quick continuation of the original attack.) Between good fencers, ownership of the right-of-way might pass back and forth two or three times in a second!

Occasionally a true double hit occurs, with no difference in time and no difference in initiative that the president can see. That is, both fencers attacked "simultaneously" and hit, either fair or foul. In such a case no score is awarded.

To sum up, in order to score you must hit a valid target, in the correct manner (thrusting in foil, thrusting or cutting in sabre), either clearly first or with right-of-way (starting first and not interrupted by your own wobbling or by the opponent's deflection or block). This is the object of the game. In other words, three factors are taken into account in scoring: where you hit, how you hit, and when.

There are occasions when one fencer hits and the other misses. Then it doesn't matter who was "right"—the hit is of ultimate importance. A beautiful attack is no good if it doesn't land.

Contrarily, a hit made in any manner, with a bent arm or by any clumsy maneuver whatever, is good if it hits clearly first on valid surface. There are no points for good form, and no penalties for poor form, as long as you don't collide with your opponent or do something that is brutal or dangerous.

Because of these regulations about clear precedence in time or initiative, and the requirement that a genuine attack must be avoided or deflected before any answer can be made, sabre and foil fencing are called "conventional." Many times both fencers are hit within a fairly short time interval. If the weapons were real both would supposedly be wounded, but that doesn't matter at all in the sport: Points are awarded according to rules. In a way, the épée is also unrealistic in that the time gap is terribly small, but both fencers do lose a point when there is a double hit, and there are no problems about doing moves in the "proper" sequence.

I will discuss in greater detail the rules for each of the weapons in later chapters.

OUTLINE OF THEORY

The rules set a framework for fencing as a sport. They tell you what you can do and what you can't do. They do not say what is the best way. Any attempt to describe a "best way" of fencing effectively, what moves to make in order to win according to the rules, is theory.

There are plenty of arguments about the rules and what they really mean. These arguments are—we hope—eventually settled by common sense based on experience: Some rules sound very strange, but the decisions of the officials should be, and almost always are, understandable.

Likewise, there can be arguments about theory, a much broader and more subjective area with difficult-to-define boundaries. Some of the arguments are very hard to prove. One would think that the test of theory occurs in the competition hall, where the winner should be the best applier of a particular idea or set of ideas about how to fence effectively. This is not always the case, but there are certain principles about which there is general agreement. Theoretically, there is a good way to fence.

I will put forth here a very general outline of theory. You can try it out, experiment, test it, question it, argue with it, change it, improve it, or throw it out entirely. The only thing you must not do is swallow it whole. Don't believe it is the truth, the whole truth, and nothing but the truth. It is just a starting place.

In fencing, everything happens at once. We can't really separate the elements. You don't fence just with your body, but with your mind, emotions, temperament, spirit, or whatever. Sometimes we talk about body/mind or mind/body, and perhaps we remember, without saying it, that "mind" includes (and is more than the sum of) intellect, reason, logic, emotion, feeling, spirit, temperament. We could have great arguments about what each of these "things" is. These discussions can be fun, but hardly ever get very far because we're trying to separate features of a whole person.

Fencing can be broadly described as a big, total, ongoing process and we might have a difficult time picking it apart. On the other hand, some analysis is worthwhile. Instead of saying that we're separating pieces, let's suppose we're looking at it from three points of view (one at a time), or noticing features that we just decide for the moment to name: physical, tactical, and strategic. Here's the bare outline:

Physical

Development of your natural resources

Set of movements for fencing

Tactical Influences
    Distance
    Time
    Relationship of blades
Strategy
    Big, loose plans for operating
    Related knowledge of anatomy/physiology, psychology, etc.

PHYSICAL

The inexperienced spectator at first sees fencing as a lot of physical activity. This is not, of course, all of the game, but you will have to spend time and thought on the physical part of it. This book contains chapters on physical training, and a large part of it is devoted to the sets of movements (slightly different for each of the weapons) necessary and sufficient to achieve your objectives. For the time being, concentrate on aspects of the game other than the purely physical. If the following sections don't make a lot of sense at first reading, come back later when you have had a little more experience with lessons and actual bouting.

TACTICAL INFLUENCES

In the sense that I use the word, *tactics* means the factors that must be working for you when you apply fencing movements in bouting. Tactics still relates to physical matters.

Distance. Two people are involved in a fencing bout. The success or failure of a particular action always depends to some degree on the distance between them. An attack by lunging, although done with perfect form, can't hit if you start from too far away. Sometimes your attack will fail if you start from too close.

We might say that this applies to every kind of fencing action. Certainly many counterattacking actions will fail at close range. The physical set of movements that you learn in class or find described later in this book must be adjusted to the distance between you and your opponent. Some of the movements are used almost entirely to get closer or farther away. Deflecting or blocking moves can be smaller at longer ranges or wider at shorter ranges.

Often when we speak of distance we mean how far an individual person can reach. Distance in this sense is different for everyone. No two people have exactly the same length of arm and leg. Thus, when you face an opponent you must think about whether or not he can reach farther than you.

You will find that there is no *absolute* advantage in being taller or having a long reach. You must simply fence according to your own physique. In many circumstances, the shorter person will have the advantage—momentarily. Nevertheless, you would be wise to "develop your natural resources": Work out so that you can reach as far as your bones, muscles, and tendons can possibly allow. Some tall people get lazy and do not do this—they give away the advantages they might have at longer distances.

Time. Distance co-ordinates with time. At a given speed, it takes more time to travel a long distance than a short one (also to make a larger move than a smaller one). Part of your tactical work is to arrange to make a smaller move at the right moment; in this way your important move can be completed before your opponent can react. This is often what we mean when we mention "timing."

The word *time* also refers to rhythm. When you make several movements in a row, some of them may be short and others relatively long; the sequence has a kind of rhythm. Take an advance lunge: The advance is usually thought of as two short counts, and the lunge as a long one. Therefore, the natural rhythm of the sequence is short-short, L . . . O . . . N . . . G. Other patterns of hand- and footwork have their characteristic rhythms. Very often the feet go in one rhythm and the fingers in another, just as when a person plays a piano, one hand plays one pattern and the other hand a different pattern.

These hand and foot patterns must be in harmony. Again you must spend time and effort practicing, mostly on your footwork, because that part tends to be slower, and in a co-ordinated action your fingerwork can be dragged down by clumsy footwork.

When you are playing an opponent, you should notice not only his reach, speed, favorite moves, etc., but also his typical rhythms. This is another feature of what we call "timing."

Relationships of blades. In the section above on distance, I mentioned a space relationship, how far apart the two fencers were. Usually there is not a very great difference in height between fencers, and we didn't consider one fencer to be much taller than the other. Neither did we think about one being at a great angle to the side: Fencers maneuver to keep facing one another, pretty much along a straight line. These matters are important, occasionally, but I won't deal with them in this general discussion.

It *is* worthwhile to think at this point where the blades are in relation to each other: above-below, side-by-side, above-and-to-the-side, etc. Just as in the discussion about distance I indicated that there were circumstances in which "you can't get there from here," I must point out that to move your blade effectively, you must always think about where it is at a certain instant compared to where your opponent's blade is.

There can be many variations in the positions of blades, in that they might be parallel at the same height or at different heights, or they might be at one of many different angles to one another. They are, of course, always moving, so that the angles change constantly. In many cases a difference of a few degrees in angle may not be important or decisive, but you need to work this out. Ordinarily, the blades are not farther apart than a few inches, a foot or so at most.

Blades are very light, and you can bring them together or otherwise change the relationship between them, fairly quickly. You can move your fingers much faster in bladework than you can move your whole body in gaining the right distance.

You may think up some other factors similar to distance, time, and blade relationship, which influence your success in the application of your physical movements. This explanation was simply meant to get you started in thinking about this aspect of theory. As I said before, you may eventually decide that a lot of revision is necessary to make the theory fit what you think actually happens in fencing. In order for it to be useful to you, the theoretical thinking has to be your own.

STRATEGY

Your physical work and the tactical applications must become almost automatic. There is hardly any time on the fencing strip for "thinking," in the ordinary sense. But when we talk about strategy, we're talking about "principles," "attitudes," or a wide-open sort of planning, and general ideas about how to fence successfully. These notions may, in turn, have an effect on what physical work you do to develop your natural resources, which of the almost infinite variety of movements are significant, and so forth.

Suppose you take up the policy called *economy*. In order to do a certain job or achieve a certain objective, it seems reasonable to try to do it with the least necessary effort. Fencing is certainly an activity in which you have a difficult enough time without wasting energy with moves that are too big or too strong. Thinking according to this principle of economy, and observing what goes on in fencing, either when you yourself are involved or when you are learning by watching others, you should be able to discover just how much motion/effort/ time you need in a particular situation. You should also notice how you lost a point or failed to score one because you spent too much strength on one part of a sequence.

This study should then reflect back on how you train. The set of fencing movements should have been built up according to an efficiency principle. Later on I will describe a set of movements for each weapon: I think these sets are as small as they can be to do the job, but if you find that they are not adequate, you should add to them.

The advantage in choosing the set of fewest necessary and sufficient moves is that you can spend proportionately more time practicing them, thereby making them even more effective. Suppose you chose another system of movements, some of which were too wide, too strong, or whatever, and practiced those inefficient moves over and over. Eventually you would be able to make them work a good deal of the time, but you would have wasted valuable effort and time when a simpler, more efficient system could have produced better results. In other words, part of the principle of economy is to avoid doing anything more complicated than you must.

Strangely enough, however, you won't really want to be absolutely efficient. You'd better assume your opponents are very clever; that's safer than thinking they are stupid. Accordingly, if you always performed with the least effort, your opponent ought to be able to figure out what you will do in the particular situation. Therefore, part of your program should be to make sloppy, meaningless movements occasionally, to confuse your opponent. The most efficient method is not to be too efficient!

Since a lot of other influences are at work, it is actually impossible for you to do the "same" actions in exactly the same way every time. There is always at least a small amount of variation, no matter how hard you try or how much you practice. This being so, you don't have to think a very great deal about deliberately showing your opponent inefficient moves—you will make quite a few of them anyway. We simply think it is ideal to have all moves under pretty good control.

In the popular conception, success in fencing depends a good deal on deceiving one's opponent. The terminology shows up frequently in our language: People in a debate are said to be fencing with words, thrusting and parrying, riposting, etc. But how can you deceive when everything is out in the open? Just as in chess, all your moves are done in full view of your opponent.

The strategic idea is summed up in the word CHANGE. You can change your physical actions and their tactical application, patterns (sequences of foot and hand movements), levels (high, middle, and low target areas), distance, timing (rhythm), relationships of blades, and so forth.

Some fencers, mostly beginners, "rehearse" their patterns before they try to hit with them, thus giving themselves away. Others will honestly try to carry out the same attack over and over. Their opponents should be able to counter these maneuvers. But suppose you did show your opponent a pattern a few times, then started the same way but finished up differently? This would be one method of deception.

In a very simple case, if you always retreat when your opponent advances, and by the same amount, you will lead him to expect that you will continue to do that in the future. If you *change* distance by advancing when he advances, by not retreating, or by retreating more or less than usual, you may deceive him—at least enough to spoil his plan. Likewise, if you change your rhythm (having set one up) by speeding up or slowing down, he may be thrown off his stride. You can also change the blade relationships just by carrying your hand a little higher or a little lower, a centimeter farther to one side or the other. You will be surprised at how much difference these small shifts make.

We can sum all this up by saying, "Don't do the same thing three times in a row." Presumably, most opponents would catch on by that time. A good fencer could even take advantage of your first repeat. But there is a higher level of sneakiness. If both of you are pretty good, and you go through a pattern twice, your opponent might think, "Oh, no, he won't do that again. Now what is he really going to do?" Then repeat the pattern once more.

The strategic aspect of fencing also includes specialized knowledge that will help to improve your performance. Basic physics, for example, tells you that when an object is at rest, you must apply force to get it moving, and you must continue applying force to keep it moving, for it will eventually stop again. You would need more force to get a more massive (heavier) object going. Next, physics tells you that a moving object tends to go straight, and you must apply force in order to change its direction. This also means that if you want to stop the object suddenly, you must apply force in the opposite direction.

Of course the human body is far from being a simple object. If you think of it as a machine, the bones go together in a complicated system of levers, ball-and-socket joints, etc., with a great many muscles pulling this way and that. Your weapon is an extension of the system, and it has peculiar properties of its own, in some circumstances acting like a lever and in others like a spring. You should take note that your opponent applies force on your blade by means of his own, pushing or knocking it here and there. Most of the time we think of the weapon as a separate object which is not very heavy but which requires varying amounts of force to get moving, to stop, or to change direction. Ideas along these lines should have some influence on the set of fencing movements previously mentioned.

Some knowledge of how your body functions as living organism, including the functions of the nervous system, might also guide you in your training program. In the next chapter I will discuss exercise, nutrition, and other factors in physical conditioning.

Here I just want to say a few words about the effects of nerve functions. We can say that there are three levels of reaction: reflexes, conditional responses, and decisions. You are certainly familiar with so-called simple reflexes: If something unexpectedly flies at your face, you automatically blink your eyes and jerk your head away. If you unexpectedly touch something much warmer or much colder than your normal surroundings, you pull your hand back swiftly, without thinking about it—without being *able* to think about it. Perhaps you have had a doctor hit you below the kneecap with his little rubber hammer, and your leg kicked.

There are a number of other involuntary reactions of this kind. We humans have such a complicated nervous system that hardly any of these reactions are still "pure" or "natural." Many of them seem to have been changed slightly by events that the individual has lived through. Certainly many of them can be modified: You can train yourself not to blink when somebody strikes at your face. Also, even if your muscles do jerk reflexively, you can learn to change the direction of the movement, which may be valuable in fencing.

In the main, however, psychologists believe that reflexes are very reliable. Within the same environment, the same action will produce the same reaction, every time. One feature of reflexes is that they are comparatively quick; another is that the speed is almost exactly the same every time, within limits. When a person is tired or sick, the reflexes might be slower or weaker, or the reflex motions might tend to fly off in odd directions. Drugs likewise might make the reactions slower, or faster but erratic. Inasmuch as successful fencing does not depend on sheer speed or sheer strength, but does require precision, drugs are harmful. Besides, as you probably know, the use of drugs is forbidden by the rules of every sport.

Much experimentation has been done with so-called "conditioned reflexes." To a considerable extent, athletic training is aimed at making movement patterns as nearly automatic as possible. A good athlete should be able to perform an action somewhat more complicated than the reflex type as fast, or almost as fast, as a simple reflex. We can name this kind of reaction a "conditional response": In similar circumstances, a person should respond very quickly and very reliably to a certain signal. These are not simple reflexes, however, but more complicated action patterns, built up with the co-operation of the higher levels of the nervous system. Therefore they are *not* as fast as reflexes or as automatic and uncontrollable.

Throwing aside the fancy words, these conditional responses are what we commonly call habits. According to our individual standards, we say that habits are good or bad. Since the surrounding conditions in fencing are fairly complicated, and we receive quite a number of different signals in comparatively short spans of time, our conditional responses, or habits, might or might not work. Your goal is to develop good fencing habits which will allow for adjustments to different conditions. As far as we're concerned, good habits are good only under certain conditions. We should have some control over them—at the cost of a little time.

At the decision level, the speed of reaction is still lower. When the situation is changing very rapidly and we are receiving a great many signals (or signals that are *not different enough* from one another), we have to make decisions. This takes more time. To put it another way, we have to wait a little longer to gather more information about what has been happening in order to make a better prediction about what is likely to happen next, and we have to make a choice between two or more alternatives, hoping to deal with the developing situation successfully.

We are always, to some extent, "living in the past." When something happens out there, outside of you, no matter how exciting it is, you do not and cannot react at the same instant that it happens. Time passes while nerve impulses travel around their circuits and muscles contract, even in a simple reflex. You might think that you're sharply aware of what is happening NOW, but what you're aware of is what happened at least a tenth of a second ago. Usually this is close enough; sometimes it isn't.

When you fence, you can try to play against the three levels of response in your opponent. You can expect, of course, that he might try to do the same to you, but if you can do something very suddenly and unexpectedly, you might trigger off one of his reflexes that doesn't help him block your attack. At a higher level, you could discover, by testing him out and observing his reactions, some of his habits, which you could then use to your advantage. Finally, you can make moves that look very much like other moves, so that he would have to take time to decide what you are going to do, and that hesitation might be just enough for you to get in.

A person who is surprised usually reacts reflexively or habitually—he may freeze or flinch, or he may carry out an action that he was already "set" to do, or, mistaking a signal for one very much like it, he will make his standard move.

Suppose you want someone to believe you when you tell a lie. First of all, you must tell the truth most of the time. Any deceptive action you make in fencing must be backed up by a number of strong and honest actions. Usually you will have to attack your opponent several times, really meaning to hit with a particular move, before you can successfully get tricky: The basic program is to try to score with reach and speed, from fairly simple setups. The second requirement for getting your opponent to believe your lie is that the lie must be as nearly like the truth as possible. It must seem to your opponent that you are again coming on with the powerful, straightforward attack that you did before.

If your real attacks succeed, your opponent may try harder to make the same blocking action work the next time, thus giving you an opening for a deception. Strangely enough, if your real attacks fail, your opponent is pretty likely to use the same response again, just because it was successful for him before.

This is merely a beginning. You will find that the game is played with many different kinds of honest attacks and false ones, and real and false responses to attacks.

We have examined fencing briefly from three points of view. Now try to see it all at once: the physical actions applied according to the tactical factors of distance, time, and blade relationships, all governed by broad strategic considerations. Assuming this theoretical framework works, you should see that you can't fence with your body alone.

Chapter 2

TRAINING

CONDITIONING DIFFERS FOR different sports. In fencing, precision, flexibility, mobility, and speed are greatly emphasized, although power and endurance cannot be completely ignored. Fencing does require considerable use of muscles that may hardly have been developed at all by other activities, and in those particular areas you will need to gain strength. Fencing does not put much strain on certain other sets of muscles, but your training should be for the whole body, to promote general well-being and give you "reserves."

A complete training program consists of three parts: exercise, nutrition, and rest.

Quite a few coaches have stressed that success comes from hard work. Maybe they mean no more than that, but certainly it is easy for a student to get the impression that if he sweats this much, he will become twice as good by sweating twice as much. Up to a point this may seem to happen, but there are limits. Among other considerations, we should think carefully about what we all know so well that we may overlook it: Fencing is a rather complicated sport—more complicated than lifting heavy weights, for example (although a good deal of skill is needed for that, too).

Progress in lifting weights is more easily measured. You could find a mathematical relationship between amount of exercise and increasing ability, but progress could probably not be graphed as a straight line. More likely the graph would show a curve, rising very slightly at first, getting steeper for a while, and then leveling off. This is a normal picture for many kinds of activities. As a comparison, children do not grow at a steady rate, such as one inch per month, but in alternating periods of very slow and comparatively rapid increase.

Another point is that different people do not progress at the same rate. In an activity as complex as fencing, one student might be improving very quickly at a certain part-skill (call it A) but not at another (B), while his classmate makes progress at B but has trouble with A. Many of these part-skills are related in various ways, and we will look for fundamental actions or postures that more or less determine whether the subsequent moves are effective.

Physical training can be divided roughly into five areas: limbering, endur-

1. *Two-way stretching: central position*

ance, power, skill practice (fencing movements), and tactical/strategic practice (individual lessons, bouting, etc.). Your "hard work" needs to be spread out reasonably, usefully, over these areas.

I assume you are not a professional athlete, and you have only a few hours a week to do all this. Therefore you must choose how to spend your time for the best results. As previously noted, your progress at first might seem very low, and a great deal of hard work will *not* increase that progress significantly.

Also, in a year-round program, you would emphasize certain areas in the competitive season and different areas during the slack season. There would be a period of building up to competitive peak, a period of maintaining the competitive level, and a period of different activities for refreshment.

Limbering exercises are those that increase flexibility of your joints. These are not strenuous, not hard work in the simple sense. I often say that beginners in fencing are too strong, meaning that they are too stiff, too tight. You will have to stretch your muscles and tendons easily and progressively, so that your joints, especially those of your lower back, hips, knees, and ankles, can bend as far as

2. Two-way stretching: opening

3. Two-way stretching: short form

4. Two-way stretching: full stretch

possible in all directions. Most of the exercises in the basic warm-up are of this type.

Your endurance, or stamina, can be progressively increased by jogging, running, or swimming at moderate speed, going a little farther each time you try. Exercise of this kind involves doing many repetitions of a single (or multiple) motion against light resistance. This can take up a good deal of time; at some point you might be wiser to put the effort into fencing drills (multiple lunging, etc.), thus improving both skill and endurance all at once.

In a fencing competition, the demand for endurance is not the same as jogging ten miles without stopping: The meet could last for several hours, but you would be able to rest between bouts, and there would be lunch and dinner breaks. Somehow you must be able to put out energy at a high rate for a fairly short time, and do it again and again and again. The ordinary kind of stamina work will help you build up reserves for this, but the management of energy output is quite different.

Power exercises call for the exertion of a very strong effort for a short period, such as lifting a weight that is so heavy that you can only do it once. For practice, you would choose a weight that you could lift, in a particular manner, three or five times in a row. This would eventually enable you to lift a heavier weight once. This is what we usually mean by *strength*. For fencing, such strength is not needed. The reason for doing such exercises is to enable you to move your own body weight faster and more easily, without so much strain—you will, in other words, have a reserve. For the most part, powerwork should be concentrated on the legs (the physical education department in your school may have special apparatus to give resistance of a chosen amount to leg-straightening and leg-bending movements). If you do this kind of exercise, you should set the apparatus for a weight that you can push or pull at least ten times.

One problem with this sort of powerwork is that it might slow you down. Your muscles and tendons may shorten and thicken so that you can't move as freely. Fencing coaches usually advise you not to do much of this kind of exercise during the season when you are building up to and keeping up your competitive level. You would, naturally, mix power exercises in with other exercises.

Power is also developed by doing fairly light-resistance exercise at maximum speed. Examples of this are short sprints on the track or in the swimming pool, series of squat jumps, "burpees," or multiple lunging. Sprints and the like are always done over and over, with a few seconds or up to a minute of rest in between.

Don't forget to warm up BEFORE doing any of these strenuous exercises! If you are "cold" you might pull a muscle, which would keep you out of practice for a while, maybe a long time.

BASIC WARM-UP

Every practice session must begin with a warm-up period. The exercises below are recommended for stretching practically every part of your body. When you are in shape, you can use just a few of them to loosen up just before a tournament begins: if you have time only for one, do two-way stretching. Follow the order listed: start by loosening your center (hips and waist), next your legs, then your arms and shoulders.

1. *Giant Circles.* Set your feet about double shoulder-width apart. Keep knees straight and feet flat. Hang forward limply from your hips—many people seem to have stiff necks at this point and don't let their heads hang. Slowly move your hands as far as possible to the right, leaning and stretching. Continue the swing upward, reaching and leaning back—look at the ceiling. Smoothly go on to the left, stretching as far sideways as you can, and so on down to the starting position. Reverse and go to the left for the second giant circle. Make 6 or 8 circles altogether, alternating left and right.

This does, in one swoop, practically everything that two or three other waist-bending exercises will do, toning the muscles of your back, sides, and belly, loosening your waist and hips. The next exercise works on the same area with a different movement.

2. *Twisting.* Standing in the same position as before, raise both hands in front of you to shoulder height. Twist your upper body around, trying to look behind you. Then twist around the other way. Repeat for about 12 counts, left, right, left, right, etc. Keep your feet flat (don't let them slip around) and keep your knees straight. Otherwise you won't be twisting your waist, you'll merely be pivoting around on your feet.

3. *Two-way Stretching.* Feet placed as before, at least double shoulder-width apart, bring your fingertips to your chest, elbows almost shoulder high. Lift your right toes and swivel that foot outward. Your left foot will remain flat and in place. As your foot turns, open your arms. When your pivoting foot is at right angles to the other, put it down flat and bend that knee—the other knee (the left) must remain straight. Bend your right knee as far as you can *without* pulling your right heel off the ground. Your arms continue to stretch out until they are in line

above your legs. Your left leg must be kept stiff, and your body should twist enough so that that left leg is definitely *behind* you. Reverse to the starting position, folding your arms, straightening your right knee, and pivoting your right foot on its heel until both feet are again pointing in the same direction.

Notice especially that your torso must NOT lean out over the bent knee. One of the most important purposes of this exercise is to stretch the hip joints. This means that the leg that is *behind* you at any particular time—since you will do the exercise in both directions, alternating right and left—should make the greatest possible angle with your upper body. If anything, try to lean backward, pushing your belly forward.

Both heels should stay on the ground. If the one on the bending leg lifts, your feet aren't far enough apart. Your bending knee should naturally stop over your shoestrings.

Notice also that your hands should be palm up as much as possible, so that your shoulders are rolled back and your chest is open. The arms slant parallel to the straight leg.

As you become better conditioned (looser in the hips), you will be able to spread your feet farther apart and lower your body more. At full stretch (Fig. 4), the foot behind you should roll over (which it should NOT do when you lunge in combat or a lesson), allowing the hip joint to bend even more. You will be able to go faster, in a regular rhythm, bouncing back from the limit of your outward motion. You might count out loud (SHOUT!) on each outward movement.

In your first session, you should be able to do this exercise at least 14 times (7 in each direction, alternating). In the second session, do the exercise 20 times. From then on, do half with your feet flat and half with the rear foot rolling over. You probably will not need to do more than 30 for a warm-up.

A variation, for an occasional change, is to do the two-way stretch very slowly, with a long expulsion of your breath on the outward movement and a long inhale on the return to the central position. Ten times (5 each way) is sufficient.

This exercise is *essential*. Most importantly, it stretches the tendons and muscles around the hip joints. It strengthens muscles on the inner sides of the thighs, which are seldom well developed except in people who have taken ballet or modern dance. You should never lunge without warming up this way, even if you're a trained fencer.

4. *Arm Swinging and Twisting.* If you are following this sequence of exercises, you will have already done some arm and shoulder loosening in connection with giant circles, two-way stretching, etc. Here are some more active exercises:

Swing your arms in large circles as though doing the "butterfly" stroke in swimming, 6 or 8 times. Reverse the direction for 6 or 8 swings.

Wrap your arms around you, cupping your left shoulder with your right hand and vice versa. Then fling your arms out and back. Repeat 8 or 10 times. If your shoulders are loose enough, the backs of your hands should touch behind you.

Stretch your arms out sideways at shoulder height. Along that line, twist as much as possible, in one direction so your palms face backward, in the other so that they face up.

5. *Jumping Jacks.* This exercise is familiar to most people. It is also known as the side-straddle hop. From a standing position with your feet together and arms hanging, jump up, swinging your hands overhead as high as you can, and landing

on your toes with your feet 12 to 18 inches apart. Immediately jump again, returning to the starting position.

In the first training session, for most people (who are not in good shape), the exercise should be done about 12 times at a moderate pace. At the next session, go for 15 or 20. These should be counted out loud (SHOUT!).

As an endurance exercise, jumping jacks can be pushed up by stages to 30, 40, 50, or even 100 (perhaps in two sets of 50, with a short rest between). Another variation is to do 15 at moderate pace followed by 10 as fast as you can.

This exercise not only works out your shoulders and lower legs, but speeds up your breathing and heartbeat. It should always be the *last* item of the warm-up, after you have gradually raised your body to a higher level of activity.

Suppose your fencing class meets twice a week. For homework, you should do your warm-up routine, plus some footwork drill (fencing movements) at least one other time during the week. Three periods outside of class each week would be fine. Once you know the movements well, you will be able to get through this practice in about fifteen minutes. The homework will definitely help you to get more out of your classwork: You will be able to take more instruction without fighting your body. Otherwise, muscles and joints that have loosened up in class will just stiffen again, week after week, and you will make comparatively little progress.

EXTRA EXERCISES FOR LEGS

A single exercise, such as two-way stretching, tends to work on just some of the many muscles you have, while other muscles do not bear much strain. For complete training, you will want to do a variety of exercises, particularly for your legs.

Two of these are super-stretchers: the sitting toe-touch (Fig. 5) and the sit-up (or lie-back) with legs folded under (Fig. 6). Perhaps in class gymnastic mats can be brought out on occasion for these special exercises, or you can do them at home on the floor, with some kind of firm pad (a folded blanket will do) under you.

For the toe-touch, keep your knees stiffly straight, and point your toes back toward your face. Otherwise try to relax as much as possible. Flop forward and bounce loosely 5 times, sit up and stretch your arms toward the ceiling, bounce forward 5 more times, sit up (breathing in), and bounce forward 5 more times. With each set of bounces you should be able to reach farther toward your toes—eventually, get to curl your fingers over them. Once you are used to doing this, you can get a partner to help you stretch even more by pushing (gently!) on your back, following the rhythm of your bounces. This way you can relax more, instead of straining to reach your toes. Your whole body, especially your neck, should be loose—with the exception of your legs. It will hardly do you any good if your knees bend. The object is not, necessarily, to touch your toes or reach beyond them, but to reach as far as you can with your legs straight.

For the sit-up or lie-back exercise, you would begin in the position shown in Figure 7. If you don't have a partner to hold your knees, you can try to lie back, lowering yourself on your hands and then your elbows, finally getting your shoulders on the mat. Most likely your knees will rise, but try to stay in that position and relax, letting your knees gradually sink down.

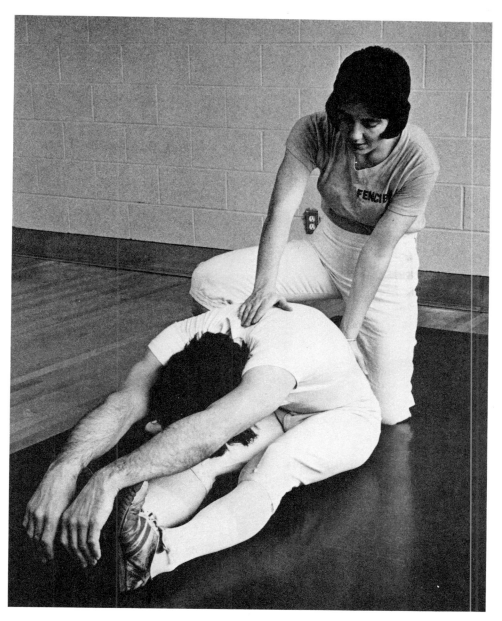

5. Sitting toe-touch to stretch back of leg

This exercise hurts different people in different places: for some, the lower back is too stiff to bend very far backward; for many, the ankles won't want to bend that way; for a few, the pain will show up first in the tops of the thighs. The best way to make progress is to have a partner hold your knees firmly against the floor, and for you to do sit-ups, leaning back as far as possible. This is not very difficult—for many people it doesn't feel as strenuous as the usual sit-up from a lying position—and after you have done 15 or 20, you will probably be looser and able to lean back farther. If you keep this up, every other day or so, you may soon be able to go all the way back until your shoulders touch the mat. Then you may also be able to lie back and stay in that position for a minute or so. The main purpose of this is to stretch the muscles at the front of your thigh.

6. Sit-up with legs folded under to stretch front thigh muscles

There are several kinds of squats and deep-knee-bends that you might do for a change, including the leg-straightening and leg-bending with apparatus, as mentioned before. You can also do hip-swings, standing on one leg and swinging the other forward, back, or sideways.

SUPPLEMENTARY EXERCISES FOR BEGINNERS

Many people will need more flexibility or strength in one part of the body or another, principally in the wrists, hands, and fingers, or the feet and ankles. For a week or two, supplementary exercises may be included in the class warm-up, and continued thereafter as homework by those who think they need them. These exercises can be fitted in almost anywhere *before* the jumping jacks, and in any order.

1. *Fist Clenching.* Close your hands into fists and squeeze harder and harder while you silently count to 12.

2. *Finger Spreading.* Stretch your fingers apart, and keep trying to spread them wider and wider while you silently count to 12.

3. *Wrist Bending.*

a. Put your palms together in front of your chest, fingers up, and push inward. Force your wrists down until they hurt, and silently count to 12.

b. Put the backs of your hands together, fingers down, and push inward. Force your elbows down, keeping your wrists pressed together, while you silently count to 12.

You should thus have bent your wrists hard in the two main directions, stretching and toughening the forearms.

4. *Rapid Squeezing.* Open and shut your hands with a sharp squeeze over and over, as quickly as you can, as many times as you can—try for 50. This is an endurance exercise. You won't need a strong grip in fencing, but you will often need to make several sudden squeezes in a row, and in the course of a tournament you will have to squeeze many, many times.

5. *Crumpling Newspaper.* Take the corner of a sheet of newspaper between the tips of your thumb and first finger. Hold your arm out at full stretch, shoulder high. Gather the newspaper up with your fingers (one hand only!) and squeeze it into a ball. Do this once with each hand. If you have small hands, use a half-sheet rather than a full double-sheet of newspaper. This is an alternative to the rapid-squeezing exercise above, and requires you to use your fingers in a variety of ways.

6. *Toe Rising.* Stand with your heels together, feet at an angle, and rise up on your toes, slowly, as high as you can, keeping your weight on the big toes. Keep your heels together. Slowly lower your heels to the floor again. Curl your toes upward and rock back slightly on your heels. Repeat 6 times.

7. *Ankle Bending.*

a. Stand with your feet parallel and about 6 inches apart. Roll one foot onto its outer edge as far as possible. If you know you have a weak ankle, don't put much weight on it. Return to starting position and roll the other foot onto its outer edge. Alternate, left and right, 4 times.

b. In the same position, roll both feet outward and return, 6 or 8 times.

c. Place your feet about 18 inches apart and roll them onto their inside edges (keep your knees straight as long as possible, but eventually bend them and bring them together), then roll out. Repeat 8 or 10 times.

8. *Toe Pickup.* Barefooted, pick up a pencil or marble off the floor with your toes, lift and hold it, put it down. Repeat up to 10 times with each foot.

9. *Treading.* Stand facing a wall and about 3 feet away. Place your hands on the wall and lean forward. You should feel a pull in the back of your lower leg if you keep your heel down. The more you push your hips forward, the more uncomfortable the pull will be. Now bend one knee, letting that heel come off the floor. Change over. Your toes will stay on the floor, but you will make a sort of treading or stair-climbing action by lifting your heels alternately. Take from 20 to 50 steps.

This helps to stretch the tendons and muscles from the heels up to the backs of the knees, with a fairly easy motion. A similar effect can be achieved by pretending to walk—with no forward motion—on a thick foam cushion while barefooted. You could get the opposite result (which you DON'T want) by wearing high heels; always wear the flattest shoes you can find.

10. *Sitting Against the Wall.* "Sit on air" with your back pressed flat against a wall, arms folded on your chest. Your thighs should be level, your shins vertical —your feet will be about 15 to 18 inches out from the wall, depending on your build. Hold this position while you count to 12.

a. Variation with heels off the floor.

b. Similar position, on only one leg at a time, the other ankle resting on the bracing knee, as if sitting in a chair with your legs crossed. This may also be done with the heel off the floor.

These are "isometric" exercises that put the muscles under nearly maximum stress for a few seconds. They will help you gain considerable strength—according to your condition when you begin—for the time spent, a few seconds a day for a few weeks.

11. *Abdominal Toning.* Fencing itself does not demand much from the abdominal muscles. Giant circles, waist twisting, and the sit-ups described earlier will help to tone them up, for general fitness. If you need more, and almost everybody does, try these:

a. Swinging Bridge. Lying on your back, place your feet flat, as close to your buttocks as possible. Lift your hips, bridging between your feet and shoulders. Swing your hips from side to side for a while. Twist your hips one way and then the other.

b. Leg Lift and Curl-up. Lying on your back (on a soft surface), raise your legs, keeping them straight. Go to a shoulder stand and then curl on over until your toes touch the mat beyond your head (in the Yoga position called the plow). Do this fairly slowly, and repeat up to 5 times.

c. Drumming. Standing, drum on your stomach rapidly with your fingertips for about 10 seconds. Also drum on your lower belly.

COOL-OFF

Just as you should warm up before fencing, taper off afterward with some kind of easy exercise. You will probably not be huffing and puffing, but you may feel tight or stiff from maintaining the strange positions, and you will want to loosen up. You could jog around the gym a couple of times and then walk, swinging your arms in various ways, until your breathing settles down somewhat.

Even better, jog and walk *backward.*

Beginners will undoubtedly be stiff or sore for at least two days after their first class. The worst of this can be avoided by walking a mile (about fifteen or twenty minutes), or swimming for about a half an hour, as soon as the lesson is over. Soaking in a hot bath later will also reduce soreness. But you should never let down completely after a hard workout; you should never, for example, ride home, eat, and go to sleep.

OTHER ACTIVITIES

Participation in other sports may contribute to your fencing, but more often the benefits seem to go the other way. I've been told by a number of people that they have noticed improvement in their skiing (snow and water), skating (ice and roller), tennis, mountain climbing, golf, etc. Fencers generally are good automobile drivers. A medical committee has recommended fencing for aircraft pilots because it trains peripheral vision, depth perception, and increases the speed and accuracy of decisive reactions.

Training for fencing should have some improving effect on those activities in which you must move around irregularly on your feet, control your balance, and co-ordinate a variety of movements.

Exercising when you are healthy is said to help you stay healthy. Fencing certainly won't cure a deficiency such as nearsightedness or astigmatism, or correct a skeletal deformity or an old injury. It can't overcome an organic disease when you've got one. But fencing may help you develop greater resistance to disease, and exercise is often prescribed to speed recovery from illness or injury.

Fencing may help to improve your over-all performance, making up for so-called handicaps.

From time to time you may get stale in fencing, and for a change you can profit from bicycle riding, soccer, dancing, swimming, volleyball, handball, games played with paddles or rackets, etc.

In Chapter 12 I mention training for more advanced fencers. But before going into work at the next higher level, you should have a good grasp of fundamentals, and a good start on your conditioning.

NUTRITION

When coaches emphasize hard work as the key to success, they make it easy for the student to overlook the importance of good nutrition. In most cases, even those fencers who are on college varsity teams do not eat at a training table. It is impossible for a coach to follow his athletes around and force them to eat some things and prevent them from eating others. This is another area in which you have to do it yourself.

If you started fencing as an aid to reducing, for example, all the exercise you could do would not take off much, if any, excess weight. You are simply taking in more food than you're using, and the excess is being stored as fat. Or, possibly, your body is loaded to a great extent with fluid. You would really have to exercise pretty hard for most of the day to achieve a very noticeable loss of weight.

People in this situation hate the word *diet*. They have *tried* dieting. Dieting means not eating enough to keep those hunger pangs away; it means not eating the stuff you like; it means eating stuff you don't like. Right? Well, it needn't be. Food that is good for you can and should taste good.

Most likely, along with eating too much, people who are very overweight have pretty strong habits: There are a number of foods for which they have great cravings, and a number that they very much dislike. Usually, their favorite foods are not as good, nutritionally, as the less-favored or hated ones.

Maybe you've started skipping over this. You're skinny and energetic, you can eat as much as you want of anything you like and never gain weight. Nevertheless, at the end of a long day's fencing tournament you might poop out or simply "lose the edge" and wind up without a medal instead of first. Championship quality (peak physical condition combined with skill) takes several years to build. Eventually you might come to the time when your technical ability and wisdom could take you to the finals of the highest competitions, only to miss out by *one touch* in each of two or three crucial bouts, perhaps because of a nutritional deficiency or imbalance.

Even though you fence for recreation and to help yourself stay healthy in the ordinary way, you would be better off to eat high-quality food. If you have athletic ambitions, you should be even more careful. Your body uses up food not only for energy, but for repairs and replacement of worn parts (cells of brain, bone, muscle, tendon, etc.).

The different types of food you need are called proteins, starches (or sugars), fats, vitamins, and minerals. You might be able to get all of these out of one food, such as potatoes (skins and all), but in order to get *enough* of one essential factor, you would have to eat a tremendous amount, thus taking in a great excess of some other element. You would be what most Americans are: overfed and malnourished. The body is a marvelously adaptable organism, and you could go along this way for years before you started to break down.

Proteins, which are made up of amino acids, are used to a very great extent to provide the materials for growth, repair, and replacement. They are also used as sources of energy, as your body is capable of converting them into sugars. People who are physically active need a very good supply of this type of food. The sources are: meat, fish, poultry, eggs, milk, cheese, yogurt, beans, squash, etc.; generally, the vegetable sources are not as high in protein content. You would need the equivalent of a quart of milk a day or more, especially if you have not yet reached your full growth.

Very probably you now have a habit of eating far too much of the starches, especially those that have been refined so that they have hardly any other nutritive value, such as white bread, white sugar, white rice, potatoes, pastry, candy, and so forth. This is all energy food, but if you don't burn it up as fuel—and as I said earlier that would take a good deal more activity than our civilized world provides—your body converts it to fat for storage.

Some fat is necessary for your body to work properly, but here again, you most likely get more than enough in your meat, poultry, milk, butter, and cheese.

Vitamins and minerals should come along with your regular food, provided you eat a variety of vegetables, fruits, and so forth. Vitamins and minerals are needed to combine with the proteins, starches, and fats and help them work most effectively. Food processing—making it white, making it soft, making it pretty, fixing it so it will keep longer in storage—unfortunately often takes out some of the vitamins and minerals.

As an athlete or just as a person who wants to feel better, look better, and perform better, suppose you decide to change a few of your eating habits. You would want to get proportionately more protein, less starch, less animal fat, and an adequate supply of vitamins, minerals, and other factors. The best meat of all, from a nutritional point of view, is liver; I'm sorry about that, but maybe you're the victim of somebody who didn't cook it nicely (try soaking it in milk for a few hours before broiling, and dress it up with herbs and onions). Otherwise, eat the leanest meat available, and if you fry it, use vegetable oil. Cottage cheese is high in protein and calcium content, low in fat. Drink skim, low-fat, or powdered milk —these don't taste as good as whole milk, but can be made into something like chocolate milk by mixing in blackstrap molasses, which adds vitamins and minerals; remember that you need about a quart of this every day, mainly for the calcium which is important for muscle-function and strong bones.

In the starch line, you can make an improvement just by avoiding the white stuff: bread, sugar, rice, and potatoes. There is nothing really wrong with a potato, except that most people throw away the part with the highest nutritional value—the skin. Boil or bake, and season with margarine instead of butter or gravy. For deserts, you should stick to fresh or dried fruits, or have uniced dark cake made with unrefined flour, honey or molasses, fruits, and nuts.

An excess of animal fat comes in meat, milk, cheese, and butter. You can't avoid it completely, but do the best you can. Make sure vegetable oils (soy, safflower, etc.) are used for frying.

THE MEAL SCHEDULE

Part of the trick of eating better is setting up a proper meal schedule. Think of the fact that when you get up in the morning, you haven't eaten for, perhaps, twelve hours. Yet many people start the day with practically no breakfast. This often leads to a mid-morning coffee break with sugary pastry, then a fairly heavy lunch, a mid-afternoon coffee break, and finally the largest meal in the evening.

Although you may not feel terribly hungry, you should have a breakfast which, without being heavy, is high in protein: two eggs and a glass or two of milk, along with fruit juice and whole wheat or rye toast. This can sustain a good energy level, if you are in school or on a sit-down or stand-around job, for several hours. The morning break is not a bad idea, but should be the occasion for another glass of milk and a piece of fruit, rather than a sweet roll and coffee with cream and sugar.

Your lunch can also be very substantial, following the suggestions above: higher in protein, lower in starches and fats. Eat meat or cheese (or both), a salad and fruit, with more milk. An afternoon break could be much like the morning one.

The evening meal, assuming you are now going to be fairly inactive—sleeping most of the time—for several hours, should actually be a light one, if not the lightest of the day.

DURING A TOURNAMENT

You have a problem when you are going into a competition with enough skill to give you a chance to get to the finals. It is rather common for a meet to wind up eight or more hours after it began. You won't be fencing for more than about half of that time, if that much, but you will be putting out a good deal of energy in total. On the other hand, you know that when you have a full stomach, you don't feel very speedy.

First you must get up early enough to have an even bigger breakfast than usual, allowing an extra hour or so for digestion before warm-up time. This breakfast might include lean meat (ham or a beef patty), cereal, etc., in addition to eggs, juice, toast, and milk.

DON'T eat or drink between bouts! When you are thirsty, rinse out your mouth and gargle with cold water, but don't swallow more than a few drops. After your first pool is over, you can drink some orange juice or hot tea laced with honey and lemon juice.

Probably, after the second round there will be a lunch break. Here's where a lot of fencers lose the meet: they eat too much and they eat low-quality food, whatever is quickly available at the nearest cafe—a greasy hamburger, french fries, and pop. They are too sluggish for the next round, which is bound to be tougher than the last two.

You might gain an edge by taking along your lunch, supply yourself with perhaps two hard-boiled eggs or a sandwich of lean meat or cheese (protein, which is long-burning fuel), a whole orange or some raisins, and the fruit juice or tea that you've brought for thirst. On a few occasions I was able to find a soda fountain where I could get a malted shake with two raw eggs beaten into it; this was easy on the stomach and gave me concentrated energy food. In addition, eating this way takes little time and you can spend the remainder of the lunch hour resting, even taking a short nap.

FOOD SUPPLEMENTS

Quite a number of writers on the subject of nutrition advise the use of food supplements, mainly vitamins and minerals in the forms of tablets, capsules, or powders. Other authorities say that you *should* get everything you need in your regular meals, and that all these extra vitamins, etc., are wasted. The first group then argues back that much of the food available on the market today is lacking, for one reason or another, in these important factors.

Certainly you would be foolish to try to get by on pills, without anything else—just because you're trying to lose weight or for some other reason. Still, an athlete might need more of these condensed food elements than the "average" adult for whom the standards are supposedly calculated. In any case, food supplements are not harmful (if you eat well basically), they may do some good, and the cost is between about ten and twenty-five cents a day.

The minimum could be calcium and vitamin C, the first for muscles and bones and the second for several reasons: lowering the number of respiratory infections or reducing their severity, speeding up the healing of bruises, etc. In addition, you could take yeast and/or liver tablets for the vitamin B-complex (good for nerves), lecithin capsules (to help your body use fats), vitamin E (also for better utilization of fats, etc.), and a combination mineral tablet. Assuming you do get some of these nutrients in your regular food, you wouldn't have to take great amounts of supplements, perhaps 300 milligrams of vitamin C (100 milligrams at each meal), one mineral tablet, three yeast, three liver, one lecithin, 100 International Units of vitamin E.

Whether all this makes a great deal of difference is uncertain. Scientific experiments to test the benefits of supplements have been done with groups of people, but the results vary from person to person. You can try the program yourself—I assume you have been going along without paying much attention to nutrition, and without using supplementary vitamins and minerals—and if you don't feel much better in a few weeks (whenever your supply of supplements runs out), you don't have to continue. In my own experience, during the fifteen years I've taken vitamin supplements, I haven't spent *any* money on medical treatment for diseases; I've lost an average of about two days a year of work because of flus or viruses; I haven't had any antibiotics or other special medications for these conditions, and only take about one aspirin a year. Very possibly I would have been just as well off without supplementary vitamins and so forth, but in previous years I did suffer more from colds and the like. However, this is merely one person's experience, and it gives no guarantee of effectiveness for you.

Certainly I don't mean for you to think that you shouldn't have medical treatment. That would be stupid. You should have regular examinations when you are healthy, and you should consult a physician for high fever, bad feeling that lasts more than a couple of days, vomiting, diarrhea, and other serious signs of disease. Get proper treatment—early.

REST

With plenty of exercise and good nutrition, you shouldn't have much trouble sleeping. Sometimes you may have a "white night" when you can't get to sleep: a glass of warm milk may help; calcium is a natural muscle relaxer. For your own sake, DON'T take sedatives (and maybe get into that vicious cycle of having to take another pill to wake up). On that occasional sleepless night, rest in one of the postures suggested below, practice breathing, and get some worthwhile thinking done—go ahead and stay awake.

I believe you can rest better, "sleep faster," on a very firm bed, such as a three-inch foam pad on a plywood slab. This takes a bit of getting used to at first, but a soft, saggy bed will not seem comfortable afterward. The firm bed gives support to your spine and inner organs; it feels cooler in warm weather because you don't sink into it. You do move around quite a lot in your sleep, and on a soft bed you have to work harder to get up out of the hole. By the way, people with back trouble are usually ordered by their doctors to sleep on a very firm bed.

Now you should think about how to rest while awake. As previously mentioned, during a tournament you will have to be very active for short periods and possibly keep it up all day long. You have many opportunities for rest, and if you don't take advantage of them, you might use up energy while not bouting—energy that you could use later on. Here you won't have time to go to sleep, but you could still relax, if you are familiar with a few good postures for resting.

If convenient, lie on your back with your feet up (on your equipment bag or a chair seat) and your hands under your head—take a blanket to the tournament for this purpose, unless you're sure there will be gymnastic mats or something of the sort around. An alternative is to lie with your feet drawn up as close to your bottom as possible and sole-to-sole, allowing your knees to sag outward. A third posture is lying absolutely straight: try to go limp progressively upward from your toes. Feel like a lump of wet clay or warm butter, spreading and sinking into the floor. These are postures you can use in bed on those occasions when you can't sleep.

At lunchtime during a tournament, after eating lightly, you might get into one of these attitudes and doze off for a nap. You will probably feel somewhat stiff when you awaken, but a few limbering exercises will have you ready for your next bout in short order.

DON'T get cold! Have loose clothing to put on over your uniform whenever you have much time to wait. Even between bouts, you can drape a towel around your shoulders. A sweatshirt tied around your waist is very good for keeping your lower back and rump warm. Sometimes competitions are held on fairly hot days, but nevertheless the surrounding air is seldom as warm as your body (98.6° F.) and you may get cold. Better to feel too hot—and then refreshed when you unwrap to bout. This coldness might not lead to "a cold," but could be enough to slow you down a bit and put you in a hole that you have to fight your way out of. Start the bout as if already in the middle of it.

When you have less time, say a wait of two or three bouts in the middle of a pool, you can rest by sitting with your legs folded under (Fig. 7). In this posture your back is straight, your shoulders relaxed, and your chest open. You can remain alert, watching what is going on, and get up soon enough to loosen up your legs. You should practice this way of sitting so that you become accustomed to it: aside from doing the sit-ups shown in Figure 6, you could use the posture for watching television, reading a book, or whatever, until you can endure twenty or thirty minutes of it. If you haven't progressed that far, sit up straight on a chair, with your back and hands in the same attitude.

BELLY BREATHING

Most people never breathe fully. This is natural, as your body instinctively does not push out all the air, saving some for an emergency. Full breathing does have good effects, however, among which is relaxation.

Breathing in, try to fill up your belly like a balloon. Make sure your waist-

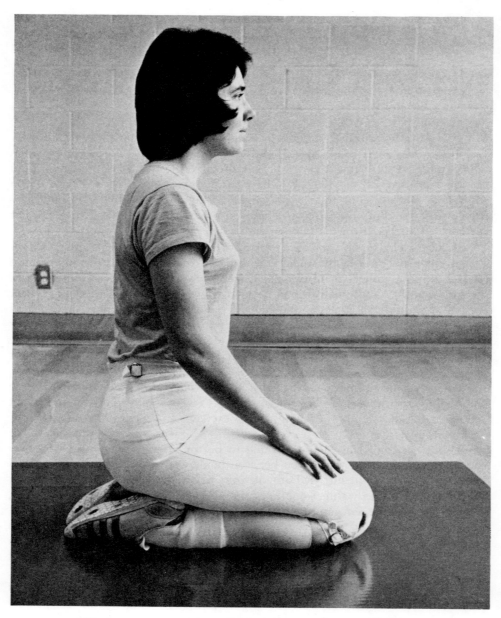

7. Sitting with legs folded under: posture for resting and breathing

band is loose so that you can expand your stomach and lower abdomen without restriction. Now slowly make your belly smaller and smaller until you are really squeezing to get the last bit of air out. At this point you might think you're empty, but if you form your lips into a small circle (as if whistling) and blow, you will probably find that you still have some air in your lungs. After you have blown it all out, relax your belly again, letting it expand slowly, and air will easily flow in through your nose. Repeat.

After a while, if you haven't been exercising, you will feel dizzy. Hold your breath for a few seconds when you're full and when you're empty. Try to slow down the inhaling and the exhaling so that each takes twenty seconds or more.

Belly breathing can be done in any of the postures mentioned above. If you don't force yourself to continue, you will change back to normal, unconscious breathing, but you will be more relaxed about it. You may fall asleep. Belly breathing for a couple of minutes can, on the other hand, get you "up" for your next bout: looser but more alert.

TRAINING EVERY MINUTE

Maybe you still think training to fence is a lot of hard work. But you can train cleverly, too. Budget your time and effort and concentrate on limbering-up exercises and skill practices (footwork drills). None of the exercises are "pure"—while working on flexibility or skill, you will inevitably develop more strength and stamina.

You don't necessarily have to set aside special times for exercise. One of the best exercises is walking. Another is climbing stairs. You should easily be able to arrange to get off your bus, or park your car, a few blocks farther away from your destination. You should easily be able to walk up, and down, a few flights of stairs, rather than take an elevator, or get off the elevator a few floors short of your destination. When you are in fair shape, you should go up and down stairs two or three steps at a time, depending on the length of your legs, in order to stretch and strengthen your muscles. When you are in good shape, you can run up—and down—several flights in this fashion. This everyday activity can cut down on the time you need to spend on warming up or specific work for leg power.

There are numerous opportunities for bending, squatting, twisting, etc., in your normal business. Use them. When you sit, sit with a straight back. When you have nothing to do, or want a moment's rest, breathe fully; eventually you will breathe more deeply, but more slowly, without thinking about it.

You might gain a good deal by merely thinking about fencing. Sit or lie at ease and review practice movements, combinations in lessons, or happenings in real bouts. Feel the event again. You can develop "muscle memory," remembering how a good action felt compared to the "same" move done inefficiently, stiffly or off-balance. You can also develop "muscle imagination" for planning how to deal with a particular opponent in a particular situation.

Fencing is an extremely varied game. Your training must be many-sided also.

Chapter 3

THE FENCING CLUB

You AND YOUR fellow fencers may wish to establish a fencing club. Your reasons depend to a great extent on local conditions.

In and around New York City, for example, there are many fencers and coaches, and numerous high schools, prep schools and colleges with fencing classes and varsity teams, along with programs offered by Y's and community centers. A broad scale of competitions is scheduled by the AFLA Division in addition to interschool and interclub matches. The new club should have no particular difficulty fitting into all this organized activity. The reason for forming a club might be simply a matter of convenience for the fencers of a borough or neighborhood, so that they need not travel so far for practice.

I am more concerned about situations that are not so favorable. There are cities where only one or two community centers or schools have fencing classes, or where perhaps there are very few experienced fencers altogether. Students might want to continue beyond the class or course offered, or the few fencers might decide that expanded activity would give them more enjoyment.

The purposes of a club in an underdeveloped area would be to spread the sport and to improve its quality in that locality. The club would be involved in furnishing instruction and holding competitions.

Let's imagine the worst—there are two or three pretty fair fencers in the town, and they aren't completely happy with exercise among themselves. They decide to offer instruction to build up a group of younger (i.e., less experienced regardless of age) fencers.

They first make an arrangement with a school, Y, or community center for a reasonable amount of space at a certain hour or hours each week. They must attract potential students by getting a notice in the newspapers, putting up posters in likely places, distributing fliers, perhaps getting mention on local radio or TV programs. Unless they are very lucky in finding a sponsor, students must buy their own equipment. This will limit the size of the class somewhat (publicity usually attracts more students than you can handle). Finally, the experienced fencers must dig in and teach a regular course in basic skills to bring the beginners up to the competitive stage.

Pioneering is always risky. Enthusiastic amateur coaches inevitably feel badly when a large proportion of students drop out. But if every effort is made to put across a simple training course so beginners can actually fence with understanding in a fairly short time (about two months), the activity will catch on. Still, it may take two years for the group to become solidly established.

Those who put themselves forward as instructors must devote a good deal of time and work to the task. Not only must they spend the hours in class each week, but they must study and practice among themselves to figure out methods of teaching. They have to be able to answer questions, spot problems, and suggest solutions.

They cannot be distracted by relatively unimportant matters such as imperfect execution by a student who is simply not yet strong enough or flexible enough. Perfectionism drives people away—students need to be praised for improvement, no matter how small, until they are far enough along to want to polish their actions. Once beginners have been in competition, even among themselves, they will be ready to start refining their technique.

ADMINISTRATION

Don't overorganize. When the group is still merely a class, no officers or committees are needed. When the group gets into outside activities such as competitions, it may need a president, a vice-president, and a secretary-treasurer.

The members will presumably see one another frequently at practice sessions, and very few business meetings will be necessary. The by-laws of the club need not be complicated, most questions can be settled informally, and special events arranged by temporary committees.

The most active committee is the Bout Committee. It schedules competitions, finds places to hold them, sends out notices, obtains prizes, assigns the presidents of juries, arrives early at the place of the tournament and marks out the strips, registers the entries, and makes up the pools. Depending on the numbers of fencers involved this can be a job for one person or it can be shared by several. Provided enough time is allowed, the task is not too hard.

Meets are the main outside activity of a club. Money is needed to buy prizes, unless they are donated, but they needn't be elaborate. Most often free space is obtainable. Entry fees collected, if any, are returned to the club treasury.

If the club engages in team matches with other groups, team captains may have to be selected. The captains are not permanent officers of the club, and captainship may shift from meet to meet. Since teams are small and the members are likely to have their own equipment, the captains merely have to get the teams together at the right time and place, decide in what order the team will fence, and negotiate with presidents, etc.

CONTINUING INSTRUCTION

Where there is a regular school class, students may want to have club sessions in which they can build on what they have learned. Most school clubs afford members the time and place for casual bouting. Here again there must be someone in the position of a teacher, although the instruction might not be so formalized as it was in class. The teacher could be the same as for the regular course and might enjoy the chance to give interested students more individual attention.

In the absence of a varsity team (more the norm than the exception in the United States), the club could form a team—supposing there was any other group with which they could have a match. Selection of the team is best done by intramural competition, so that the best three or four fighters, regardless of form or other standards, would represent the club.

The teacher, perhaps assisted by advanced students, should be able to bring these club members, who are voluntarily involved beyond the requirements of a course, up to a fairly good level. Should there be a better fencer or two in town, he or she could be invited in to improve the youngsters even more.

In the case of activity started by two or three advanced fencers working through non-credit classes, students may move up through beginner and intermediate courses into club activity. The club organization, or classes established in a Y or community center, will be able to obtain for its members special prices for direct shipment of equipment from the suppliers, an advantage over retail buying. The club, aside from having started and maintained volunteer classes, will be able to arrange meets and other activities. In time some of the new fencers will attain a good level of quality through club practice sessions and bouting with the original leaders.

COACHES' TRAINING PROGRAM

Enterprises of this kind sometimes bring about a considerable increase in fencing activity in an area. Two or more clubs may come to exist where there were none before.

A problem arises. Fencing can't expand beyond the capacity of the coaches available. Those who did the pioneering will reach their limits with a few hours a week devoted to helping beginners. The next step is to train more coaches.

Other commentators have claimed that the way to develop fencing in the United States is to have colleges establish training programs for people majoring in physical education, who would then be able to go out and start classes in other colleges and secondary schools. This is not feasible.

College administrators quite rightly do not see any sense in allotting budget, space, time in their programs, etc., while demand is low. The total membership of the AFLA is about 6,000. Physical education majors have little incentive to specialize in fencing when they will most probably not be called upon to teach it. The great majority of colleges that offer *any* fencing classes (perhaps 20 per cent of all colleges) have no more than one or two courses scheduled—introductory and advanced! Schools that already have fencing classes are reluctant to up-date their programs, either by fielding a varsity team or buying electrical foil equipment, and schools that do not offer fencing are equally reluctant to purchase the initial set of twelve or fifteen outfits.

Fencing must be built up by volunteers, amateur coaches. When there are several clubs in schools and community centers in a region, with a number of meets being held, persisting for a few years, then college administrators are likely to be impressed. Then, maybe, a professional instructor will be hired. Then, maybe, a college will certify a program for P.E. majors and minors.

Meanwhile our pioneer teachers are getting overloaded. There is no sense in putting out more publicity to attract more students. Now the leaders must try to get their advanced students to instruct.

Clinics. By this time the original band of teachers should have developed a pretty good, workable lesson plan for beginners as well as methods of presenting the material. The new coaching candidates will have been trained by these methods. A clinic can be offered, running for about four sessions of two hours each, to give the younger group a clear idea of how to go about conducting a class, how to work with an individual student on the simpler movements, etc.

In the coaching clinic on foil, one session can be on the basic sequence, the second on the disengaging sequence, the third on beating, and the last for review, teaching practice, etc. Since new coaches will deal with absolute beginners, these sessions need not go into every particular. The progression must be clear. An elementary coaching clinic can be followed up a few months later by an advanced clinic on secondary intentions, countertime, and composite attacking.

When these beginning coaches set out to establish new classes, the experienced leaders should try to visit them frequently. It is frightening to face a class alone for the first time. The older hands should be available for consultation.

Assisting. In some cases it will be possible for new coaches to serve for a while as apprentices, occasionally acting as substitutes when the regular teachers wish to take an evening off. Thus, the trainees can find out how problems are met in real class situations. There is no better way to learn to teach.

Team Instruction. The new coach, completely on his own, has a very tough job. A preferable arrangement would be for two or three to work together. They can switch around from time to time from leading to assisting.

Students benefit from this arrangement, getting two or more styles to practice against (no two fencers are exactly alike in size, speed, natural rhythm, preferred attacks, etc.). A team of coaches can also demonstrate with ease and can actually bout with each other to give beginners an idea of what more advanced fencing is like.

The meritorious service of amateur coaches should certainly be given some recognition. A cloth emblem for the sleeve of the fencing jacket, reading "Amateur Coach" (or something of the sort), could be awarded to those who have established a class or assisted for a month or so after attending a coaching clinic. A certificate might be given or the coaches' names mentioned in the club newsletter (which is a good thing to have, if the fencers in an area are numerous enough and somewhat scattered).

This system has growing power. Out of every crop of beginners a few should be willing to teach—or help—when they have finished their basic training. Those who first learned to teach in this kind of program can, in turn, supervise clinics and train a later wave of elementary coaches. Groups can be established in more places to increase the next crop.

The limit is the indefinable level of knowledge and skill of the leaders. At some point the number of people will become large enough to support a fencing master; a professional instructor. Even so, since the expert cannot work directly with more than a comparative few, the maintenance of a corps of amateur coaches will be essential. Such a system produced good results for fencing in

Japan, where the leading was actually done by a master who resided in America most of the year (the late Torao Mori) and the drill and practice was supervised by amateurs in his absence. In the United States, a similar program has been very effective with judo and karate, in which one of the requirements for the black belt is teaching service; probably there were no college classes in these sports fifteen years ago, but now P.E. majors can take judo and karate for specialties. I see no reason why the same shouldn't be true for fencing.

COMPETITION

Competition is the goal of training. Besides, interest and participation are greatly stimulated by meets. Beginners should get into meets as soon as possible, if for no other reason than to find out what they're like. If necessary, an original group in an underdeveloped area should split in order to create two clubs in opposition.

One club can challenge another to a team match. A club can invite other groups to an individual meet on its home ground. The host group must make the arrangements for space, officials, prizes, perhaps refreshments, etc.

On these occasions publicity for fencing can usually be obtained, more easily in small cities than large ones, through newspapers, radio, and TV. Spectators should be welcomed: announcements should state that admission will be free; seating should be provided, and some kind of guide sheet for spectators should be distributed. The presidents should speak clearly, with gestures, so the audience can get an idea of what is going on. Fencers who are not entered in the meet should be ready to explain the action to visitors. It should be remembered that spectators may become fencers or supporters of the sport in various ways.

AFFILIATION WITH NATIONAL ORGANIZATIONS

Amateur Fencers League of America (AFLA). Anyone interested in fencing can join the AFLA. The present secretary's address is Ms. Eleanor Turney, 601 Curtis Street., Albany, CA 94706.

Your group may fall within the area of an already organized AFLA Division. If not, when you have ten solid members over the age of eighteen, including enough over legal age (twenty-one in most states) to fill the offices of divisional chairman, vice-chairman and treasurer, you may ask for a charter as a new AFLA Division. This will put you in regular communication with the national governing body for amateur fencing.

Members are entitled to receive the national magazine, which comes out six times a year. The AFLA will also supply material on the Junior Olympic Development Program, on request.

You can then hold AFLA-recognized competitions in your area. Among these might be Qualifying Rounds for the National Championships. Qualifiers may enter the Nationals directly, or by way of the Sectional Championships.

National Fencing Coaches Association of America (NFCAA). Membership in the NFCAA is open to both amateurs and professionals. Those of you who become volunteer teachers might wish to join. The present address for information is in care of Castello, 30 East 10th Street, New York, NY 10003.

Contact with these national organizations may be helpful to smaller groups in isolated areas. Even without entering, fencers from your area might be able to attend Sectional and National Championships and come back with much useful information, especially in the form of motion pictures, as well as impressions gleaned from talking with top competitors and AFLA officers.

Progress in your own locality, however, depends entirely on you. The work must be done by your club or division members, and the results may not be immediately apparent. But I believe you will find enjoyment in officiating, teaching, and administrating as well as in salle bouting and formal meets.

Part Two

FOIL

Chapter 4

RULES AND THEORY

In CHAPTER 1 I discussed in broad terms the rules and theory of fencing and compared the three weapons of modern sport fencing. Now we can proceed to a more detailed study of the sport.

Review and take to heart the advice on safety given in Chapter 1. Imagine and look for every possible factor and situation that might cause an injury, no matter how slight. Avoid it before it happens. NEVER point a foil at anyone unless: (1) he is completely uniformed, with mask on, and (2) he *knows* you're pointing it at him—he might take off his mask at just the wrong moment. Know where the point of your foil is at all times: carry it either by the handle, with the blade pointing straight down, or by the tip; if it is tucked under your arm or slanted over your shoulder, you might poke somebody behind you in the eye. Don't fool around—fencing is a lot of fun but only if it's done properly.

The technical limitations on the foil are that the blade must not be more than 90 cm. long, the guard must not be more than 12 cm. in diameter, the length of the hilt (everything from the front of the guard to the end of the pommel) must not be more than 20 cm., and the total weight must be less than 500 grams (about 1.1 pound). There are specific tests to insure that the blade is neither too stiff nor too whippy. Usually the weapons and replacement parts supplied by manufacturers are well within these specifications: blades are a centimeter or two under the maximum; you cannot buy a commercially made guard of the full size, etc. A foil may weigh as little as ¾ pound (375 grams), considerably less than a loaf of bread.

The foil is a thrusting weapon only. When we say "hit" we mean that the foil tip touches the opponent's body with at least a tiny bit of forward motion along the line of the blade. If the blade slides along against the body, or slaps, there is no hit at all.

There are two kinds of hits: those that touch good target, and those that touch "foul." The good target includes the neck, the front of the torso to the tops of the hips and down the groin lines (forming a V), and all of the back above a horizontal line drawn around the tops of the hips. The foul areas are the head (the mask, including the bib, which must not be too long or too wide), the arms, the rump and the legs. These areas are defined anatomically, but in reality it is impossible for a judge to be absolutely sure about a borderline hit; in electrical foil, too, it is impossible for the current-conducting overjacket to cover the valid target exactly, no more and no less, in any and all positions. We must accept the judge's call or the machine's registration—if the electrical overjacket is obviously too small, the fencer should not be allowed to begin a bout wearing it, but if it is too long, he may accept the risk.

The foil strip is 2 meters wide (or may be slightly narrower) and 14 meters long (Fig. 55). It is marked with two guard lines, each 2 meters away from the center, and warning lines 1 meter from each end. (If there isn't enough room for a full-length strip, with some extra run-off space at each end, the rule is that the fencer may retreat 5 meters from the guard line and is entitled to a warning when his rear foot reaches the warning line, before a penalty touch can be called against him.)

Suppose you are retreating and your rear foot crosses the warning line. The president is required by the rules to call a halt, tell you that you are on the meter mark, place you with your rear foot exactly on that mark, place your opponent out of attacking range, and then command the action to resume. If you retreated very rapidly and went over the end line before the president could call a halt, you would still be entitled to be replaced at the warning line—no penalty touch should be awarded against you. After being warned properly if you go over the end line with both feet, you are automatically touched.

On the other hand, if you have retreated past the warning line without going over the end boundary but then manage to chase your opponent back until you are at least at your own guard line again, the original conditions are re-established. You are entitled to another warning if you retreat back that far—assuming nobody has been legally touched in all this running back and forth. Nevertheless, if you *don't* regain ground to your guard line, but only a few steps, and then retreat past the end, you are *not* entitled to another warning.

The president is supposed to call a halt when a fencer puts one foot outside the side line, and replace the combatants halfway between the side lines. Fencers often drift one way or the other, and it's perfectly okay—it may be good strategically—as long as they stay in bounds. If a fencer goes off the strip with both feet in the course of an action, he is first of all vulnerable to an immediate shot by his opponent, while any hit he makes after going off will not be counted. If no good hit has been scored, the fencer who has gone off will be penalized by the loss of 1 meter of ground (commonly, his opponent is advanced 1 meter).

It follows that if a fencer's front foot is already behind the warning line and he goes off the side with both feet, the above-mentioned penalty will put him behind the end line, and he will lose a touch.

The normal bout ends after 5 touches, and the time allowed is 6 minutes. There is, however, a provision for overtime: If the score is tied when the 6 minutes are up, the score becomes 4–4 (if it isn't already), and there is unlimited overtime for the deciding touch. If the score is uneven when time expires, points are added to *both* sides to make the score 5-something. For example, if the score is 1–0, 4 touches are added to the 1 to make 5, but the *same* number of touches are added to the zero, as well—the score sheet will show 5–4. Trick question on the final exam: How many touches do you have to score to win a foil bout? Answer: One, provided the opponent doesn't score any.

Fencers ordinarily have no way of knowing how much time is left in a bout except at the very end when the keeper of the clock signals the president that 1 minute of fencing time remains; the president then calls a halt and informs the fencers. The clock runs during action only. You can call for time out to adjust uniform, change weapons (you're expected to have at least one spare in good condition), or try to recover from an injury, but unnecessary stalling will be penalized.

In addition to the above limitations, body contact is forbidden; using your off-hand (left, if you're right-handed) to cover your target or interfere in any way with your opponent's blade is also forbidden as is ducking your head or raising your leg into the path of your opponent's attack so that he hits foul. Fencing is supposed to be a skillful game in which you lightly touch with your foil tip and use only your blade and guard to prevent touches against you.

Right-of-way is determined by the president, and you have no appeal. According to the rules, if one fencer hits clearly before the other does, that hit is "right," good or foul, and stops the action, blanking out any later hits. If both fencers are hit practically at the same time, the one who started his action first is "right."

That might sound simple enough, except that when you are a beginner things may happen faster than you can see or feel. You could very well believe that you started first and hit; against a very good fencer, you might not even notice that your blade was tapped out of line on the way. The president will see this, however, and say that your first movement was deflected (parried), and that your opponent then made a correct thrust without delay. Indeed, you will have made a single motion, as far as lunging is concerned—not breaking or faltering—but your blade did not travel in a smooth line because your opponent knocked it aside, lightly, and it then flipped back onto the target. Meanwhile your opponent started his point forward, so he is first *after* deflecting your blade for an instant.

There is one situation in which the foil tip does not have to move forward against the target. A fencer can extend his arm, blade in line with his opponent's body; then the opponent moves forward and pushes his body against the foil tip that is just sitting there; a touch is called against the opponent. In this case, the blade-in-line must be out there before the opponent lunges, or whatever. The blade-in-line is a potential threat, established before the opponent begins an attack by moving his own point toward target.

FOIL PLAY

Keeping the limitations and conventions (right-of-way) in mind, we can outline some of the basic possibilities and see where they lead us in actual play.

1. Either your opponent is close enough for you to reach him (or for him to reach you)—or he isn't.

2. Either your opponent is open—or he has put an obstacle in your way (a blade in line).

3. Either your opponent is moving—or he is standing still. And if he is moving, it's either toward you or away.

This sounds pretty simple. The trouble is, nobody has perfect judgment about how far away the opponent is, whether the blade is really in line, etc. Also, as previously mentioned, there is always a time lag between what you saw (1/20th of a second ago) and what is really happening NOW. Moreover, nobody has perfect self-knowledge about how far he himself can reach, etc. But let's pretend that you and your opponent are evenly matched in physique, in seeing ability, in reaction speed, and in the basic skills of fencing—he just doesn't know as much as you do about tactics and strategy.

1. If your opponent is not close enough for you to reach him, either move toward him—or wait until he comes to you—and attack. (You may also be moving or standing still, and if moving, either toward him or away, so you have to keep changing your estimate of whether you can reach him or not. The distance between the two of you will be different every second, or every split-second, and can change because of his move, yours, or both. Suppose you back up 3 inches and he moves forward 6 inches: The result is a net decrease in distance.)

    a. The manner of your attack depends on whether your opponent is open or not. If open, your attack can be "direct."

    b. When your opponent comes close enough, or you go close enough, but there is an obstacle in your way, remove the obstacle as you attack. One example of this is to wait for him to attack you, which would mean that his blade would be in line, aimed at you, and you could remove it and make an answering attack of your own (parry-riposte or time thrust).

2. If your opponent is just about within your reach but moves away before you can start your attack, chase him. If you attack and he runs away, chase him some more.

3. If your opponent moves toward you and you don't care to attack or answer his attack just then, move away. You aren't required to meet every attack he makes—you may avoid it, if you can.

These are not the only alternatives, and there are exceptions in every case, but it is good for the beginner to have an aggressive attitude and seek chances to attack as often as possible. The modern game strongly emphasizes attacking. In a lot of borderline decisions—aside from those cases in which the rules definitely give the preference to the attack—referees seem to call more often in favor of the aggressive-looking fencer.

I hope you agree that you aren't perfect. You aren't 100 per cent efficient, therefore you won't score a touch with each and every attack you make—some your opponent will jump away from, some he will knock aside, and some will miss simply because you aren't accurate enough yet. Also, I'm sorry to say, some won't be seen by the officials, or will be called wrongly, so you really need to hit good target perhaps seven or eight times to get five touches on the score sheet. Most likely you will have to attack at least five times, perhaps ten times or more, for every hit you achieve. That makes a total of thirty-five or more attacks required to win the normal bout.

This doesn't mean you should be stupid and reckless. Remember that time lag between seeing and doing: As the distance is BECOMING critical (close enough for somebody to reach), not AFTER, you should be either already attacking or keenly aware that you are inviting your opponent to attack you. Practically speaking, you should begin your attack an instant before you're in range, or else have a counteraction in mind. Watch the distance, practice estimating. Don't get too close—it's better to fall short on your attack, and be able to go on, than to overshoot (you would then have to use two moves, one to draw back and one to push your foil tip into target). Keep moving. Never sacrifice your balance or your relaxation for a chance of hitting: If you miss, you'll probably be hit before you can recover. Stay loose.

These and other strategic considerations have some bearing on your training objectives: to increase your reach, so you won't need to get so close to your opponent; to increase your mobility; to improve your accuracy, so your efforts won't go to waste; to increase your speed, etc. Training will give you several ways of attacking and deflecting attacks. This plus variations in timing, distance, etc., will keep your opponent guessing as to what you're going to do next. Don't forget, though, that he'll be trying to fool you, too.

Next we can examine the set of movements that should enable you to play a winning game within the requirements of the rules.

Chapter 5

BASIC SEQUENCE

THE EARLIEST PRACTICE for foil play should be done without the weapon in hand. You must think more about your foundation, that is your feet, legs, and torso, and the large movements of your arms, before you become concerned with how to manipulate the foil.*

First Position. The first position in fencing is simply standing with your heels together, your leading foot (the right, if you are right-handed) pointed directly toward your opponent, the other at right angles to it, your head up, and the palms of your hands turned outward (Fig. 8). Stand proudly but not rigidly. This position is also called "attention."

Guarding/Inviting. From first position move your rear foot a good way (at least 18 inches, for the normal person) backward. Bend both knees equally—pretend to sit on a stool that is exactly halfway between your feet (Fig. 9). Your weight should be the same on each foot. Raise your arms so your fighting hand (the right, for right-handers) is about chest high, the other somewhat higher, elbows pointing downward and bent easily. Your foil hand will be flat and naturally palm upward, on a straight wrist. This stance is called *guarding/inviting Sixte* (six) (Fig. 12).

It is important that your front knee, as well as your front foot, should always point foward. It is important that your torso and head be erect and that your shoulders hang naturally down and back without strain, not hunched up and bowed; your chest should be open, not caved in. Hips and shoulders must be level, and you should have no more weight on one foot than on the other.

A variation is to have the foil hand at the same height as the elbow or very slightly below it. We call this *guarding/inviting Octave* (eight) (Fig. 11). In both cases you should be able to stand with your leading shoulder touching a wall, your front foot and back heel against the baseboard, and the outside of the thumb of your foil hand also touching the wall. You will *not* be turned sideways

---

* In European training programs, *six months or more* may be spent on conditioning and foot-work before the student gets to handle the foil. I think that kind of program is largely a waste of energy. Students can develop form and stamina while they are really learning to fence. But we'll spend a couple of hours on fundamentals and keep returning to basic drills throughout the courses outlined in Chapter 11.

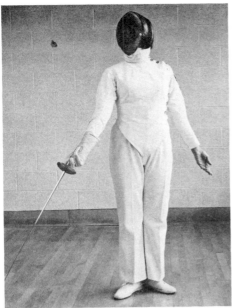
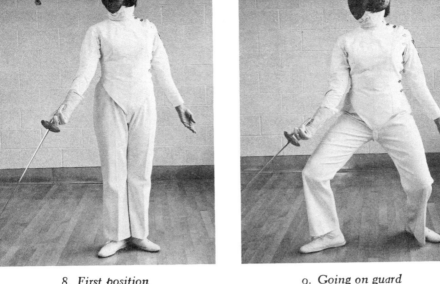

8. *First position*　　　　　　　　9. *Going on guard*

to your opponent (with your back flat against the wall). In good guarding/inviting, your chest will be at an angle of about 45° to the wall.

Very often these positions are referred to as "guards." Don't forget, though, that when you guard one way, you are still open to attack—you are *inviting* an attack—from another point of view, *at the very same time.* You should never hold any "guard position" stiffly.† If you are so far from your opponent that he can't reach you, you are not required to be in any special position—you can stand up and relax—but be ready to go on guard at any instant when he comes closer.

The third useful basic attitude is the *low invitation* (Fig. 10). In this case the fighting arm is down, hanging loose, perhaps as a rest from the other positions. You can move and attack, but you are wide open to your opponent's attacks. Keep in mind that in order to block or deflect his attack easily, you would have to take a little more time to move your hand up, approximately to guarding/inviting Octave or guarding/inviting Sixte.

Practice moving from first position to guarding/inviting Sixte, guarding/inviting Octave or low invitation and back. Practice changing from Sixte to Octave and from Octave to Sixte.

Advancing. When you wish to approach your opponent or chase him while guarding/inviting, move your front foot forward 3 to 6 inches, *no more,* and bring up your rear foot exactly the same distance. Don't allow your weight to go over your front foot. Don't drag your back foot—move lightly and quickly, but don't bob up and down. Don't take steps bigger than 6 inches. If necessary, take several small steps to get where you want to go.

Retreating. When you wish to go away from your opponent while guarding/inviting, shift your rear foot backward about 3 to 6 inches and then move your front foot backward exactly the same distance. Don't allow your weight to swing onto your rear foot—you may have to retreat again and you'll find that foot is stuck to the ground.

† The well-known command, "On guard," merely means "Be alert" or "Look out!" It is not the position that saves you, but your vigilance and ability to move.

10. Low invitation

Extending. Assuming you found yourself in a good situation to attack, you would first *aim*. From your inviting stance, extend your fighting arm, reach forward, and squat an inch or two lower (Fig. 17). Your arm should be right over your front foot and knee, but not higher than your chest. Keep your hand palm up. Don't throw or jab so that your shoulder hunches. Pretend that you are offering your opponent a dish, balanced on your hand—don't spill it. Don't lean forward; "sit" a little lower instead.

Sometimes you won't hit by extending, and you may need to *recover* your arm. From full stretch just let your elbow bend downward a trifle and you will be guarding/inviting. Don't jerk your hand backward and don't let your elbow tip outward. Keep your wrist straight at all times.

Practice extending and recovering. Then practice extending and advancing at the same time, and extending with retreating—remember to sit lower as you extend.

Lunging. Sometimes after you have aimed by extending, you might carry your foil tip to the target by advancing, but most often you will attack by lung-

11. *Guarding/inviting Octave*

12. *Guarding/inviting Sixte*

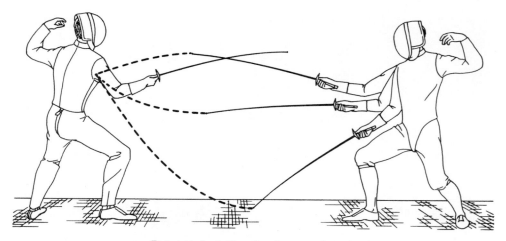

13. *Point paths in lunging from each invitation*

14. *Lunging practice: leaning*

15. Lunging practice: stepping out

ing. To lunge, start pushing with your rear leg, jamming the heel to the floor. Before your front foot gets pinned down by your weight, take a long step, leaving your rear foot in place. Your body, although it will remain erect, will *drop* forward. Your rear leg must snap straight. When your front foot comes down on its heel, still pointing forward, then that knee will bend until it is over your toes. As you lunge, your rear arm should be dropped backward above your rear leg, helping to drive you forward.

All this happens in a fraction of a second, as a single continuous movement. It's much faster to demonstrate than to describe, and you'll probably have to practice many times before your coach is satisfied.

Many books and coaches make it seem as though the first bit of the lunging process—after starting the hand forward—is to lift the front foot, toes first. This is *not* the way fencers lunge. As the body starts forward with the beginning of the push from the rear leg, the front *heel* comes off the ground, then the foot is flipped so that the heel strikes first at the end of a long step. It is a natural move, since that is what happens when a person walks: His weight moves and his foot rolls off the ground.

Lunging (first extending) is the key move in foil play. You must stand (guard/invite) so that you can lunge easily at any instant, and you must lunge so that you can recover. The slightest lack of balance control will spoil the whole

16. Lunging practice: finishing

thing, and your effort will go to waste. It is worth practicing carefully, smoothly, and patiently a thousand times.

Recovering from Lunging. Suppose you don't reach when you lunge, either because your opponent is farther away than you thought, or has retreated. Your recovery will be *forward,* to a lower version of guarding/inviting Sixte, with your feet farther apart than usual: Quickly bring your rear foot forward a few inches and let your arms bend.

Other books and coaches will tell you to recover backward. They claim the object is to get away from a riposte. The truth is that nobody in top competition recovers backward EXCEPT when he has lunged as a *fake.* A good foilist who goes all out for a hit can't possibly recover backward fast enough to escape from his opponent's riposte. And if the attacker *doesn't* go all out, he probably won't hit in the first place.

There are three possibilities: (1) He hits, action ceases, and he can stand up any way he likes; (2) he is parried (his attack is deflected) and he must expect a riposte, in which case he is much safer in good solid low lunge position; (3) his opponent retreats out of range without riposting or counterattacking, and the attacker would be foolish to give back the ground he has gained with his threat—he recovers forward.

So there's no reason to recover backward except, as I say, when you've faked. In that case you would have lunged very short; merely bring your front foot im-

17. Extending and squatting

mediately back to your normal guarding/inviting stance. But learning to lunge fully and recover forward will do you a lot more good. Eventually you should be able to lunge three times in a row at least, without wobbling or stiffening up.

Appel Lunging. This involves slapping the ball of the front foot on the floor. Thus, lunging can be taken in two short parts: As you start to lunge, move your foot forward and tap and immediately move it onward to the full lunge position.

18. Seesaw exercise: front hand will
swing up; other hand, down

19. Seesaw exercises: torso stays straight,
weight does not shift

The appel is not a stamp, and it isn't intended to startle the opponent—a good fencer doesn't pay the slightest attention to stamping or yelling. Neither should stamping be used nowadays to signal for "time out"—the president is most likely to regard it as some kind of maneuver. If you want time out, get away back out of your opponent's range or off the side of the strip and say so in a loud voice.

The usefulness of appel lunging cannot be demonstrated very well to rank beginners, but it does come in handy fairly soon. Refer to Chapter 8 for actions that might be co-ordinated with appel lunging. For the moment, let's say that appel lunging helps lighten up your footwork and leads into hopping.

Hopping.

a. Forward. In advancing, the front foot steps and the rear foot follows. In hopping, although the front foot is lifted first, both feet land at the same time. From a stance with your knees only slightly bent, hop forward a few inches on the balls of your feet, bending your knees more as you land. Don't jump up in the air—*drop* forward.

b. Backward. Standing with knees slightly bent, lift your rear foot and hop back, landing on your toes and sinking in.

Those are the main stances and moves—except for manipulation of the foil —that a beginner needs. They must be practiced over and over again singly and in combination: advance lunge, retreat lunge, hop-forward lunge, hop-back lunge;

20. Lunging: early phase

extending before advancing, with advancing, between advancing and lunging, on the hop, etc. The importance of this practice cannot be overemphasized. There are very few physical problems in fencing that can't be traced back to faults in the foundation—the stance—or errors in footwork.

SPECIAL EXERCISES FOR LUNGING

Lunging is such a peculiar move, and yet so important, that it may be worthwhile to approach it several different ways. The following practice methods might help you get some of the essential feel of lunging.

Falling Out. Stand in first position. Extend both arms, your fighting arm in the direction of your opponent. Pretend that your back foot is glued or clamped flat to the floor, and your back leg is in a cast—it will not bend. Now push your lower belly toward where your front foot and hand are pointing. Soon you will begin to fall, and you will have to step out to catch yourself. You should end up in lunge position. Notice two features: (1) Lunging involves pushing the hips forward; (2) lunging doesn't fight gravity—you don't go up at all, but down, falling into it (Figs. 14–16).

Seesaw. Stand as if in low invitation, but with your rear arm much higher than it should be when you're really fencing. Keep your head, spine, and legs absolutely still—don't shift your weight—as you move your arms in seesaw fashion,

21. Lunging: intermediate phase

22. Recovering forward after lunging

one going up as the other goes down. Swing your arms loosely and lightly. After three or four swings, follow the upward movement of your fighting arm by stepping out on your front foot, snapping your rear knee straight. In other words, lunge. This should give you the swooping feeling that lunging should have, and help you build the habit of dropping the rear arm back when you lunge.

Lunging should feel as if you are scooping or reaching upward, at least a little. In many cases your fighting hand may not rise at all (it may actually proceed straight forward at the same level), but it *feels* as though it rises because your body drops down. Your hand doesn't fly above your shoulder, your shoulder goes below your hand.

Now, remembering the feel of these two exercises, try lunging from low, from Octave and from Sixte. Be sure to start extending your fingertips outward ahead of your front foot. The lunge should be a smooth flow, led by your hand, When lunging from guarding/inviting Sixte, the upward swing of your hand would be very, very small—your fingertips would, however, be higher than your wrist (don't cock the wrist up).

Repeat these exercises a number of times in your early homework sessions, and compare with standard lunging practice. You will, of course, need to warm up. As time goes on and you gain better condition—more flexibility—you will be able to step out farther and lower, without bending the rear knee or letting the rear foot roll over.

COMMON FAULTS AND CORRECTIONS

Guarding/Inviting. The worst fault is for the front foot and knee not to be pointed in the direction of movement. Usually they turn inward (to the left, for right-handers). Check yourself frequently. Your coach will probably tell you dozens of times, but he can't be with you every minute.

Beginners usually don't have enough strength and flexibility to keep their knees apart and well bent. You must keep trying to get your knees apart so that, with your feet at right angles, each knee is over its foot.

Weight is often misplaced, more commonly on the rear leg. You must get the feeling of being *centered* between your feet.

The torso gets distorted mainly because the hips are tilted one way or another. Keep reminding yourself to sit naturally straight, as though on an invisible stool. Ordinarily, if you can get your hips leveled, your chest will be open, not caved in or pushed out, your shoulders will not be hunched up. Keep feeling for stiffness within yourself and turn loose. The easy way is very often the right way.

Make sure you keep your elbows pointing down (although your arms are only slightly bent) while guarding/inviting. The fighting arm, in particular, should not be held with the elbow tipped outward. Keep your foil hand palm up throughout practice.

Advancing. The most noticeable error here is that the beginner rocks back in order to lift his front foot and rocks forward when he brings up his rear foot. The step is much too large. If you take very short steps, lightly and quickly, you can avoid rocking.

With a short, light, quick step, the chances are that the back foot will not drag, an error frequently seen.

After just one step you may find that your front foot and knee have turned in. Other parts might have gotten out of alignment too. Correct yourself. Next time make sure that you step directly forward and do not lose your guarding/inviting form.

Retreating. Many beginners rock when they retreat, also. Take very small steps. Make sure your front foot and knee do not turn inward. Pick your feet up and put them down. Don't let your weight go back over your rear leg. Spread your knees.

Extending. The worst error here is that the beginner jabs stiffly and his shoulder hunches and rolls toward his chest. His whole arm tends to turn over—if he were balancing a bowl of water on his palm, it would be dumped on the floor.

This hard punching motion from the back of the neck often twists the torso around slightly, and the front knee tends to turn inward. Any so-called lunge following is likely to be poor, off-balance.

Another common error is to lean. The beginner *tries too hard* to hit, throws his weight on his front foot, often straightens his rear leg, tilts his hips, etc. You can't lunge well after that.

Remember, extending is meant for aiming at, not hitting, your opponent. Let nothing rush you, panic you, or tempt you. Extend smoothly, squatting an inch or two straight down, a hundred times or so, slowly at first and gradually faster.

Lunging/Recovering. Your arm should at least *begin* to extend a split second before you lunge and should keep extending until it is stretched. It should be straight (but never stiffly locked) before your front foot hits the floor.

The worst thing that can happen in lunging is for your front foot and knee to turn inward. This is dangerous in that your moving weight may result in a sprained knee. Aside from that, you'll probably miss as your body turns with your foot and pulls your arm out of line.

Another common fault is "pulling" the lunge—not lunging fully. The beginner seems to try to go in two directions at once, he nearly falls over, his body folds in the middle, and his bottom sticks out. You must practice lunging a great deal without the intent to hit, as though there were nobody there to stab back at you. You must not overreach (lean) to hit; *nor* hold back.

In recovering, first, don't recover too soon. Many beginners recover before they have lunged fully. Secondly, the beginner often tries to heave himself up to a regular guarding/inviting position instead of sinking more. The beginner may alternatively pull his rear foot too far forward and at the same time let his front foot and knee turn inward: He then loses balance despite his low center of gravity.

The remedy, of course, is to lunge and recover smoothly and *straight*. Go very slowly at first and don't try for a tremendously long lunge. Gradually work up to a faster, longer lunge, but still one from which you can recover—forward.

Appel. Don't stamp with your whole foot. Just slap the floor quickly with your toes in the middle of lunging.

Practice shifting your weight momentarily on your rear foot, extending your front leg, and patting the floor sharply with the ball of your foot. But when you really appel lunge you must not rock backward.

Hopping. Hopping is not jumping. Almost all beginners go up in the air. Practice by starting with your knees straight and suddenly bend your knees—try to pull your feet up while your body floats in the air—as you skip forward or back.

DRILLS WITHOUT THE FOIL

For general correction of faults you must simply repeat the moves while your coach or another advanced fencer comments on your mistakes. This practice will first of all gradually build up the flexibility and strength you need to stand and move correctly. Second, you will naturally find the most efficient ways of moving. Third, you will get the feel of the right movements and learn to spot your own mistakes.

Part of your training will consist of 10- to 15-minute drills for each hour of classwork. PROVIDED you have a good idea of the moves, you should also drill yourself outside of class. Homework pays off. Use a mirror if you can.

Blind. With your eyes closed, and either on the commands of your instructor or by your own decisions, you should be able to do all the basic moves. From first position, go on guard. Change from Sixte to Octave to low and back again. Advance. Retreat. Extend and recover your foil arm. Hop forward. Hop back. Extend (squatting), lunge, and recover. Appel lunge and recover.

Drill yourself on the combinations of footwork and the co-ordination of extending the arm, or changing guards, with footwork. You will eventually be able to do very complicated series of moves with your eyes closed.

Instructor: It will immediately be apparent that beginners look better with their eyes closed than with their eyes open. I suppose this is because they are more cautious and because without the distraction of sight they pay more attention to internal perception of balance, movement, etc. In combat, of course, sight is for observation of the opponent, and a fencer should never look down to see what his own feet and hands are doing.

A person who cannot stand up with his eyes closed is extremely rare and deserves medical attention. Among normal people facility in moving around while blind varies, but it can improve with practice.

Arms Behind, Blind. Fold your arms behind your back. Repeat all your footwork keeping your head and body erect. This drill should always be done with the eyes closed. It is excellent for balance. In fencing the arms should be free, and this drill will help you to control your body without using your arms for balance.

Silent. For silent drill you must have an instructor or somebody who will make moves to which you will have to respond, without being *told* what to do.

The instructor and pupil (or line of students) face one another. There is a certain space between them which should be kept the same BY THE STUDENT. Instructor and student go on guard. The instructor may then make one of the four moves: advancing, retreating, dropping his foil hand (or moving it far to one side or the other), or extending his foil arm.

If the instructor advances, you should retreat in order to keep him from getting closer to you. If he retreats, you should advance the same amount. If he drops his hand or moves it to one side, he is abandoning his guard completely, and you should extend (or extend and lunge, if you've gotten that far with your lessons). When he returns to guard, recover. If he extends at you, you should retreat, since at this stage you don't know any other way to avoid an attack—giving a little ground when attacked is not a bad habit for a beginner to develop.

Instructor: In this drill, which can be carried on for five or ten minutes with breaks for loosening up, use a variety of moves. In earlier lessons the pace will be fairly slow. You need to concern yourself only with correct form. Thus, students can begin to fence the first day: i.e., you will try to confuse them with an unpredictable series of moves, and they try to win the game by responding perfectly.

If, for example, when you extend and they also extend or advance or fail to retreat fairly soon, they have obviously lost; if you drop your hand and they do not extend (they often imitate by dropping their hands too), they know immediately that they have made a wrong response and have missed an opportunity to attack.

BASIC MOVEMENTS WITH THE FOIL

Holding the Foil. Your weapon should be held very lightly and loosely, cupped in your hand as if you were holding an egg—still in the shell but uncooked. You'll make a mess if you crush it. The manner of holding each of the two recommended grips, the Cetrulo (Hern style, or "Spanish offset") and the French, is shown in Figures 25 and 26. Your thumb should touch the pad inside the guard. Your wrist must be STRAIGHT! The pommel or butt end of the weapon should lightly touch your forearm.

The rules of fencing call for an attachment around the hand to keep the weapon from being cast among the bystanders by a strong action of an opponent's blade. The thong shown in Figures 23–25 meets this requirement and gives support as well, allowing you to use more delicate fingerwork. It should not, however, be too tight.

The shank of the French blade should also be bent so that the weapon will line up naturally with your forearm. This is described and illustrated in the chapter on teaching (Chapter 11).

First Position. When you stand in first position (attention) your foil arm, which remains straight, must be lifted slightly to keep the foil tip off the floor. Otherwise, first position is as previously described.

When you also have a mask, it will be held in the other hand, preferably with the mask face toward your chest and the bib upward, with your fingers around the mask tongue.

Saluting. Keeping first position except for the movements of your foil arm, raise your arm to point at your opponent, partner, or instructor. Then bend your elbow, bringing the guard of your foil to your chin (your forearm and blade should be vertical). Finally, swing your foil tip downward until you are in first position again. If you are not engaged in a formal bout, you will then put on your mask by sticking your chin into it and pulling the tongue back over your head (make sure the bib is pulled down over your throat before going on guard).

In a formal bout saluting is expanded from three moves to nine. After saluting your opponent turn slightly to the left (unless you are left-handed; then to the right) and salute the officials and spectators on that side, then salute to the right, and finally your opponent again.

There is no particular "right" way of saluting. There is no need to make it flashy or elaborate. The idea is to show respect for your opponent and the people watching, as well as respect for yourself—therefore the "wrong" way is to be sloppy, to stand in a slouch with your feet apart, to wave your foil around haphazardly or, worst of all, to neglect to salute. If you fail to salute neatly in the presence of a fencing master or a president, you're likely to get a sharp reprimand.

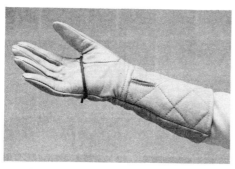

23. *Thong around hand to aid in holding French foil*

24. *French foil through loop of thong*

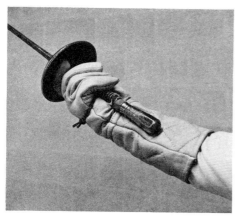

25. *Holding French foil*

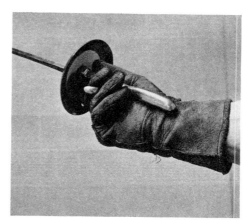

26. *Holding Cetrulo (Hern style) foil*

At the end of a lesson or practice session remove your mask, again salute your teacher or partner, disarm yourself, and shake hands. At the end of a formal bout you must salute as previously described for the beginning of such a bout, before shaking hands.

The rest of the postures and actions will be the same with the foil as without it. Just remember to keep a very light grip and a straight wrist.

COMMON FAULTS AND CORRECTIONS

Check your guarding/inviting again by standing next to a wall. Your foil tip should touch the wall, whether in Sixte, Octave, or low.

Your instructor will undoubtedly keep reminding you about a "broken" wrist and a tight grip. You must remind yourself, too, until you get the feel of holding the foil easily and naturally while you perform the other movements.

Instructor: At this stage many of the earlier mistakes will reappear. The pupil becomes fascinated by the weapon, worries about it and clutches it, wants to punch with it, etc. Tension seems to spread from the hand to the shoulders and all over. Use a bit of drill without the foil (blind, arms-behind blind, and silent) again, and a good deal of blind drill with the foil. The fundamental postures and movements are not automatic yet by any means and require continual practice. This work will pay off later. If at all possible, students should have a chance to observe advanced fencers with good form practicing and bouting so that the goal of light, smooth, controlled action is realized.

SIMPLE DIRECT ATTACKING

The teacher is in a sense a "dummy" who presents certain uncomplicated (at first) situations to which the pupil must respond. The teacher also points out mistakes, and gives praise when moves are made correctly or are getting better. You simply can't learn to fence without the aid of another fencer who is considerably advanced.

The term "simple direct attacking" refers to moves in which the foil tip travels by a straight line (or a smooth curve in one plane) to the target. A simple direct attack takes *one* move. There are just three simple direct attacks: extending alone, extending and advancing simultaneously, and extending and lunging in a single continuous action. Each of these can be done from low, Octave, or Sixte.

You need two conditions in order to be able to make a simple direct attack: (1) Your opponent must be close enough, and (2) he must be wide open. Look for this situation and practice attacking smoothly and promptly.

INDIVIDUAL LESSON

In the lesson outlined below, student and instructor perform their parts as in a play or musical duet. Most often the instructor leads and the student must make appropriate responses. The pupil should not be reprimanded, however, for hitting in good form by making an aggressive move not specified as part of the lesson: i.e., in B.1. below, extending and lunging instead of waiting for the target to come into range.

I. *Attacking on Favorable Change of Distance*
  A. Range: Extending plus about 6 inches
    1. Extending, Opponent's Initiative

Instructor	*Student*
Open	Guarding/Inviting Sixte
Steps forward	
	Extends and squats, allowing target to come onto foil tip

    2. Extending, Student's Initiative

Instructor	*Student*
Open	Guarding/Inviting Sixte
	Advances
Stands still (*fails to retreat*)	Extends, squatting

  B. Range: Extending plus advancing plus about 6 inches
    1. Extending and Advancing, Opponent's Initiative

Instructor	*Student*
Open	Guarding/Inviting Sixte
Steps forward	
	Extends, advancing

2. Extending and Advancing, Student's Initiative

Instructor	Student
Open	Guarding/Inviting Sixte
	Advances
Stands still	
	Extends, advancing

C. Range: Lunging plus about 6 inches

1. Extending and Lunging, Opponent's Initiative

Instructor	Student
Open	Guarding/Inviting Sixte
Steps forward	
	Extends, lunging*

2. Extending and Lunging, Student's Initiative

Instructor	Student
Open	Guarding/Inviting Sixte
	Advances
Stands still	
	Extends, lunging*

II. *Attacking on Opening*

A. Range: Extending

Instructor	Student
Blocking line of direct attack	Guarding/Inviting Sixte
Footwork, if any	Keeps distance
Opens line	
	Extends, squatting

B. Range: Extending plus Advancing

Instructor	Student
Blocking line	Guarding/Inviting Sixte
Footwork, if any	Keeps distance
Opens line	
	Extends, advancing

C. Range: Lunging

Instructor	Student
Blocking line	Guarding/Inviting Sixte
Footwork, if any	Keeps distance
Opens line	
	Extends, lunging*

Instructor: **W**henever possible, if you see the student making an error, such as hunching the shoulder before extending or moving a foot before starting to extend, step back out of range. Tell him how he gave himself away (telegraphed his move).

Otherwise, about one-third to one-half the time do not give the touch even when the move is correct. It is unrealistic for the student to expect to hit every time. He must learn not to strain, stiffen, and lose balance trying too hard, overreaching for another inch or two in hopes of making a touch. If he falls short, he must recover and try again.

This rudimentary lesson can be elaborated in several ways: (1) Occasionally extend at the student (as in silent drill), and he should retreat; (2) if he does

---

* Appel lunging may also be used.

*not guard properly, as though foil tip and shoulder were against a wall, attack
through the opening; (3) sometimes extend your foil tip outside his guard so he
will recognize that this is not a real threat and that he can attack in contact with
your blade; (4) extend at him and then withdraw your arm or shift your point off
line, opening the way for his attack; (5) by retreating, lead the student to lunge
two or three times in succession.*

*Lunging range is the standard, and for each pupil the actual range would in-
crease with practice. The student needs a number of repetitions, and often the
early minutes of an advanced lesson should be devoted to these simple direct attacks.*

BLIND LESSON

After just a little practice you should be able to take a lesson with your eyes
closed. The first individual lesson pretty much follows the silent drills, and you
can act upon what you see. In a blind lesson, when the line is not blocked you
will have to be told to advance, etc., to keep in range, but on the word "Now"
you should simply make the move—extending or whatever—as prescribed. When
the line is blocked you should be able to feel the blade, and the break of contact
will be your signal to go—you'll have to loosen your grip in order to be sensitive
to blade contact.

*Instructor: The blind lesson must be slower and less complex than the regular les-
son, but can be developed for practice of such combinations as hop lunging, appel lunging, etc. Again the student should not be allowed to hit every time, but
hits should occur more frequently than in a sighted lesson because the student
cannot know whether he has been short or out of line when he doesn't hit. Not
knowing what will happen, he must conserve his balance and relaxation, feel
whether his lunge (or whatever) is correct, and recover, waiting for the next opportunity. Command as little as possible, but mention errors in form: unequal
distribution of weight, hunched shoulders, and the like.*

STRATAGEMS WITH SIMPLE ATTACKS

Maybe it seems to you that simple direct attacking is *too* simple and
wouldn't succeed in combat. Truly, one of the hardest things to do is to hit with
a simple attack for this requires full development of your lunging ability, high
speed, and excellent control (timing). Beginners very seldom manage to do it.

Your coach will not have allowed you to start bouting yet, but you should be
able to understand the possibilities of hitting with a simple direct attack. These
"tricks" depend on footwork:

1. Suppose you see that your opponent follows you pretty regularly. When
you advance, he retreats. Set up a fairly slow rhythm. Then a change of pace, a
rapid advance or a hop forward, may gain enough ground for you to hit by lunging. But you must not make a jerky or jumpy move that would tip him off too
soon.

2. Given the same type of situation (your opponent follows when you retreat), watch his front foot, and extend lunge smoothly and swiftly just as his
foot starts to lift for advancing—he won't be able to back up until that foot

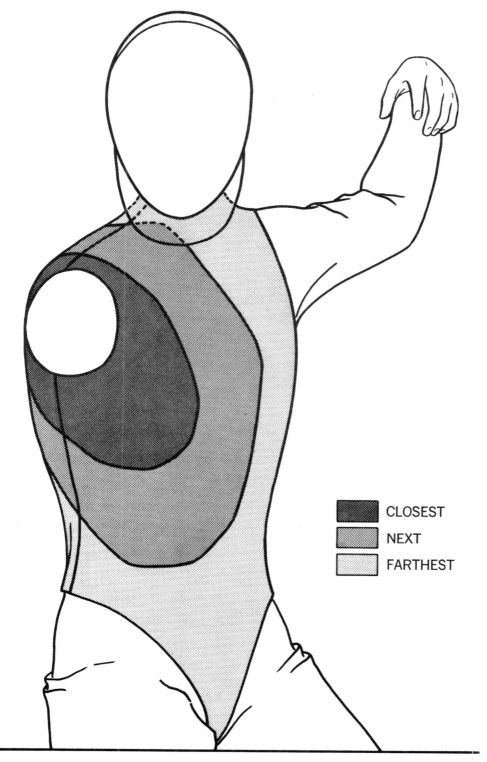

CLOSEST

NEXT

FARTHEST

27. *Target divided for preference in combat: closest area around armhole; next requiring two to six inches more penetration; farthest. Hits to back are comparatively rare, to the rear side impossible unless opponent turns*

touches the ground. For this trick, you need the footwork combinations of retreat lunging and hop-back lunging.

The second example is the best trick of its kind for beginners. Many of your opponents in your first competition will not be alert to how far you can lunge and will be ignorant of their own lunging range, so they will advance one step too far before they even begin to think about doing anything effective, such as aiming at you or beating your blade. Attack *just as* they move into your range.

3. Suppose your opponent attacks you. He extends and lunges. You can merely retreat out of range and attack as he recovers. If he has been taught to recover backward, the chances are he is *extremely vulnerable* at that moment. By advance lunging or hop-forward-lunging you can reach him. Your practice pattern should be retreat attack or hop-back attack, or to be complete about it, advance (to invite his attack), retreat (to avoid it), and attack when he breaks. (This, by the way, is Method No. 1 for *responding* to attack—simple, but difficult in timing.)

4. You may see that your opponent attacks by advancing clumsily (rocking) and lunging, or by lunging and then making an additional forward motion of his foil, jabbing, or falling. Notice that his foil tip starts forward, pauses, perhaps draws back, and then comes on again. He makes at least two separate moves to attack. Your basic action is to retreat—but suppose you *extend* and retreat at the same time? Then you may have your blade aimed at him before he makes his second move, and he may come right onto your tip. You'll both be hit, maybe, but the score should be against him because he was responsible for a double hit. His attack was not continuous.

Your action is called "stop thrusting." It *cannot* be done against a genuine simple attack because your extended blade must be out in line *before* the attack begins. As described above, the opponent made two separate forward motions, and the stop was done before the second. The stop cannot be done against a composite attack that doesn't falter (that is done, essentially, with one lunge). But it can be done against any attack of two or more moves when there is some break, hesitation, or lapse of time before the final motion because only the final motion is the attack.

Don't try it too often. The president might not see it your way.

NOTE WELL: In combat you must be alert to this fact: The instant you come within your opponent's reach without threatening, you *are* inviting. Your opponent might or might not attack. With a sluggish or suspicious opponent you may have to offer a great deal before he will attack. You may have to get dangerously close or show him a lot of target, or both (hence, it's better to do the attacking). Nevertheless, in every circumstance, it's better to know *you're inviting unless you're attacking* (provided the distance is favorable to one or both fencers).

THE IDEAL LINE

For competitive success it is very important that right from the beginning you get a feeling for "the ideal line." This is a line from your shoulder socket to a spot on your opponent's chest about an inch to the side of his armpit.

When guarding/inviting Sixte the ideal line usually runs from your shoulder through your hand—more exactly, through the point where your blade goes into your bell guard. You extend along this line. The rest of your body must be

28. The ideal line: shortest distance at the end of an attack

adjusted to make forward and backward movement of the hand on the line as easy as possible.

Another line, drawn through your rear heel and front foot, should be in the same vertical plane as the ideal line; that is, the line of your feet should pass under the striking spot on your opponent's chest. Your front knee also should be pointed under the same ideal line. This way your whole body will be aimed at all times, whether you are attacking or not. The narrowest movements will be needed when you wish to strike.

Your hand will move forward on the ideal line when you attack. Your foil tip will come onto the line, and usually you will try to hit that spot on your opponent's chest very near the shoulder seam of his jacket, the closest target (Fig. 27).

Depart from the ideal line at your peril. If your opponent is taller, your line will slant upward, and if he is shorter or crouches lower than you do, your line will slant downward a little. If you lower your hand against a taller opponent, he will have an advantage in attacking your upper body. A smaller opponent will be able to get underneath if your hand is too high, and yet you should not lower your hand too much.

Your foil tip will swing in arcs away from the ideal line and back to it again. For example, in guarding/inviting Sixte your tip starts above and to the outside (the right, for right-handers) of the line, goes onto the line when you extend, and lifts up and out immediately when you recover. Movements of the foil tip are accomplished often by finger action alone—but sometimes by finger action together with rotation of your arm on the ideal line as an axis.

When you lunge your body drops below the original level of your ideal line. Therefore, the line will shift from approximately horizontal to a slight upward slant. If your hand falls below the line, your foil tip will be carried lower also; you may hit foul on your opponent's leg or not hit at all. But even worse, you are in much greater danger from his counterattack or answering attack (riposte).

Should you wish to hit in the "low line," with your target spot just under your opponent's armpit, you must not tilt your torso forward so that your ideal line slants down. You must squat or lunge so your shoulder will be approximately on the same level as the striking spot.

While still a beginner you may have a chance to watch some advanced fencers at play. You will immediately notice that they do not always carry their hands on the ideal line—in fact, their hands may seldom be on the ideal line but above, below, or to one side. Probably, however, you will be able to see that when the time comes to attack, counterattack, or parry-riposte, their hands *do* come to the ideal line, and usually with *forward motion*.

After a few years of practice, even if they are never told about it, fencers develop an exact feeling for the ideal line, and although they are completely open (not guarding/inviting) most of the time, they are quick to try to gain control of that central line the instant there is an opportunity to attack, counterattack or parry-riposte. Precision and accuracy in this regard make the difference between a beginner and an advanced foilist.

PRACTICE IN COUPLES

In class, the instructor will have very little time to spend with each pupil. A great deal can be accomplished through careful practice by the class members with each other, starting with the simplest moves and situations. You really need to do the basic actions many, many times in order to have them at your command in future competition.

1. *Silent Drill.* Refer back to the description of silent drill (p. 63). This drill can be done in couples. Decide who will be the leader. If you are the leader, you face off with your partner, set a reasonable distance, 3 to 4 meters, and go into guarding/inviting. (The follower should use the three inviting variations, Sixte, Octave, and low invitation, an equal number of times.)

The leader has 4 moves to make: advancing, retreating, lunging (with recovering, of course), and uncovering (dropping his foil hand or putting it far to one side or the other). To these the follower must respond by retreating when the leader advances, advancing when the leader retreats, retreating when the leader lunges, and lunging when the leader uncovers.

The first objective is to keep the original distance. That is, the follower must not allow the leader to get any closer or farther away. The second objective is to take advantage of an opening by lunging when the leader uncovers. The third objective is to retreat out of range when the leader attacks—the follower should retreat at the first sign that the leader is extending his arm. This kind of practice will help you master a few of the most important actions in fencing.

Go slow at first. Both the leader and the follower should try to make the moves correctly, smoothly, without losing balance, and without needing to stop to regain good posture or distance. You should change partners often in order to get used to the individual style of different opponents. Practice should go on for about a minute before you break to loosen up.

2. *Drop-the-glove Game.* When you have been given foils, you can immediately start another practice that will help you to extend your arm swiftly and accurately the instant you get a visual signal.

Choose a partner of your height. Guard/invite facing a wall, close enough for your foil tip to touch the wall when you extend fully. Your partner holds a glove against the wall as high as he can reach above the point where you will strike. Tell him when you are ready. He drops the glove.

Your objective is to extend (squatting) and pin the glove to the wall. After 5 or 10 tries trade places with your partner.

You may not catch the glove once in your first ten tries, but play the game again another day. When your score is seven out of ten at full reach, you won't need this kind of practice any more. (If you catch it seven times out of ten right away, you're either very fast or you're standing too close.) A few fencers can catch the glove even at lunging range.

Instructor: Check once in a while to see that pupils are keeping good form and really stretching their arms.

3. *Timing In.* When you and your partner both have full protective equipment, you may practice against each other. One will be the "dummy." You will stand so far apart that even your longest lunges will not quite reach. The dummy stands in first position, lifts his foil from the elbow so the blade is at a fairly steep angle, and slowly sweeps it from side to side. At such long range the blades shouldn't meet. The active partner merely has to "time" the dummy's swings and lunge. The objective is *not* to hit but to *finish* lunging, blade aimed at the target, before the blades come together. The dummy then steps back and the active partner recovers forward. The action is repeated about 6 times—the active partner should be able to choose whether he will lunge when the dummy's blade is swinging from right to left or from left to right, and do about 3 each way. Then the partners switch roles.

After this has been practiced in its simplest form the dummy changes to large clockwise circles, moving his foil from the elbow, until the active partner has lunged 5 or 6 times. The dummy then makes counterclockwise circles.

Change partners as often as possible. *Don't* practice with your best friend all the time. You need to work against people of different sizes, right-handers and left-handers, people who are naturally quicker or slower, smoother or jerkier.

The dummy may mention any glaring faults he sees in his partner's stance or movement. The active partner should make a simple direct lunge—at the right time—and shouldn't be disturbed when the blades come together but should recover properly when the dummy steps back.

WARNING: The dummy must remember that his moves in this exercise are not suitable for combat. He should not be guarding/inviting. When two students practice with one another they must *avoid* as much as possible any situation in which the dummy is really practicing *to get hit*. It is one of the coach's jobs to make mistakes, as an advanced dummy.

Practice is just that—practice. It is not bouting. It is not free play or loose play. You need a lot of practice in simplified situations or you'll never be able to do the more difficult things. You should practice at long range so that attacks fall short (which is safer even when both partners are masked and jacketed) by an inch or so.

Instructor: Demonstrate practice in couples beforehand, thoroughly, and issue warnings. Circulate through the class when practice is going on. You'll have to remind students about form again because now that they are really facing one another, armed and uniformed, they will show all the old signs of anxiousness or eagerness. You will probably have to remind them to stay farther apart. Dummies may be swinging too fast or in an erratic rhythm, or may push too hard when the blades meet.

OCTAVE

All of the above lessons and practice will have been done from guarding/inviting Sixte. Use of actions from guarding/inviting Octave should be deferred a bit, then worked out as variations on a known theme. Individual lessons, blind lessons, and practice in couples will follow the same scheme.

There is no reason, of course, to imitate your opponent at any time. If he is guarding/inviting Sixte, you may use Octave and make simple direct attacks whenever convenient. If he is in Octave and you are in Sixte, he is open for a direct attack and you merely need to get close enough (or get him to come to you).

Chapter 6

DISENGAGING SEQUENCE

"ENGAGEMENT" IN FENCING means contact of the blades, and originally most attacks began with engagement. "Disengaging" thus means breaking contact.

Modern foilists rarely *engage* in the first place—they fence "open." Therefore, we now consider that a disengagement is a shift of the foiltip to threaten target by: (1) *moving* from a blocked line to an open one; (2) *avoiding* the opponent's attempt to engage, beat, or bind; or (3) *releasing* from a pressing engagement.

By disengaging you maneuver your foil tip over or under your opponent's guard to make (or maintain) a threat. You should definitely extend your arm when you disengage in order to avoid your opponent's attempt to "take" your blade, or when you release from contact. If you have already threatened him by extending (probably with an advance, or just as he closes distance by stepping toward you without threatening you), you would disengage to avoid his blocking move. Sometimes—you should not expect it to be very often—he will succeed in pushing your threat aside, but will *freeze*, in which case you can disengage without pulling your arm back.

DISENGAGING EXERCISES

Standing. In first position lift your foil hand to chest height keeping your arm straight. Loosen and squeeze your fingers gently: Make your foil tip drop and rise, down and up, about 3 inches. By changing the way you move your fingers you can make your foil tip go in *ovals*, clockwise, and counterclockwise. Remember these must be ovals, longer from top to bottom than from side to side, *not circles*, and no more than about 4 inches high.

Instructor: Stand before the pupil, about 7 feet away. Move your blade in this pattern: right to left; left to right; clockwise; right to left; counterclockwise (i.e., the traditional parries of Quarte, Sixte, counter-Sixte, Quarte, counter-Quarte). The student's task is to avoid contact by dropping and raising his foil tip or making (vertical) ovals. This must be done by fingerwork, not by moving the arm or

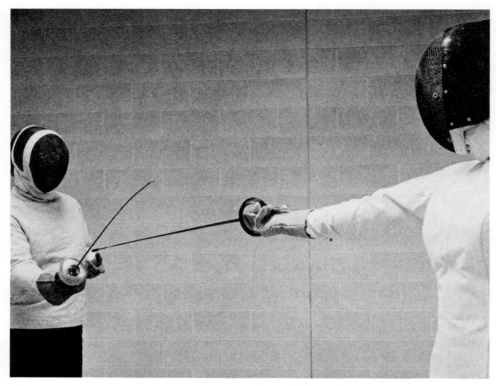

29. Disengaging exercise: blade in line

bending the wrist, and the student's arm must remain stretched. The five-move sequence may need to be repeated 3 to 5 times.

Sinking. Stand with your feet as far apart as they would be in guarding/inviting but with your knees straight. Have your foil arm extended and your rear arm in its usual attitude. As you make five movements with your foil tip—(1) down-up, (2) down-up, (3) counterclockwise, (4) down-up, (5) clockwise—sink about 1 inch lower on each move by bending your knees. At the end of 5 counts you should be in a fencing half-squat, knees well bent, and foil arm stretched out. Now lunge, and after checking on the correctness of your position, recover.

Instructor: Again standing before the student, who is in the starting position described above, move your foil in the five-count pattern while the pupil gradually lowers himself to a half-squat. If he does everything correctly, step back and allow him to lunge. Check his position and allow him to recover. The sequence may need to be repeated 3 to 5 times.

In Half-squat. Take your normal guarding/inviting position. Extend your arm. Repeat the five-count pattern. Lunge. Recover. Did you make any mistakes?

Instructor: Tell the student to go on guard and extend, aiming. Lead him through the five-count pattern. If he has done everything correctly, step back and allow him to lunge. Make any needed corrections and allow him to recover. Repeat 3 to 5 times.

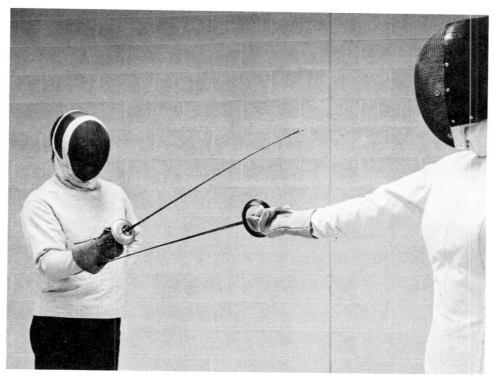

30. Disengaging exercise: dropping foil tip

SIMPLE INDIRECT ATTACKING

Like the simple direct attacks (Chapter 5) the "simple *indirect* attacks" are done in one move. The chance to make a simple indirect attack comes when your opponent tries to strike your blade—or if he has made contact, when he tries to push it sideways.

Your opponent is not attacking you. Remember, an attack is a movement of foil tip toward target (at a reasonable distance). His foil tip is not coming toward you, it is moving sideways. Therefore you need not be afraid. You have an excellent chance to attack *him*. You can take the initiative. The important thing is for your point to go forward—that is, for your arm to extend.

Deceiving an Attempt to Take. If you can see your opponent start trying to "take" your blade—to beat it or push it, or even to make light contact (engage) —you should immediately begin extending and dipping your foil tip. This action should avoid the attempted "taking" and at the same time start your attack. Depending on how far away you are, you may hit by extending only, by extending and advancing simultaneously, or (most frequently in combat) by extending and lunging in one continuous movement.

Instructor: Stand close enough for the student to be able almost to reach your chest by extending. Swing your foil from right to left across your chest. The pupil should extend, deceiving. Repeat several times with advances and retreats be-

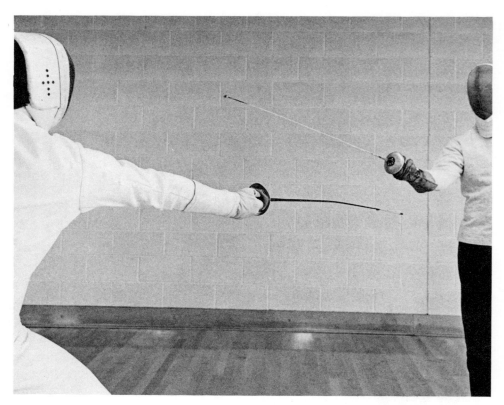

31. *Deceiving: extending, aiming at wrist*

32. *Deceiving: lunging to higher spot*

tween, moving your blade from side to side or in a clockwise or counterclockwise circle.

Similarly, set the situation so the student must extend, disengaging and advancing. Then arrange for disengage/lunging.

Releasing from Pressure. Suppose your opponent's blade does contact yours, either because you can't move fast enough to deceive or because you *let* him engage. Then there may be sideways pressure on your blade. Release, EXTENDING. Loosen your fingers so that your blade will slip under-forward-away from the contact and go on to threaten target, initiating an attack.

Instructor: Catch the pupil's blade with yours and press or bind. Change the direction of pressure frequently in the course of several repetitions. The student practices releasing—with extension—and should co-ordinate footwork appropriately.

COMMON FAULTS
AND CORRECTIONS

Upon seeing that his opponent is about to strike his blade, or upon feeling the shock, a beginner often flinches, withdrawing his arm. You should practice extending at the first sign of movement from instructor or opponent.

A beginner may also withdraw his arm because he doesn't believe he has room to disengage without snagging his foil tip on his opponent's arm or leg. This might be—but shouldn't be—true. Actually, you should be well beyond extending distance. Extend *first* and then disengage, for practice: The disengagement need not be so large in that case. Eventually you will extend and disengage simultaneously.

Another error is to avoid the opponent's attempt to take or to release from pressure without extending at all. The beginner is defensive, doesn't like anyone to strike or push his blade, but overlooks the opportunity to attack. Nothing positive is achieved. Keep your eye on target and aim at it whenever it is within range.

Again, upon contact you are likely to stiffen. You may resist pressure. Of course if you can see the attempt to take coming, you can at least *start* to extend and disengage. Even though you aren't fast enough to deceive completely, you will be releasing.

You must be as loose as possible in shoulders, arm, and hand at all times, and alert to the opportunities for attacking. If you aren't surprised, you will probably not stiffen up.

A very serious fault is to thrust hard. Your elbow will lock and twist outward, your shoulder will hunch up, your fingers will clutch, and your hand will turn over (thumb up). As a result, you will often miss even if you manage to deceive or release. You must practice slowly at first and achieve smoothness.

Your instructor will no doubt mention errors to you as soon as you commit them, but you should correct yourself and remind yourself until actions are automatic. The important thing here is to be *aware* of how it feels to make the mistake, and aware of how it feels to do the action correctly. Once you know the difference and have some success with correct actions, the bad habits will fade away.

BLIND LESSONS

The best general corrective measure is the blind lesson. When you have your eyes closed you can concentrate on being as loose as possible. You will then be more sensitive to light pressure. You depend on the instructor to tell you if you need to advance, retreat, lunge, or whatever, but you should be able to release in the right direction.

Instructor: The blind lessons must be confined to disengagements from pressure. Vary the sequences by applying pressure in different ways, at different ranges, calling for different kinds of footwork. The speed should be fairly slow, but a steady rhythm should be avoided, and there should not be too much repetition. The pupil shouldn't be allowed to hit every time.

PRACTICE IN COUPLES

It is possible for students to practice together, one partner taking the instructor's place in attempting to take the blade or pressing. This should always be done at long range so that most attacks fall short by an inch.

The dummy must be conscious of the fact that his moves are *not* good moves to make in combat. He should not be in fencing position (guarding/inviting), and must realize that his arm movements are wide and slow. He should keep well away, and not let attacks reach.

The active partner who insists on getting too close must be corrected, otherwise the dummy just keeps retreating. The dummy should mix up his arm moves, side-to-side and circling. He may remind his partner about basic faults in extending, lunging, etc. The active partner should stretch all the way out, lunging fully.

COUNTERING SIXTE

Now for a new idea. If a right-handed fencer is guarding/inviting Sixte and causes his foil tip to move in a *clockwise* oval, he is said to be "countering" Sixte. (The left-hander guards/invites Sixte as though a wall were to his left, and counters Sixte by making a *counterclockwise* oval.) This move is similar to one of the ways of disengaging, as you can see. If an opponent's blade is nearby, contact may occur. First think about how to use this movement in attacking.

Attacking on a Blade in Line. A blade aimed at you gives you a chance to attack.

Your opponent is no longer in any guarding/inviting position. His point in line is of course an obstacle that must be removed. That is IF you wish to attack, and if your target is within reach by lunging.

You do have a choice between attacking or not attacking. You may wait for some other situation. Just stay out of his reach and see what develops.

But suppose your opponent has his blade extended at you and is standing still. Possibly he is daring you to lunge. If you did you would run into his point.

A very poor fencer may have his blade aimed at you but with his arm and wrist bent. He just doesn't know what he's doing and doesn't realize that he is extremely vulnerable.

In either case, you must extend swiftly, countering Sixte at the same time, and continue right on into your lunge. You should have thus "scooped" his blade out of your way in the midst of your attack.

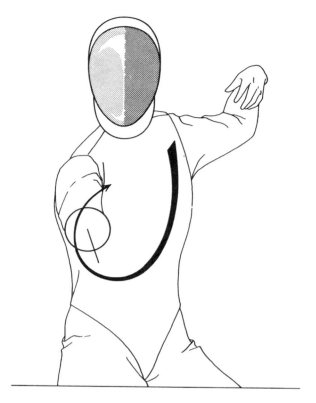

33. *Countering Sixte: your foil-tip path, if right-handed*

34. *Time thrusting by countering Sixte: early phase*

35. *Time thrusting by countering Sixte: finish*

We call this a simple attack since only a single move is needed (i.e., extending, twirling your point, and lunging, all blended together). It is an indirect attack since your foil tip can not take quite the shortest possible path to the target, but no time is lost. The essential movement is extending and lunging.

Instructor: Give your blade in line at long range. The student must reach out, gather it up, and lunge with his hand in Sixte. Allow the hit the first two or three times, then avoid about half of his actions by stepping back.

At a slightly later stage the pupil may be led to lunge, countering Sixte, 3 times in a row, falling short on the first 2. In such a sequence your blade is replaced in line by disengaging as you step back, and the student must counter-Sixte with his recovery forward to keep from getting hit.

Still later a more complex sequence can be developed: Originally you are open, and at favorable range the student makes a straight lunge, whereupon you step back. As the student recovers, you try to take the blade or (having succeeded in doing so) press. The student must then make an appropriate indirect attack (disengaging). But you again retreat, this time placing your blade in line. The pupil must counter-Sixte as he recovers and lunge for the third time. Thus, the student does all three of the simple attacks in a row: simple direct; deceiving or releasing; taking the blade.

Time Thrusting. Suppose your opponent attacks you. His blade is aimed at you and is coming toward you. I hope you haven't made the mistake of getting so close to him, or letting him get so close to you, that you have no time to react. *Extending* (squatting), counter-Sixte.

You should thus scoop his blade out of line, diverting it past your upper

36. *Countering Sixte: attacking on a blade in line, early phase*

37. *Countering Sixte: attacking on a blade in line, finish*

back as you put your own blade in line. He should run into your foil tip. You won't need to lunge or advance—so you shouldn't. Your opponent does most of the work.

This is the second basic method of responding to an attack. It is called "time thrusting by countering Sixte." It is classed as a counterattack* because it is done in the midst of an opponent's attack. It is not a *defensive* move because it strikes back at the same time that it removes the opponent's threat.

You should also practice co-ordinating this arm-and-finger move with retreating or hopping back, in case you meet an opponent who is very swift and has a long reach.

Instructor: Make a simple attack slowly, allowing the student to extend and counter-Sixte. He should begin his action at the first sign of your attack and must let you come onto his foil tip rather than leaning, stepping, or lunging. Gradually increase speed. When the pupil is used to the move, actually attack from a realistic distance.

Later you may check your motion before running onto the foil tip and step back. The student should lunge in pursuit, still holding the blade in Sixte.

At a more advanced stage, stop your motion and release your blade into line as you step back. The student should counter Sixte a second time, lunging. Thus, the student learns to act properly as the range shortens and lengthens.

COMMON FAULTS AND CORRECTIONS

These are *simple* actions and thus must be made in one move. It is an error to hesitate once you begin. If you have not yet learned to extend and stretch your foil arm smoothly, following up *if necessary* by advancing or lunging, you must continue your practice on those basic moves, co-ordinating them with the finger-work for countering Sixte. Make sure your foil tip starts forward ahead of anything else. You must extend and keep extending without stopping halfway.

If your hand turns over so your thumb is on top when countering Sixte, you will be much less successful. Practice carefully to counter-Sixte palm upward, loosening and squeezing your fingers so your foil tip makes an oval (actually a forward spiral).

You should *never* withdraw your arm as you counter-Sixte. For practice you might start with your elbow right against your ribs so you can feel more definitely that your arm goes forward while your foil tip swirls. Think of countering Sixte when your arm is straight, or almost so. The action is 95 per cent extending, 5 per cent countering.

BLIND LESSONS

Instructor: As before, a student will probably do much better with his eyes closed. Blind lessons in countering Sixte will be divided between attacking on a blade in line and time thrusting against an attack.

Start in engagement of Sixte. Tell the student that when contact breaks, the opposing blade will be coming in line. Tell him whether the blade will be merely

---

* The word "counter" is used several ways, as in the terms "counterparry," "counterattack" and "countertime." The other counterattack is the "stop thrust." Recently the term "stop thrust with opposition" has been used in the rule book to replace "time thrust."

extended and waiting, or attacking. Then break contact and give the blade. The
pupil can do the move, lunging or not as the case may be.

From disengagement you will have to say "Now" to inform the student
when the opposing blade is in line.

Blind practice can be expanded by stepping away from the attack or stop-
ping before you run into the foil tip on the time thrust. If the student is correct,
you may say, for example, "Your direction is O.K., but you're short—lunge." The
pupil should feel whether he still has contact, and if not, should counter-Sixte
again before continuing.

PRACTICE IN COUPLES

1. At long range the dummy stands and extends, aiming at the active partner, who must extend, countering Sixte, and lunge. Repeat 5 or 6 times. Then
the couple switch roles.

The dummy must not stiffen his arm, grip his foil tightly, or raise his hand.
The active partner must be allowed to make his move as easily as possible, although it will be obvious that the dummy could often block the move.

2. At long range the dummy lunges. The active partner extends, countering
Sixte, and thus executes a time thrust. Repeat 5 or 6 times. Then switch roles.

In this case, the dummy gets extra practice in making long, smooth, easy
lunges. His arm should remain loose.

Remember to change partners as often as is convenient. There is no better
way of getting used to handling different people in combat.

READY? FENCE!

You can now begin to fence.

If you could always do everything described so far in this book perfectly, at
the right times, and in the right situations, at your top speed, and could keep it
up all day, you could be champion of the world without *knowing* any more.

Since nobody is that good and fencing so simply would be dull, more techniques will be given. However, your instructor may now allow you to bout. Fence
regular bouts for 5 touches. If you and your opponent can't agree about who hit
first, or who had right-of-way when both of you were hit, forget it and continue.
Don't waste time arguing.

Remember the manners and formalities of fencing. Salute before you begin,
and after the bout is over, salute and shake hands. If you are hit on valid target,
say "Good." If the hit is on invalid target (foul) let your opponent know, and if
you're not sure, say so.

Don't fence with the same opponent every time unless you have no choice.
Don't keep choosing your best friend for a partner. In a class there are usually
plenty of other people available. You must have practice in figuring out exactly
when and how to move against adversaries of all sizes, speeds, and styles. If there
are advanced fencers around your school or club, challenge them to bouts. Fence
with them as often as possible. You will improve much faster by fencing with
better opponents. Seek out left-handers, especially if you are left-handed yourself.

Think over what has happened after each bout. Try to remember the moves
and try to figure out why you were successful in hitting, why you failed to hit,

why you were able to remove obstacles, and why you were hit. Use the explanation of theory (Chapters 1 and 4) to guide your analysis.

It's worthless to explain a loss by saying, "He was better than I," or "He was faster." The answer is likely to be, "I was too close," "I was too stiff and couldn't get started when the chance came," "I was off-balance and couldn't move the right way," "I telegraphed my attack by moving my body or my foot instead of leading with my fingers," "I was too far away," or "I didn't extend," or something like that. Then you know what to correct, exactly how to improve.

Similarly, analyze your good actions. Remember how it felt when you succeeded.

Spot your opponent's habits, especially his bad ones, so you can take advantage the next time you meet him. Remember, though, that he might improve—don't be overconfident. Make sure you too improve—preferably more than he does—by drills, lessons, and intelligent bouting.

Keep trying, in spite of your panic, to use the moves you have practiced. It takes guts to lunge fully and correctly—you will feel awfully exposed—but pick reasonable-looking opportunities and do it. Even when in doubt, do it. *Often.* That's the way to learn to judge distance and timing.

YOUR ATTACKS AND RESPONSES

The above lessons and exercises were done from guarding/inviting Sixte. Together with the moves described in Chapter 5, they give you three ways of attacking and two ways of responding to attack.

The three ways of attacking are: (1) simple direct (subdivided into attacking from low, Octave, and Sixte); (2) deceiving or releasing; and (3) countering Sixte against a blade in line.

The two ways of responding to an attack, *which you should have invited in the first place,* are: (1) retreating out of range (to attack as your opponent recovers); and (2) time thrusting by countering Sixte.

These, with many footwork patterns, give you enough possible variations to keep your opponent guessing. I would recommend that you skip from here to the next chapter to learn another easy method of dealing with an opponent's attack.

ACTIONS FROM AND TO OCTAVE

There are, however, a number of actions that also belong in this chapter: those that start or end in what we call the Octave (eighth) position and involve some fingerwork. You can deceive or release from guarding/inviting Octave, you can time thrust, and you can attack on a blade in line. Deceiving or releasing is fairly simple, but the other actions are rather subtle, more difficult to do than countering Sixte, and are, therefore, riskier.

Recall that when guarding/inviting Sixte, your forearm and blade slant upward a bit, remaining to the right (if you are a right-hander) so that your foil tip appears to be on your opponent's left shoulder. When guarding/inviting Octave your forearm and blade are approximately level, and your foil tip appears to be at the left side of your opponent's waist.

This would block his attempt to hit you in the flank—under your arm—provided his blade was on the right side of yours (which it usually isn't). Guarding/inviting Octave may disturb some opponents who will worry about what

38. Time thrusting in Octave

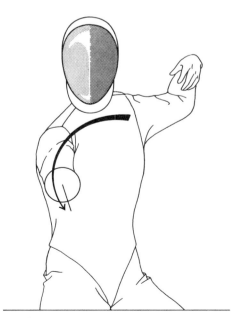

39. Sixte to Octave: your foil-tip path
from behind, if right-handed

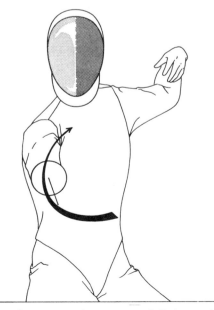

40. Octave to Sixte: your foil-tip path
from behind, if right-handed

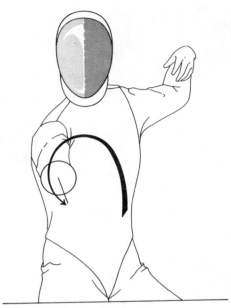

41. *Countering Octave: your foil-tip path from behind, if right-handed*

kind of attack could come from there. But to many it is an invitation to attack you in the high lines. You would be better off to think of Octave as an invitational attitude rather than a guarding one.

Simple Indirect Attacking. In attempting to press or beat your blade when you are in Octave, your opponent must lower his blade and will often lower his hand. You should already have had plenty of practice in deceiving such actions coming from different directions, and you should be able to disengage toward the opening target of his upper torso. Not much practice should be needed for understanding the technique required.

Roughly speaking, when your opponent tries to take your blade, there are only two ways he can go—clockwise or counterclockwise. That is, his point must travel in a circle, or part of a circle, one way around or the other. You can either anticipate which way he will go because you have studied his habits, or you can try to slip your blade through the tiny hole that often exists in the middle of the circle.

Time Thrusting, Octave to Sixte. When you are in Octave and your opponent attacks, you may move back out of reach and lunge at the instant he starts to recover (the first method of responding to attack). If you do decide to counterattack, *extend* and lift your foil tip in what appears as a half-oval (you might think of it as the second half of countering Sixte) clockwise (for right-handers) upward from 6:00 o'clock to 12:00. This should carry his blade to point past your upper back while your blade goes toward the ideal hitting spot on his chest right next to the shoulder seam of his jacket. His lunge should bring him onto your point. You will be extending in Sixte with your palm upward.

Attacking on a Blade in Line. Similarly, when you are in Octave and your opponent is merely standing there with a blade extended at you, you may decide to attack by taking his blade out of the way with a swing of your foil tip from Octave to Sixte. You will do this while extending and lunging in one smooth motion, so that your foil tip makes a long half-spiral forward.

Countering Octave. You can counter Octave by making an oval with your foil tip, up-down, counterclockwise for right-handers. This action, done while extending only, works as a time thrust, carrying your opponent's blade to point past your lower back. Similar fingerwork can be used to attack along a stationary blade in line, while lunging. Countering Octave is, however, quite difficult to do properly—successfully and without excessive effort.

Sixte to Octave. Now you can see that you could begin by guarding/inviting Sixte and time thrust or attack on a blade in line by making a counterclockwise half-sweep to Octave.

The Octave position is anatomically weak. If you try to parry or block, you may be too slow, your opponent may be able to force his way into your flank or, taking advantage of your stiffening up, disengage (deceive or release) to your high lines. You *must* extend while making these spirals or half-spirals.

Octave is a good position from which to attack. Your blade is not so easily available to your opponent at the beginning of your action. Attacking or time thrusting from Octave to Sixte occupies the ideal line; even though you don't catch the blade as you wish, you still have a fair chance of deflecting your opponent's blade with your guard.

Instructor: Lessons will be similar to those given before. Progress ought to be more rapid, since students will have more facility and understanding. Practice in couples will help bring Octave actions into the competitive repertoire.

Chapter 7

BEATING SEQUENCE

IN THE RULES of fencing and in discussions about the sport, the word "defense" is often used. I wish that word weren't in your vocabulary. Defense, as such, is useless. Think about it. If your opponent attacks and you merely deflect his blade, he will attack again and again and again. Eventually he will hit you, or he will drive you off the end of the strip, which gives him a point against you. Repeating this process, he will win the bout.

The only way to stop your opponent is to hit him first or with right-of-way. Therefore, instead of thinking of his attack as something against which you must defend yourself, think of it as an opportunity to hit him. Every situation in fencing, *within distance*, offers such an opportunity. His attacking you is just one of those situations. I have mentioned before that it would be a good thing for you to set up the situation so that he attacks you when and how you wish.

No matter how you manage to deflect your opponent's attack, you should not think of it as a defensive move that you will then follow with a separate move that will hit him. Rather, you must think of the deflecting/hitting as a single action. Train that single action into your muscles. You should be able to count, "ONE!"

If you hear or feel it as two, even as fast as "onetwo," you should spend some time practicing to get the blend. You have already become acquainted with an example, extending/countering Sixte as time thrusting, in which your foil tip travels forward in a smooth spiral, gathering up the blade and reaching to threaten all at once.

Unfortunately, we are forced to use words and a language structure that break up the continuous happening into unreal pieces. When you throw a ball against the floor, it bounces and rolls until the energy you gave it is exhausted. This is all one event, but in describing it we have to use a number of separate words, perhaps saying that it bounced this many times and rolled so far, etc.

Now I want to talk about a method of deflecting/hitting (or at least deflecting/threatening) which is a single action but which, for a while, I must describe as two. The deflecting part is called *beating*, a tapping or slapping motion that throws your blade across the line of your opponent's. The blades inevitably bounce apart. Just as you can pretty well determine where a ball will go when you bounce it on the floor, you can learn to bounce your blade toward target—you don't have to carry it all the way there, any more than you have to carry the ball to its ultimate destination.

Have a friend hold out his hand, palm up, next to yours when you are guarding/inviting Sixte without a weapon. (If you are right-handed, his hand should be to the left of yours.) Read this next sentence very fast without stopping: Flip your hand and arm over to slap his hand and unwind while you extend. Try it again. While extending, rotate your arm and hand counterclockwise very swiftly so that your palm pats his and then turns upward again.

Sorry about that—I could show you the move in two seconds, but it's difficult to describe. Now if you were both in fencing positions, he with his arm extended, palm up, and his fingers pointed at your chest, and you as before, you would slap his hand and end up with your arm extended, palm up, your fingers pointed at *his* chest.

This could be used for a reaction exercise. If you make a big move, your friend should be able to take his hand away before you touch it. You can't afford to take the time to raise up your arm or move it sideways—away from his hand—in order to hit his hand hard. You would also give his hand a push rather than a bouncing pat.

From another viewpoint, your hand and arm should move forward *along the ideal line*, rotating, with that line as an axis, a half-turn (from palm up to palm down) counterclockwise and immediately clockwise from palm down to palm up. Your arm must not swing away from the ideal line.

Duplicate this situation with weapons in hand. Your partner extends his blade at you from a suitable distance. His ideal line is alongside yours. Beating with the blades will be much easier than slapping palms: flip your blade over like a windshield wiper. His blade should bounce down to your left, and yours should bounce onward to aim at him. For convenience, I'll call this process "beating Quarte," but whenever I use the words "beating" or "beat" I always mean beating *while extending*.

Beating doesn't hold the blade away from you, as countering Sixte does, while you make your shot. If you don't threaten your opponent instantly—sooner than that, at the same moment, with the same action—his blade will naturally spring back into line, and you will have lost a chance to take the right-of-way. Very possibly you will be hit.

A second reason for beating, whether your opponent's blade was in line or not, would be to shock him, startle him, and make him flinch or stiffen momentarily. But he might not do what you expect. Your attempt to beat may be too heavy and wide, and give him a chance to deceive and attack. It is better to beat mostly to remove a blade in line—in particular, a blade that is coming at you. For the time being, let's agree that you will NOT use beating to lead into lunging.

To beat well you must first have a very loose hand and arm. Squeeze the foil handle sharply and immediately let go. Actually a large part of your body will share the work because your arm has muscles attached to the middle of your chest, your neck, and down your back, as well as to your shoulder.

In traditional terminology, this beating is called a "beat parry of Quarte," which is one of those phrases that fixes your mind on the *defensive* aspect of the total action. The word that should always be coupled with it is *riposte*. Functionally, there is no such thing as a parry without a riposte, and we should always think of parry-riposting as a unit. The rules define the parry as "the defensive action made with the weapon to prevent the attack from touching," but you must remember that what really prevents the opponent from touching you is touching him first or with right-of-way.

While on this subject, you may note that the rules mention deflecting the threatening blade, and although they warn that "mere grazing of the blades is not considered as sufficient," they do not otherwise say *how much* the blade must be deflected. Well, don't try to argue with a president or director about this loophole in the law. It is understood among fencers that a blade should be deflected enough so that it no longer points at any part of your body, and if the president says you didn't deflect it enough, you didn't, and that's that.

Neither do the rules say *how long* the threatening blade must be put out of line. The prevailing opinion of officials seems to indicate that any time at all, no matter how short, is sufficient, just so the person who did the deflecting attacks (ripostes) "immediately," without hesitation.

As a side light, the rules do mention a situation in which one fencer makes a composite attack and his opponent merely "finds" the blade on one of the feints. This *finding*—presumably *any* noticeable contact—is considered to be a good parry, deserving to be followed by a riposte. You might conclude that a very light beat, done very early in the opponent's complicated action, would be enough to capture the right-of-way. This implies that you would have to contact his blade while he was still quite far away, which is of course what you can do by extending/ beating.

What part of your blade strikes your opponent's, and against what part does it strike? That depends on how far apart you are, how nearly straight his arm is, how far your arm has extended before the blades come together—and I trust you understand that you would have extended some. The beat occurs on the way. But in any case, you can deflect his blade sufficiently even by beating with the forward third (nearest the tip) of your blade against the inner third (nearest the guard) of his. But make sure you don't beat against the guard itself.

(I must point out that this notion disagrees with the ancient and cherished "principle of defense," which says that the so-called "weak" outer third [*foible*] of the blade cannot "dominate" the so-called "strong" inner third [*forte*]. This is simply not true in all instances, although it is apparently so when the blades are considered as levers. You might say that a one-ounce weight would not make much impression on a man, but when the one-ounce weight is a bullet fired from a gun, it certainly will: The impact of the weight is greatly increased by its speed. The front end of your blade is light, and can be flipped quite easily. By demonstration we can show that a tap of the foible against the forte *will* move the threatening blade out of line. The beat must be followed immediately by, or better still be a part of, an attacking motion because the blade that has been tapped will usually come back into line and may hit. But the same is true with any parry. Finally, and most significantly, the beat is recognized as effective by competent officials everywhere and need not be hard, so long as it is sharp.)

After you have had a considerable amount of practice in beating/riposting, you should try to co-ordinate beating with a rapid retreat or hop back. This is not easy, as the foot-work may spoil the firmness of the beat. A good way to master this is to do the footwork first: Invite your opponent, retreat quickly the instant

42. *Beating Quarte, extending: attacker's blade has been beaten downward*

he begins to attack (or even looks like he might), and parry-riposte when he is in full flight. Beating doesn't take much strength and mustn't be heavy, but it is always sharper when both your feet are solidly on the ground.

Instructor: It is very important that the arm unwind fully after the beat occurs. If the student chokes his weapon when his hand is palm down, the riposte will be delayed, at best. The riposte may not get off at all or it may miss. The hit should be made exactly as though the student had extended in Sixte.

Notice that this way of parry-riposting sweeps the upper lines twice. Even if the beat is deceived—which is hard to do when there is no preliminary shoulder hunch to give it away—the riposte is made closing the Sixte line, and a deception should not succeed. But the student must practice following through whether or not the blades come together.

A blind lesson will be helpful. At the word "Now," when your blade is in line, the student should beat Quarte, extending (or extend, beating Quarte, if you prefer). Alternatively, you may engage him in Sixte and disengage into line. He must parry-riposte the instant he feels a break of contact. Later sometimes deceive his beat, disengaging to Sixte so he will be sure to close that line in riposting.

The intermediate or advanced student can beat with a retreat or hop back. He may also be allowed to lunge on the riposte in such a situation, assuming his retreat was actually what caused the attack to fail and his beat lunge is timed on his opponent's recovery.

In the past, instructors often spent several class periods in a row on a complex defense system, showing several "guards," parries from each guard position to every other, counterparries, sets of two or three parries in a row, etc. Drills in parrying were prescribed.

Students thus trained in *defense* were slowed down for months because riposting was taken up as a separate topic after all the parries were learned. In combat such students tended to freeze on the parry and could be hit by remises and redoublements (see Glossary).

Even if you adhere to the French or Italian or some other "school," you would benefit from learning one parry-riposte at a time. When the first and most useful, from Sixte to Quarte and hit, is pretty well absorbed, you can go on to the next, etc. An additional advantage of beating for deflection is that you start out *not* pushing or clinging to your opponent's blade.

Response-beating Quarte. If your opponent beats your blade on the inside (from the left, if you are a right-hander) and your hand is soft, your natural reaction will be to clench your fingers. This reflexive action can be turned into an answering beat with an extension. When two fencers beat extend (parry-riposte) back and forth, they are said to be "exchanging."

You must have some practice in beating back when your blade is beaten. You must extend, as always, and when your arm is stretched out it mustn't be tight because if your opponent beats again, you must be able to react quickly.

After the first beat extension the exchange may be continued for two more beats with arms stretched out. Your elbow will give slightly when you beat and stretch fully for each riposte. Notice that when somebody Quarte-beats your blade, it goes down and to the outside. Your arm will remain on the ideal line, however, if your hand is soft. Now when you beat in response, your foil tip goes upward (Figs. 43–44).

Instructor: Beat Quarte and threaten any spot from the student's elbow level up. The student should have a loose hand, and should answer with a beat (extending) done mostly by finger action. By continuing the exchange to 4 or 6 moves, 2 or 3 on a side, you will condition the student to avoid stiffening his arm and leaning forward. He should let touches come to him—there is a fine line between full reach and straining or overdoing.

COMMON FAULTS AND CORRECTIONS

Probably the most common mistake in beating Quarte is to move the hand downward or sideways (to the left, for right-handers)—off the ideal line. You should have chances to play around with the blades and see that displacement of the hand is not necessary and is wasteful: Moving sideways, your hand can't go forward as swiftly. You should also find that your accuracy is not as good: Having thrown your hand out of line, you must bring it into line again (throwing the blade out of line instead does not disturb accuracy because the blade, which is much lighter, is easily and naturally returned to line with the arm). Once you have proved to yourself that extending/beating is more efficient than your instinctive reaction, you can practice in different situations until your execution is automatic and refined.

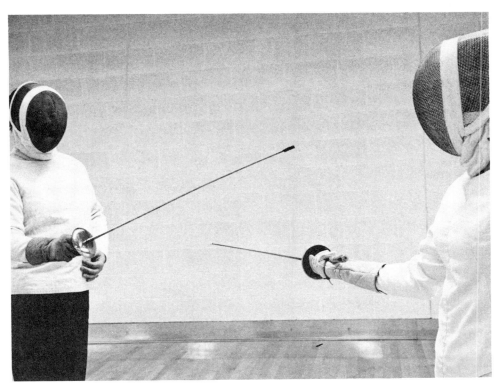

43. *Response beating Quarte: teacher beats*

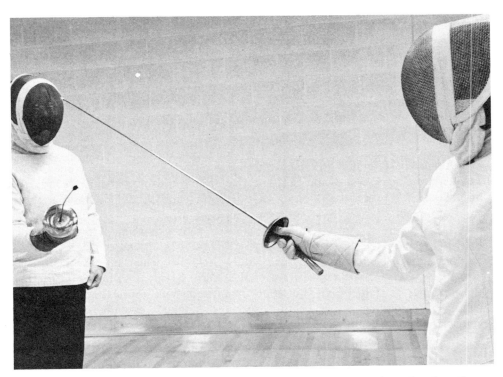

44. *Response beating Quarte: pupil beats back. Similar method to beating Quarte from Octave*

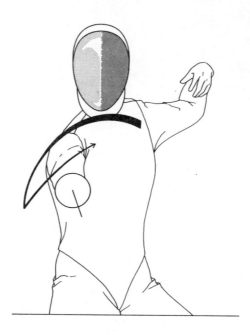

45. Beating Quarte from Sixte: your foil-tip path from behind, if right-handed

(The "classic" parry Quarte is done by moving the foil hand sideways. This is similar to an inherent defensive reaction: A person with no training whatever will very possibly parry Quarte just as well as a novice or intermediate fencer with several months of lessons who is startled by an attack in combat. He will push the threatening blade to point past his chest.

So much practice is needed to make the traditional Quarte parry-riposte work well that you should avoid the method altogether. Top competitors do not use it in anything like the way beginners are taught. Champions normally show that they have gone beyond their training, and parry-riposte by beating/extending.)

A subsidiary fault is to beat without extending. Beating force comes from a momentary contraction of muscles, one that should last only a split second. Your arm should flip over loosely—along the ideal line—and should be loose at the instant of impact.

The arm must unwind fully, completing your extension. Think of drilling the tip into the target by twisting clockwise (if you're right-handed).

Sometimes beginners jerk their hands backward when they beat, which is certainly negative. Another variation of this kind of fault is to freeze on the beat; the arm may start to extend but then doesn't continue onward and doesn't unwind. Try extending *before* beating. As your opponent extends, extend loosely, your blade alongside his, your hand palm up—then flip your hand over and back.

PRACTICE IN COUPLES

Parry-riposting. At long range the dummy lunges. The active partner extends, beating Quarte, the instant he sees his partner begin to move. Then the active partner retreats and the dummy recovers forward. After 5 or 6 repetitions they exchange roles.

When this routine has been practiced well for a week or so it should be done at lunging range, so the dummy will hit—lightly, on the forward surface of the target—if the active partner doesn't beat properly and soon enough. The active partner should score, but the dummy should also spring his foil tip back onto the target in order to impress on his opponent that hitting is the most important thing.

Both partners should try to get lighter and lighter. The dummy practices to do the smoothest possible lunge, without telegraphing. The active partner practices doing the neatest beat thrust.

Response Beating. At extending range plus a couple of inches, the dummy beats Quarte, extending. The active partner, extending, answers beat with beat. They return to guard and start again. The exchange may be prolonged to 4 beats, 2 for each partner—and the second pair of beats should be done with arms extended.

The dummy must be very relaxed and avoid giving any clue about when he is going to begin. The active partner must also be loose in order to respond quickly and lightly.

For a later variation the active partner could start by lunging directly, and the dummy could make a beat riposte (too far away to reach) to which the active partner should answer.

"Patty-cake." This is strictly an *exercise*, just for loosening your hand and arm. Neither partner extends or tries to hit. At moderate range they merely stand and beat back and forth a few times, agreeing on who will start. Obviously, the situation is not realistic, but some students get too excited by the routines described above and become too tight to perform well. A light rhythmic exchange at medium speed, with no threats being made, may help. Certainly it will build up the endurance strength of your hand, which has to squeeze and let go several times in succession.

Instructor: Demonstrate the varieties of practice, emphasizing lightness, good form, accuracy in aim (without straining to hit). Issue the usual warnings about protective uniform and safe distance. Circulate among the pairs, making the necessary corrections.

Remember to change partners as often as possible. Everyone is different. You must learn to fence with all kinds of opponents, and you begin by practicing with all kinds of partners.

Beat Lunging. Don't. Refer to the next chapter.

BEATING QUARTE FROM OCTAVE

You can beat Quarte as a parry-riposte from the Octave invitation. This part of the beating sequence might be deferred to the time when other actions from and to Octave are studied, but the action is similar to that shown in Figures 43–44. The situation might come up without planning in classroom bouting as you become familiar with the slight variations of beating Quarte according to distance, timing, and blade relationships. The same scheme can be followed, but the

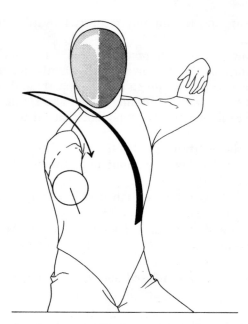

46. *Beating Quarte from Octave: your foil-tip path from behind, if right-handed*

work will be reviewed much more rapidly because by that time you should have a good deal more ease and developed ability.

With your hand in Octave you could approach your opponent or allow him to get close enough to you for an attack. Since you don't extend at the instant of this decrease of distance, you're inviting. As he begins to lunge, shoot your hand forward and at the same time flip your foil tip *up* and across. Your blade should cut across the line of his, and bounce onward to target (Fig. 46).

The normal blade relationship here is that your opponent's blade is coming in above and to the left of yours, if you are right-handed. However, if you are considerably taller than your opponent, you would have to make your "windshield wiper" swing in a big enough arc to beat his blade farther downward. Alternatively, if you are considerably shorter than your opponent, most of your Quarte-beats would be thrown upward—this also applies to practically all cases when you are stretched out in a low lunge and your opponent is still in the regular stance.

WARNING: Beginners get too fond of beating! This is what they thought fencing was all about before they started: banging blades together movie-style. Try to beat as rarely as you can, almost always as a response to attack (which you have invited) rather than as a means of getting a reaction. Of the three methods of dealing with an attack, use the retreat lunge about 20 per cent of the time (1 out of 5), time thrusting by countering Sixte about 40 per cent of the time, and beating/extending about 40 per cent of the time. Incidentally, of all the methods you use to score, you should probably try to use attacking a good deal more than 50 per cent of the time—perhaps as much as 75 per cent.

BEATING SECONDE

When you are guarding/inviting Sixte and your opponent attacks in a line below your hand, the choices available to you at this stage (assuming you have skipped over time thrusting from Sixte to Octave for the time being, as I recommended) are: (1) postponing matters by retreating out of reach or (2) time thrusting by countering Sixte, which works very nicely at good distance.

Notice that if you and your opponent have about the same length of arm, you can touch his upper chest while his foil tip is still a couple of inches from your waist. In other words, attacking to your low target is a longer way for him to go.

But you might feel that those moves which you already know are too weak or too refined. Perhaps you will discover that officials don't see things your way, and you will want to do something more impressive. Beating Quarte won't work because it only sweeps the *upper* half of your target. As an alternative, you can beat Seconde.

Beating Seconde is like beating Quarte except that your hand and arm must turn about twice as much, until your thumb is downward. Again your hand flips over and unwinds while extending along the ideal line. Beating Seconde should deflect the attacking blade to point past your lower back, and your unwinding thrust should threaten a high target. As before, the blades should strike sharply and bounce apart.

This action is not as easy as beating Quarte. You must be loose enough to rotate your arm all the way over—it is easier to do when your arm is extended. Start with your palm upward and shoot your hand forward, lightly whipping your blade over (palm to your right, if you're right-handed) and return on the twist clockwise along the line to the hitting spot.

It is very worthwhile to practice this maneuver without the weapon. Stand with a wall at your side touching your shoulder. Keeping your hand flat but loose, reach out and slap the wall and unwind to full stretch. You should hear two distinct sounds very close together, the slap of your palm and a tap as your thumb hits the wall on the reverse twist. Repeat this a number of times, sitting low in your stance and squatting an inch lower as you extend and slap. Then try the same kind of exercise with your weapon against a blade held out for you by your partner.

One thing happens in beating Seconde that is actually an advantage but can cause a problem. When you wind your arm up, your shoulder naturally rolls up and over (your elbow is not, at the instant of the beat, pointing downward). This tends to make your back hunch, make you lean forward (sort of folding in the middle), and makes you rise up altogether. You must not let this happen.

In the chapter on training I mentioned an arm-twisting exercise to loosen your shoulders. Now pretend that your tailbone is a spike—think about driving it down so it is stuck in the floor, and don't let it pull out. Keep your head up and your back straight. You should be able to stretch your arm all the way out, twisted over so that the pinky side of your hand is upward. It is much easier when you do it very lightly and very quickly.

The advantage? Well, you may still instinctively feel that you need to bend your elbow to make a defensive action. Remember that your opponent must travel farther to reach your waist than he would to reach your upper chest. Now

47. Beating Seconde

48. Beating Seconde: another view

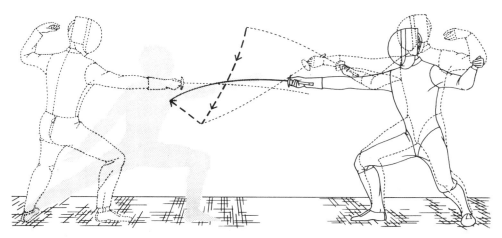

49. *Beating Seconde: foil-tip path from the side. Further penetration after impact comes from bringing your blade onto ideal line and unwinding shoulder*

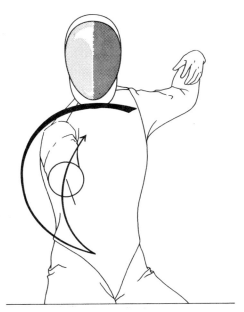

50. *Beating Seconde: your foil-tip path from behind, if right-handed*

notice that your straight arm is shorter when it is "upside down" than when it is unwound to the palm-up attitude. The difference is drawn up into your shoulder. Even though your arm should be straight by the time the blades strike, you do have more to extend—out of your shoulder.

As far as using extending/beating Seconde in combat is concerned, you should set up for it by raising your hand to a higher version of the Sixte attitude at the same time that you allow the distance to decrease. If your hand is high enough, practically any spot your opponent might threaten would be below your hand. Of course, you don't want your invitation to look too phony. Just give him a glimpse of your lower ribs, which are ordinarily screened by your elbow.

A good feature of beating Seconde is that it sweeps all lines *twice*. When done lightly and swiftly it can hardly be deceived, but if it is, your unwinding motion will almost always catch the opponent's blade (in Sixte). In this regard, remember to practice and practice to complete the whole action, WHETHER the beat occurs or NOT. If you beat hard, expecting that shock, and the other blade isn't there, you will swing far out of line and very often freeze. Either do the whole thing or nothing.

Instructor: Lessons, sighted or blind, would be much the same as for beating Quarte, except that the student should invite with a slight raising of his hand as well as an advance.

Beating Seconde is excellent for training, in that the foil arm must turn completely over and unwind completely. The "unwound" attitude is the way the arm should always be when extending in Sixte or Octave. By this time you should be into an intermediate course, but still a few students will be punching, with the thumb getting on top when they thrust. Making them turn the arm all the way over, thumb down, and unwind completely should cure that.

Used in a beat-lunge combination, as described in the countertime section of the next chapter, it should cure the collapsing lunge in which the student tips over, folding at the stomach and sticking out his behind. Practically all lunging should be done in this unwinding fashion, "screwing it in," even if started with the palm upward.

Inasmuch as beating Quarte is done by flipping the arm (the elbow does tip out somewhat) and hand in a similar manner, but with about half as much twist, practice in beating Seconde brings about improvement in beating Quarte, which is, after all, a more useful action.

PRACTICE IN COUPLES

You can work on beating Seconde routinely with a partner in the same way you did with beating Quarte. You cannot exchange or play Pattycake because the necessary actions for the dummy are too difficult to bother with. Your instructor should be your only partner for this kind of exchanging practice. Your student partner can simply replace the blade in line for you to beat quickly 2 or 3 times in a row, for purposes of loosening up. Otherwise, the dummy lunges and the active partner parry-ripostes by beating Seconde.

We are now through with the description of the *elements* of foil fencing.

You should, by now, have had some real competitive experience—not just bouting with your classmates—from about your second or third month of training. Repeated participation in tournaments will improve your performance. I generally feel, by some kind of vague subjective standard of my own, that a student improves about 25 per cent with his first competition—that is, his lessons right afterward are noticeably better, and his classroom practice and bouting are better.

This doesn't mean that you don't need more lessons or more practice. The competitive experience must be reviewed with your instructor, and you must always prepare for the next meet. There is a great deal more to fencing than this **or** any book can cover. You may have to spend from two to five years to reach the upper ranks, or longer if you expect to get into the international class.

Perhaps you are one of the many who do not care about competitive values. You may fence for enjoyment or for the satisfaction of knowing that you are becoming more skillful and knowledgeable. You should find that the more you study and practice, the more fun you can have at higher and higher levels, when you are better and can match yourself against better opponents, even in casual club fencing. A few students do not want to bout at all—they prefer to take individual lessons as though for a kind of dance. As a teacher, I certainly enjoy this approach, too, but I happen to like the improvised dance of free play or bouting, which requires adaptation to different partners. The meanings of the lesson patterns, however, are derived from competitive conditions, and without some tournament experience it is doubtful that you would understand the patterns.

Chapter 8

COMBINATIONS AND CONTINUATIONS

THE FIRST COMBINATIONS offered here are called "secondary intentions" and "countertime." These are often thought to be advanced maneuvers, but the ideas are not hard to grasp. The samples given show that you merely need to link together in chains the moves that you know from the earlier chapters. No new skills are needed.

VARIATIONS ON EXCHANGING

In Chapter 7 I discussed response beating Quarte. That was an example of exchanging in which your opponent, extending, beat your blade from the inside (the left, if you are right-handed), and you answered by Quarte beating/extending.

With your partner set up a practice routine in which you first extend and advance, aiming at his forward upper chest. Assuming you both fence with the same hand, he beats Quarte. You response beat Quarte. Repeat a few times and trade roles. (This can't be done when one of the partners is left-handed, and the coach will have to help the left-hander practice response beating Quarte.)

Increase the distance so that the active partner must lunge. Again, the dummy parry-ripostes by beating Quarte, and the active partner answers as before. Pay particular attention to the fact that the lunge should be complete. The active partner must not rock backward when he parry-ripostes in reply to his partner's parry-riposte. Neither must the active partner lean or push any farther forward, straining to reach when response beating/extending. In these practices the important thing is to do the move properly, lightly, and quickly, without losing balance or tightening up in the least.

Increase the distance still more so that the active partner must advance lunge. The sequence continues as described in the last paragraph. The partners should not insist on hitting, but try to get the moves smoothed out. The speed will gradually increase as you repeat the sequence over and over—don't worry about it. Do remember that the dummy must retreat a couple of times at the end of the pattern in order for the active partner to recover forward in good form.

Now consider another variation. When your partner beats your blade from the inside, you do not necessarily have to answer with a beat in the opposite direction. You can use countering Sixte. Start over at the closer range: extend and advance. The dummy beats/extends, and the active partner counters Sixte.

In terms of physics, countering Sixte involves less work than response beating Quarte because your opponent's beat throws your blade down, actually starting it around in a loop. All you need to do is raise your foil tip, completing the counter of Sixte (you're already extended, right?). Dummy: Please co-operate—when you beat, extend at your partner's front upper target and have your arm and hand soft.

Work this type of exchange out at lunging range (plus an inch so nobody hits) and at advance-lunging range.

These, like all actions, need to be practiced dozens, scores, maybe hundreds of times under easy, agreed-upon conditions before they become reliable in combat. Try them over and over with a variety of partners. Use them as part of your warm-up before a competition.

There is one more basic possibility. In the two combinations described above, your opponent hits your blade from the inside. Suppose he hits it from the outside (your right, if you are right-handed)? Practice this: You extend and advance, and your partner time thrusts by countering Sixte—not lunging. Notice that if you extended properly, palm up, with soft fingers and arm, your partner's action skimmed your blade out of line—but not your arm. Also, his force tended to make your hand turn thumb upward.

The easiest answer is to twist your hand back to its palm-up attitude, replacing your blade in line at the same time. This will deflect his blade sufficiently. Don't exert sideways force, simply rotate your hand and arm straight along the ideal line, which they should have been on from the time you first extended. If you feel an urge to thrust forward, the desire is valid, but don't strain or lean—you can get enough additional reach by squatting an inch or two lower. This maneuver can be somewhat clumsily described as a response opposition in Sixte.

With this move it is possible for a lefty and a righty to practice together. Suppose you're right-handed: You shouldn't be able to get at a lefty past his guarding/inviting of Sixte by going on the outside (from your viewpoint, on the right side of his blade). Therefore you must disengage extend where he is open, on the left side of his blade. He beats Quarte his way, knocking your blade to your left, and extends at your upper chest. Remember that if your grip is soft and your arm loose, your arm shouldn't be thrown out of line, but your thumb will come on top. Re-line your blade, screwing it back in.

If you're left-handed and your opponent has you blocked out, disengage to his upper chest on the right side of his blade (from your viewpoint). When he beats your blade to the right, quickly replace your blade in line, turning your hand palm upward again.

This pattern should be practiced at the three sample ranges, extending/advancing, lunging, and advance lunging. Remember that when you are in a lunge your ideal line slants upward somewhat. Before you start the pattern, aim your eyes at that spot on the forward surface of your partner's chest right next to his armpit, extend at that spot, and don't let yourself be distracted by his blade action. In your mind you should continue to go *through* that spot, whether your body moves or not.

To recap, you have a choice of two responses to a beat from the inside, and one response to an action from the outside of your blade. Don't worry about what else *might* happen, and don't be bothered if something goes wrong in combat. These are very basic situations. Once you have them down cold, you will find it much easier to work out answers for special conditions or surprises. What you are working on at this stage is how to keep on going when your original attack is caught by your opponent's parry-riposte or time thrust.

SECONDARY INTENTIONS

The term "secondary intentions" refers to a situation in which you don't intend to hit with your original attack. You *let* your opponent parry-riposte. In fact, you *get* him to parry-riposte. This means that you make your original attack a little short or a little slow or both—you don't go all-out (but maybe 95 per cent) to hit.

If you have developed not only the longest and fastest lunge you are capable of (at this stage in your progress) but also an ability to estimate how far away the target is (or will be), you can decide beforehand that you will attack an inch or two short. That means: Start from farther out.

I mentioned in Chapter 1 that if you mean to tell a lie, you must: (1) tell the truth most of the time, and (2) make the lie as nearly like the truth as possible. The success of your secondary intention attack must be based on your showing your opponent, earlier, that you really do attack straight and strong. Your opponent must be convinced of two things: that this is another real attack and that he can successfully deflect it. Still, he should not be so scared that he runs away.

Your earlier honest attacks will provide you with valuable information about your opponent's habits—what he likes to do in certain situations. You can anticipate to some extent what he will do the next time you launch what looks like the same kind of attack. He might parry your blade to the right, or he might parry it to the left, and you can expect him to repeat these moves. You will also find out about his timing: how quickly he parries and how quickly he ripostes.

You must be ready to handle his answering attack (riposte). You must parry his riposte and immediately riposte yourself. This time (second intention) you *do* intend to hit.

In outline form:

Fencer A	*Fencer B*
Attacks comparatively short and/or slow	
	Parry-ripostes*
Parry-ripostes†	

It is possible to carry the exchange one step further, so Fencer A's riposte is also not intended to hit, allowing another parry-riposte by Fencer B, and finally a parry-riposte by Fencer A. We could call this "third intention." In a broad sense we can speak of anything beyond the first as *secondary*.

One frequently hears about champion fencers consistently playing in fourth or fifth intention, but planning really does not extend that far. At championship speeds nobody could (or would, if he could) plan a fourth or fifth intention. The risks become increasingly greater as the exchange goes on. Champions are just so

---

* Fencer B might time thrust instead.
† Fencer A might also time thrust on his opponent's riposte.

perfectly balanced and in control that they can exchange five or six times without falling apart. These (higher intention) exchanges are examples of excellent training in responding almost automatically.‡

Here's how you would work out secondary intentions, using moves you already know:

Variation 1 (fencers both right-handed or both left-handed)

Fencer A	*Fencer B*
Simple direct attack to high line	
	Beats Quarte and ripostes (direct)
Beats Quarte and hits	

Sub-variation (a)

	Tries to take in Sixte
Simple indirect attack, high	
	Beats Quarte and ripostes
Beats Quarte and hits	

Sub-variation (b)

Simple direct attack, high	
	Beats Quarte and ripostes
Time thrusts by countering Sixte	

Sub-variation (c)

	Tries to take in Sixte
Simple indirect attack, high	
	Beats Quarte and ripostes
Time thrusts by countering Sixte	

Sub-variation (d)

Simple direct attack to high line	
	Counters Sixte, extending
Response opposes in Sixte ("screws it back in")	

Sub-variation (e)

	Tries to take in Sixte
Simple indirect attack, high	
	Counters Sixte, extending
Response opposes in Sixte	

‡ Here we have another use of the word *counter*: the riposte, after parrying a riposte, is called a counterriposte. In a third-intention exchange, we could talk about A's attack, B's riposte, A's counterriposte, B's counter-counterriposte, and A's counter-counter-counterriposte (which hits).

Does some of this sound familiar? These are pretty much the practice patterns described at the beginning of this chapter, expanded to include those cases in which the important action starts when your opponent tries to take your blade. The main difference is that you try to *plan* the sequence beforehand.

Otherwise, after a lot of practice, you might make a real attack (meaning to hit), get parried, and manage to achieve the same result by your trained response. The *plan* gives you a little extra margin of safety and sureness about scoring.

More examples can be made up. For instance, if you carry your hand quite high in attacking, you may use Seconde beat. You could use *any* attack originally, and any parry-riposte or time thrust that would fit your opponent's reaction. You would have to make up special patterns if you were right-handed and your opponent left-handed, or vice versa, but the idea is the same.

Variation 2

Fencer A	Fencer B
Beats Quarte, extends and advances, "all at once"	
	Beats Quarte and ripostes
Beat lunges (beats Quarte)	

Sub-variation

Beats Quarte, extends and advances	
	Beats Quarte and ripostes
Counters Sixte and lunges	

In the outline, "all at once" means that the combination must be done very quickly. Nevertheless, you would start the beat a fraction ahead of the extension, and the extension would be a fraction ahead of the advance. The sequence, in actions of this kind, is always fingers-arm-feet.

You will see when you try these sequences out that they must speed up as they go. You must start at something less than your highest speed, but go all out on the second move, changing pace. Otherwise your opponent's riposte might hit you (we'd better assume he's accurate).

Having extended on your false attack, you can't waste time pulling your arm back to parry and extending again. In this respect, beating works fine (since your arm bends only slightly when you beat after extending), or you can time thrust at full extension. You save time by making smaller movements, more than by trying hard to go faster.

Most of the time you *won't* have to lean or shift farther forward when you counterriposte. Your opponent usually comes to you as he ripostes. *Don't strain.*

You do need to know how he will most likely react. You have to figure him out. You might have to blast him a few times with all-out simple attacks or beat lunges to convince him that your first actions are real. You may lose a touch or two, but remember: If your opponent has succeeded with a certain parry-riposte, he will be confident and will more probably use that move again.

Variation 2 is more reliable than Variation 1. When you suddenly beat-extend-advance, your opponent may be so startled that he doesn't think of doing anything tricky. He will probably do the most instinctive thing—answer the beat directly: parry Quarte and riposte.

LESSONS

Instructor: Explain and demonstrate the first and easiest variation as one example of attacking in secondary intention. This is almost identical with exchanging in lunge position as described in Chapter 7, except that the student consciously lunges short and may expect to hit on his counterriposte. Only a few repetitions are necessary, and about half of these can be done blind.

Stress that lunging short means starting from farther out, not choking the movement.

Go on through the sub-variations in the same way, giving about 3 repetitions with the eyes open and 3 blind.

Variation 2 demands advance lunge or hop lunge footwork. More practice will be needed. A very fast competitor with a lot of confidence in his estimates of his opponent's reactions might carry out this type of secondary-intention attack with an appel lunge.

With these actions no routine practice in couples should be assigned. Students should work out their timing in bouts or free play. The reason, of course, is that the dummy would be practicing stereotyped responses and impeding his own progress. Students will readily see the possibilities of secondary intentions, and will soon use them in tournament play.

An extra dividend is that the student will now reduce the frequency of his strained, too-strong attacks. He may discover what you've been trying to tell him all along: A loose, smooth lunge is better, and really faster, than what he has been doing. Often enough the lunge—planned to lead into a secondary exchange —hits.

COMMON FAULTS AND CORRECTIONS

Since secondary-intention attacks are made up of basic actions linked together, difficulties usually come from faults in the fundamentals. If you can't lunge without losing your balance, you won't be able to parry your opponent's riposte or do a counterriposte. Fortunately the idea of making a false attack helps —you won't be making the excessive effort that might throw you off balance, and you won't be straining to hit, so you will have a looser arm and thus be able to beat riposte or time thrust.

Countertime

The term "countertime" refers to a maneuver in which you get your opponent to counterattack. This means you make a *preparation* against which he will stop thrust or time thrust. We'll think only about the stop thrust because it is more usual. The situation should be familiar because many of your beginner opponents will almost instinctively stick their blades out at you when startled.

Keep in mind, whenever you come within your opponent's range he may attack. If you're *not* attacking, you're *inviting*.

Your preparation would be any move or moves that might set up your attack. An attack, you will remember, is an immediate threat to target, the advancement of the foil tip toward its goal in a single continuous motion, no longer than lunging. But advancing to lunging range is preparation. Taking the blade is preparation, whether by beating, pressing, or binding or whether it is meant to remove a blade from line or to get a reaction. Extending, when you are beyond lunging range and must take one or more steps to get close enough, may be preparation.

When you must make two or more moves to reach your opponent there might be a pause between them. He might stop thrust before your final move (the real attack) rather than wait and parry-riposte on that attack or retreat from it. If you go ahead and lunge, you will run into a blade that was extending in line before your final move, and you will be wrong. Consequently, for a countertime action, you must make a false preparation, a real one, and then your attack.

In outline:

Fencer A	Fencer B
Prepares (falsely)	
	Stop thrusts (extends)
Removes obstacle (real preparation) and attacks	
Variation 1	
Fencer A	Fencer B
Advances to lunging range, inviting Sixte or Octave	
	Extends
Lunges, beating Quarte	
Sub-variation (a)	
Advances, inviting Sixte	
	Extends
Lunges, countering Sixte	
Sub-variation (b)	
Advances with high hand in Sixte	
	Extends
Lunges, beating Seconde	

Your opponent might actually begin to lunge as you false-prepare. If so, you must carry through your plan, but it can be very messy if you are too close. Make sure you advance or hop forward just to your maximum lunging range, and that your *finger-arm action leads* any additional footwork you do.

Ordinarily a beginner/novice or even intermediate opponent, will not stop thrust unless he is surprised, and you may think that merely advancing will not trigger off this habitual reaction. You're probably right.

We must backtrack a little and think about what might have happened *before* your important preparatory advance. The pattern you are trying to develop depends on earlier events. As an example, you could work on a change of *timing*: Do a few comparatively slow foot movements, setting up an easy rhythm in your opponent's mind—THEN suddenly advance, using a definitely quicker and shorter step. You could change direction: Get your opponent to follow you with a retreat and retreat, then advance. You can combine a speed-up with a reverse in direction.

Very likely you will have had to try this or a similar preliminary sequence of movements to find out what surprises your opponent and whether or not his habitual surprise reaction is to stick his arm out. Some people, when startled, jump back and flail their blades around—others explode into a lunge. You might have to sacrifice a touch in order to make sure: Hop forward and lunge, colliding with his point.

The better fencer can't be scared so easily, and his actions are more refined. When he stop thrusts, he more often knows exactly what he's doing and what might happen because of it.

Supposing your opponent does *not* accept your invitation by extending his blade, beat lunging will sometimes carry you through.

Merely advancing may not be tempting enough for your opponent. He may be suspicious of such an obvious opening. If so, you might give him something more interesting to deal with. As you advance, counter-Sixte with a *bent* arm, your foil tip moving in a slightly larger oval and a bit slower than usual. It should look to him as though you were trying to take his blade. He will have the momentary satisfaction of deceiving your counter-Sixte as he stop thrusts.

Variation 2

Fencer A	Fencer B
Advances, countering Sixte	
	Deceives, extending
Lunges, beating Quarte	
Sub-variation (a)	
Advances, countering Sixte *high*	
	Deceives, extending
Lunges, beating Seconde	
Sub-variation (b)	
Advances, countering Sixte	
	Deceives, extending
Lunges, countering Sixte	

You can see how you would have to change pace, speeding up as you go, or else your opponent may reach you. You move into his range to set a trap, but he might bite instantly. If you hesitate, you give him time to follow his extension with a lunge.

In Sub-variation 2 (b) you must counter-Sixte twice, and the second must be as you have been trained to do it, *extending* and spinning your foil tip much faster, after the first time around with a bent arm. Your lunge must be timed to follow your last taking, but without delay.

You must, as you can easily imagine, have good control over your footwork. Countertime actions require you to be able to advance lunge or hop lunge quickly and without wobbling. It is even possible that, with a very tall or very fast opponent, you may have to hop back as you take his counterattack. As far as the footwork is concerned, your preparation should be absolutely finished in the shortest possible time—that is, you must be completely ready to lunge.

Countertime actions might very well be done when the opponent already has his blade aimed at you. In variations of the first type, he may not expect you to advance without trying to take his blade, and your delay in taking would spoil whatever plan he might have. In variations of the second type, he should be very pleased to deceive (*derobement*) your first, false, supposed attempt to remove his blade, but not ready for your real preparation, which should put his blade aside just as you attack.

COMMON FAULTS AND CORRECTIONS

Like secondary intentions (and attacks in countertime might be thought of as forms of secondary intentions), most of these sequences are made up of basic moves. The worst faults can often be traced back to loss of balance, stiffness, poor stance, and the like. Now that you see a reason for being able to advance lunge nicely, you may wish to practice just that, all by yourself, through the set of drills: arms behind, blind; without the foil, both blind and with eyes open; and with the foil.

The new action here is countering Sixte with a bent arm. After going to such a lot of trouble to learn to counter-Sixte extending, this may bring about a relapse. The important thing is to work the foil by finger action, not by waving your arm around, or even by moving your wrist. Planning ahead, as with secondary intentions, should help you to do this move correctly. Sometimes it is smart to half-extend while countering Sixte to draw a stop thrust or attack, in order to offset the tendency to bend your arm even more. In preparing to beat Seconde, it is good to raise your hand an inch or two at the same time.

These actions must be practiced many times to achieve smoothness, the right timing, and accuracy. Try to get the feeling of a tune or rhythm that fits the sequence. Speed will come and can be adjusted to the opponent's reactions, provided you are as loose as possible at every instant.

LESSONS

Instructor: The lessons on countertime should follow the tabulations given with two kinds of false preparation and three kinds of real preparation. Each variation and sub-variation should be repeated 3 or 4 times fairly slowly until the student has the feeling of the rhythms—slightly different for each pattern—and sequences of movements.

The best corrective, as usual, is found in repetitions with the eyes closed. After this, further practice with eyes open will refine the actions.

No practice in couples should be allowed, for the same reason as applied to secondary intentions. A fencer should not practice to be hit. In class bouting, if a student finds that his partner is vulnerable to actions of this kind, he should practice succeeding with them to his heart's content. The instructor may take note of the student who is being hit, give that student a week or so to discover his trouble for himself, and then if he hasn't, tell him and show him how he is being trapped.

The same hand sequences should be practiced in another very useful way: The student retreats with his opponent's first threat, and then parry-ripostes or time thrusts. For example, he might retreat countering Sixte with bent arm (thus luring the opponent to deceive and lunge) and then remove the blade in line, extending. The handwork is virtually the same. Ordinarily no lunge would be needed. These are cases of inviting the attack, expanded somewhat for more skillful students who can do a couple of preliminary steps, an advance to invite, a retreat with perhaps some false handwork (the bent-arm counter-Sixte or a sweep up from low to Sixte) to make the opponent happy about being able to deceive it, thus drawing him out further, and the conclusive parry-riposte or time thrust.

Both secondary-intention and countertime attacks are ways of (1) getting close enough to lunge and (2) getting your opponent to extend his blade. In Chapter 7 I said you should not beat lunge, and that is generally a good policy. Now you have examined a few situations in which a beat lunge was suggested. My advice is, basically, to beat lunge only when you have lured your opponent to extend his arm—even better, to overextend, leaning and tightening up.

COMPOSITE ATTACKING

Composite attacks are *first*-intention attacks with two or more blade actions. A composite attack begins (as you come into lunging range—the preparatory footwork is assumed) with your foil tip moving toward the target, but the attack deceives (avoids) one or more attempts by your opponent to parry. Thus, the early part of the motion is thought of as a false threat, and is called a feint. Here we are continuing the study of disengaging that began in Chapter 6.

When you want to use a composite attack you must achieve two things. First you must discover how your opponent tends to react to attacks: He may parry, time thrust, or retreat. If he parries, he may have a favorite way. Secondly, you must convince him that your first action, the feint (by extending or extending/advancing), is the real attack.

The problem might turn out to be fairly simple. Perhaps your opponent has been pretty thoroughly taught to try to parry on just about any movement of a blade toward him, and perhaps he has been trained to parry in a particular way—for example, from Sixte to Quarte. If this is so, you can figure out what to do.

In case he does not react eagerly to a feint because he is either sluggish or cautious, you must prove to him that you are ready-willing-and-able to do simple attacks, direct or indirect. Either you will hit or you will be parried. If you hit, your opponent will tend to parry harder and faster next time. If he succeeds with his parry, and especially if he hits with his riposte, he will tend to repeat that parry-riposte in the future. Do not be dismayed if you have been hit this way—you have paid the price for useful information, and you have set up for an attack with a feint.

IMPORTANT: In any composite attack, your first move must be emphasized. This doesn't mean it must be hard or jerky; it means it must be *long*. Your opponent should believe you are going to continue in that same line with a lunge and hit him if he doesn't parry. If you feint by extending only, you must extend as far as you possibly can. Don't rush it and choke your action—send your foil tip in there.

Even if you advance at the same time, advancing is no substitute for extending, it is an addition. Stretch your arm to the utmost, squatting a little lower whether you advance or not. Then your lunge will be fairly short in comparison. The timing is LONG-short. (BUT, since the entire attack takes maybe a half-second or less, the long part should be about $\frac{3}{10}$ths of a second. We're not strolling along here.)

Feint Disengaging. Let's say your opponent guards/invites Sixte, and tends to parry either from Sixte to Quarte or by countering Sixte with a bent arm. (A more advanced fencer might do any one of a number of things.) Let's say, too, that both of you are right-handed.

Deceiving Parry Quarte. As you get to lunging range, extend smoothly and swiftly, palm up, toward the right of your opponent's bell guard. When he starts to parry, drop and raise your foil tip by finger action, lunging at the same time.

Don't think of going *around* his guard—think of letting his blade pass above yours while you dip under. When your foil tip rises, going forward all the time, his blade should be to the right of yours.

In combat, you can't wait to *see* his parry begin. You will have to anticipate. Have confidence in your feint. Go ahead without hesitation.

Parrying Quarte is the most common reaction. (This is not beating Quarte, as you have been told to do it in Chapter 7, but a sideways swing of the hand, an almost instinctive movement that often goes too far, leaving your opponent wide open.) If you have the right range, make a deep feint and lunge without delay; you must hit before your opponent can do a second parry.

Deceiving Counter-Sixte. Some beginners favor the counter-Sixte parry. They are not in the majority because countering Sixte is not as natural as parrying Quarte, but you should practice deceiving it.

You can lead your opponent by feinting higher than in the previous example, above his bell guard, directing your foil tip toward his front shoulder. As his blade starts to circle, drop and raise your foil tip in a counterclockwise oval (assuming you are both right-handed), lunging. You should hit his upper front chest while his blade is to the left of yours.

With these composite attacks you can co-ordinate more complicated footwork. First you must be able to carry out the easiest situation, from a standstill. Remember, extending should lead foot action, and your arm should be fully extended by the time you *finish* the advance, appel, or hop forward.

Starting from beyond lunging range, you may try making your feint with an advance of just the right length. Next co-ordinate these attacks with appel lunging. Then try the attacks with a hop forward on the feint.

You should also practice retreating or hopping back, starting the attack just as your opponent lifts his foot to advance.

LESSONS

Instructor: Up to now your students have been lunging immediately on the attack, with earlier actions being preparatory (such as very quick beats or invitational advancements). Most students have to be slowed down again for composites. Lunging must be delayed a bit. At first these attacks must be broken into two distinct parts, the straight feint and the disengage lunge, so the blade does not become entangled with the opponent's sleeve or leg.

Very soon, however, the sequence must become a smooth flow from beginning to end. There must be no hesitation whatever between the feint and the "final" motion. There is really no final because the action is a unit. The whole attack must be continuous. Otherwise the opponent might stop thrust correctly before the lunge.

You should give lots of practice on the most common situations: (1) advancing to range, attack, and (2) retreating to draw opponent in, attack. Other footwork combinations may be deferred to later sessions.

Appel lunging proves especially useful to the tall, long-limbed fencer. Having a very long lunge, he should not get any closer than he can reach with his best lunge—and yet when he extends at that range his feint may not be deep enough to excite a parry. Also his lunge may take too much time, and the opponent may be able to parry. But if the bean-pole fencer advances or hops forward to make a deeper feint, he nullifies his lunging advantage. Appel lunging creates a more impressive feint and cuts the period of vulnerability. Of course, a great deal of practice is required.

Blind lessons are not helpful in this instance. These attacks depend upon precise direction of the foil tip and careful estimation of distance.

Practice in couples is not recommended either, except among very advanced students who, when they are dummies, will be intensely aware that they should never make such parries. The instructor has his work cut out for him to give each student sufficient drill. It is then up to the students to find (or create) their opportunities in bouting, and to try these attacks with a variety of opponents.

COMPOSITES FROM OCTAVE

When your opponent is in Octave, a high straight feint might get him to parry either Quarte or Sixte by half-circle, without extending (he might actually pull his fist back). Your deceiving actions would be similar to those already described.

Suppose your opponent has a habit of going into Octave invitation and then countering Octave as a parry, without extending. The first half of his motion is practically the same as parrying Quarte, and your deception would be similar—a tiny clockwise loop or spiral going forward. I've said before that Octave is a comparatively weak position; countering Octave is a poor parry (though time thrusting by countering Octave can be effective). Even if your opponent catches your blade, you have good chances. Driving in, you might hit before he can clear the line; he might freeze so you can hit with a continuation, either angling around his block or releasing to hit upper target; he could very well parry too wide and thus miss his riposte, giving you time for a quick extra jab to any available opening before he can replace.

Instructor: These would be advanced variations on the Octave actions discussed earlier. Novices seldom use low-line actions, and your students should not have to deal with them in early competitions. If their opponents do go into Octave invitation, you can tell your students not to worry: The main objective is to hit, and when there is no blade in line, the first choice is the simple direct attack.

Another choice would be to beat Seconde, lunging. This powerful action done against a weak position might disarm the opponent, which would negate a follow-up touch. Done lightly but sharply, with emphasis on driving the point toward target, beating Seconde will very often paralyze the opponent for just the split-second needed—his parry will be too late or inadequate.

Probably you, the instructor, were taught the "one-two" and the "double." These involve two deceptions and may start from an opponent's attempt to take the blade or from pressure (engagement). Students who can deceive after a straight feint should have no special trouble in learning these attacks when they are ripe for them. The timing is virtually the same, LONG-*short. It is extremely important to make the first disengage extension as deep as possible.*

The one-two, deceiving the lateral high-line parries, Quarte-Sixte or Sixte-Quarte, is by far the most useful of these more complex maneuvers. Doubling the counter-Sixte would probably be next in utility. Very few fencers counter-Quarte well without a lot of training, and the double need not be highly polished—in any case, the novice will have some difficulty in predicting when his opponent will try to counter-Quarte, so a secondary-intention scheme would be more valuable.

Teaching the "one-two-three" or the "double-double" is of little value except perhaps as a formal exercise to give students more facility with the shorter combinations. These attacks rarely, if ever, succeed in modern competition and therefore are not attempted. You will more frequently see two one-two's in succession, with footwork of advance-lunge-lunge (recovering forward between lunges) or patterns even more dazzling.

Your students can do very well without these complexities. It would be better not to know them. Training time can be more profitably spent on refinement of the less-involved actions, making them smoother, longer, and faster.

CONTINUATIONS

There are a few moves that are done by beginners and by quite advanced fencers, but not often by intermediates; they are termed *remises* (and sometimes called "insistences," "replacements," or, vaguely, "continuations"). Beginners, having overbalanced forward in attacking, do them desperately because relaxation and fine control have been lost. Advanced fencers more often remise by calculation. A remise may be successful at either level, but it is risky at best.

Suppose you attack and your opponent parries, but for some cause he does not riposte or delays his riposte. You *could* hit him by thrusting to farther target areas, perhaps angling slightly around his block.

The rules say that this continued thrust or remise is a new attack. If you have a bad habit of remising just because you are falling off-balance and can hardly do anything else, you must train yourself not to do it. The rules, and the interpretations of the great majority of presidents, are much in favor of the riposte over the remise. In other words, if your opponent parries your attack, your remise would have to be *very* clearly ahead of his riposte—he would have to delay quite a bit.

My own preferences would be for the exchange or the secondary intention. Certainly you should not be overextended, straining forward, and unable to parry against your opponent's riposte.

The term *replacement* is often applied to the situation in which the original shot swings so that the blade lands flat on the target, without forward motion, and then the attacker changes the angle and digs in. This is seen by officials as two moves, and the opponent might score first.

Of course, if you have domination over your opponent's blade, for example with superior leverage in Sixte, you're perfectly right to "insist." Ram it in there. This happens sometimes when you take the blade and your opponent tries to resist but is in a weak position; at other times when he takes your blade and loses domination. With experience, you can feel when you have control. But don't deliberately try to set up power struggles of this kind.

Similar to the remise, except that the new attack is not made in the "same" line but by disengagement to an opening elsewhere, is the *redoublement*. One very common example, often occurring automatically without any apparent thought by the attacker, is when the opponent parries Sixte and the attacking blade slips on under to the flank. On other occasions, your opponent might very well freeze on the Sixte parry, pulling his arm back and raising his hand, and if you release you should be able to hit his exposed flank—you have a doubly good chance because if he ripostes from that bad position, he is more than likely to bring his blade down flat on your head or shoulder. If he tries to parry Seconde, he has a long way to go.

Just in case you're going to have a written exam and have become confused about redoublements, remises, replacements, and ripostes, here's another one: the *reprise*. This is a whole new complete attack, done when your opponent has retreated and perhaps parried, or perhaps even tried to riposte (but from too far away). The usual feature of a reprise is that the attacker recovers forward from his lunge and lunges again, or otherwise chases his opponent with renewed threats. The footwork pattern might be advance-lunge-recover-advance-lunge, etc., co-ordinated with feints or takings. Sometimes presidents will apply the term reprise to an attack in secondary intention.

INFIGHTING

You should not try to fence close. This is very daring, and though you might get a lot of excitement out of it, you will also lose a lot of touches.

When two fencers approach each other in normal stance and get to a distance a few inches more than arm's reach, the attacker should hit with a direct shot if he doesn't telegraph. The distance is too close for anybody's reaction-speed to allow a successful parry. Very often both fencers thrust simultaneously—after all, the time is right for both of them—but assuming both touch, neither has right-of-way. Both fencers *should* choose the aggressive strategy because the odds are very much against a reliable defense.

Infighting does occur, and it occurs rather frequently. Infighting is what happens very commonly after the original attack. Sometimes it looks like a nice exchange, and sometimes it is a burst of furious jabbing.

Imagine that you set up and tried an attack in the first intention, but somehow your opponent managed to parry. You should have launched yourself out into a long lunge. You can fight on in that low position, or you might recover forward into a low squat. Your choices have already been discussed: You can try to parry your opponent's riposte and make a counterriposte, or you can try to remise, redouble, replace, or just plain jab (several times, as fast as you can).

In general, it is good policy to stay low. You may twist your body or move one foot (usually the rear one) around or sway your body a little this way or that in attempts to avoid your opponent's thrusts. The rules do not allow you to put your head, back arm, or even your fighting arm in the way of your opponent's point; a hit on one of these normally "foul" areas might be called good because of your interference.

To have any chance of hitting in close fighting, your foil arm must be bent. That is, after the original attack and parry-riposte have missed for whatever reason, both fencers are usually so close that an extended arm would put the foil tip beyond target entirely. You can certainly continue to parry, but your ripostes will be short pokes. Keep your elbow down and close to your ribs as much as possible. Parry by flicking your blade right or left, as needed, and snap your point forward again and again.

If your opponent stands up higher, trying to throw angled shots at you from above, you must raise your fist for better coverage from your bell guard. You should certainly sit up absolutely straight, because any bowing merely gives him better chances to dig into your back (upper shoulders). Also, with your opponent standing tall—on straight legs with feet together—you might find openings to his flank or lower belly.

Now think over the reverse situation. Your opponent attacks and you parry-riposte but you miss—or you aren't sure: Never stop fencing until the president yells "Halt!" First of all, any time you parry-riposte you should squat in order to have your blade go at the target nearly horizontally, not slanting downward. Taking that for granted, let's suppose he came in a bit farther than you expected, or you happened to have moved your front foot forward when you riposted, and thus both of you are closer than arm's reach.

Unless he has lost balance—which we don't ordinarily expect an opponent to do—you shouldn't try to hook in a replacement. You must withdraw to parry, but there's no reason why you can't beat Quarte and riposte with a bent arm or block Sixte very briefly and riposte from there by directing your point with your fingers and jabbing a little forward.

Get lower, as low as you can with your back and head up straight. You can go into the deepest of deep-knee bends, but don't get up. In the long run, over many, many such encounters, very probably the most touches will be made by the lower fencer. Even though he lunged, your opponent might not stay down, and when he stands up, you have better chances, as previously explained.

Don't try to back out. Sometimes after a short exchange of this kind, one of the fencers can't stand the heat and backs off. Assuming that you are playing at bent-arm distance and you then retreat, you are vulnerable to a very fast extension. If your opponent tries to get away, your squat should not be so low that you can't lunge fairly quickly. You should be able to catch him, but if an extension or a lunge won't do it, chase him as fast as you can before he has a chance to settle down. Physically and psychologically, he is bound to be off-balance for a second or two.

Whatever else you do, don't crowd in. After the original lunge, perhaps with a forward recovery (and the original parry-riposte or other response), neither fencer should advance any more. Good and legitimate fencing can go on at close quarters, but fencing is supposed to be done with the weapon and only the weapon. Any fencer who makes body contact will very probably be penalized. Even your wrist should not touch his arm or body. Often enough, hoping to save himself or wanting desperately to get it over with, your opponent will move into a clinch. At that point, relax. Don't wrestle or push him away.

One further possibility is that he might move forward and sideways, not colliding with you but seeking to get past you and/or off the strip, at which point a halt should be called. Pivot with him and keep on stabbing. He is the one at fault, and you have the right to one immediate final shot.

Very often the president or director will stop the action after a very few moves of infighting. It is extremely difficult for him to follow the time or right-of-way, even with the electrical apparatus which, in the absence of raised extension lights, may be obscured from his view by the fighters. When human judges are used, it is very difficult for them to see all the moves that might hit.

Theoretically, the action should be allowed to go on as long as the combat-ants are not in body contact. However, the president is perfectly justified in calling a halt very quickly when novices are involved because of the danger of bumping, hard hitting, or broken blades which might cause injuries.

You should not spend a lot of time practicing for infighting. The principal game is the long-range game, and the usual phrase seldom goes beyond attack, riposte, counterriposte. Work on that long-range game. In case the all-out attack brings you to close distance, *stay in* and keep on playing lightly, trying to place your point: hit-hit-hit.

One of the obvious differences between today's foil play and that of thirty years ago is the much greater frequency of simple attacks and ripostes, direct and indirect. Fencing is now predominantly a game of *footwork* (for the purpose of achieving the exact attacking range at exactly the right time). Blade direction is extremely fast and accurate, but less complex than it used to be.

Chapter 9

THE LEFT-HANDER

ONE OF THE problems all fencers eventually encounter is that of the left-hander. Maybe you are a left-hander yourself. All lessons and practice in couples will be at least a little different, sometimes a great deal of trouble, when a left-hander is involved.

Your instructor, if he is right-handed, should teach with his left hand once in a while. You will have to go over a few examples of the basic attacks and counterattacks. You must then seek out left-handed partners and practice and bout with them until you are more at ease.

TESTING THE MASTER EYE

Quite a number of people claim to be ambidextrous. They say they do some things with the left hand, other things with the right, or do equally well with either hand. Perhaps these people are born left-handers. Right-handers are in the majority by about ten or twelve to one, and have built things to suit themselves. The left-hander does have to learn to be somewhat ambidextrous. (Some things accidentally favor left-handers. The typewriter, for example, has the most frequently used English letters on the left side of the keyboard.)

Which hand should the so-called ambidextrous person use for fencing? When in doubt, there is a simple test for eyed-ness. Stretch out your arm and stick up one finger. Pick out a vertical line on the wall across the room, and hold your finger so it covers the line. Now close your left eye: does the finger seem to shift to the left? If so, you are left-eyed. If the finger doesn't seem to move, you are right-eyed.

Try again, closing the right eye: if the finger doesn't shift, you are left-eyed, but if it does, you are right-eyed. The *master* eye guides your aim, and if you close it, the view seems to shift.

I have had students who were right-handed and left-eyed, and vice versa. These people fence with the hand they prefer, regardless of which eye is the master, but I advise the ambidextrous person who is left-eyed to use his left hand.

51. Left-hander vs. left-hander: time thrusting in Sixte

He will probably be more accurate that way, even though he has practiced a lot of fine co-ordinations, like writing, with the other hand.

Many left-handers seem to be awkward. Maybe this is due to the prejudice of right-handers, but possibly some person or group has tried to convert the natural left-hander at an early age. This might have interfered with normal development of co-ordination. Let's let the left-hander be left-handed, especially if he is left-eyed.

Left-handed fencers do very well. In the U. S. National Championships of 1963, seven out of nine of the finalists in men's foil were left-handed—although the two right-handers placed first and second. Left-handers have frequently been champions, however. Probably the greatest foilist of modern times, Christian D'Oriola of France, who was World Champion six times, is a southpaw.

LEFT VS. RIGHT

If you are a left-hander, don't be lazy and sloppy just because you have an "advantage of numbers." (As there are fewer of you, right-handed fencers have less of an opportunity to practice with you.) You must train as hard as anybody else, working on form and accuracy. The better right-handed fencers eventually get enough experience with left-handed opponents, and if you don't fence really well, you will never get beyond the second rank—the finals, or even the semifinals, of the Nationals.

Actions to Avoid. You must avoid exposing your back or flank (left side). If you lean forward or to the right when lunging, your left shoulder, neck, and

52. Left-hander vs. right-hander: attacking flank

upper back will be open. Lunge properly, head up, along an invisible wall on your left.

Don't attack deep to your right-handed opponent's left side, which is far away and where he can beat Quarte, opening you up. Only very rarely should you move your hand to the right at all.

When you parry Sixte or counter-Sixte, don't withdraw your arm. You may keep your opponent from hitting high, but you will soon have him coming underneath. Even a high Quarte parry is inadvisable, but neither should your hand get too low on the inside.

Instructor: From the very beginning, the left-hander needs special attention. He will rarely have chances to do simple direct attacks against right-handers. His simple indirect attacks should almost always go to the flank.

His counter-Sixte may meet too much opposition, and should also be turned to the flank. He may tend to move his hand sideways in beating Quarte, and you must stress that he only needs to beat very lightly to make a right-handed attack to his chest skid off. In beating Quarte and Seconde he may have greater success in turning his attacks or ripostes to the flank.

Secondary intentions and countertime sequences have to be adjusted considerably to suit the left-hander. They are best demonstrated if you use your left

53. *Right-hander vs. left-hander: attacking in Sixte opposition*

hand, and then variations against right-handers can be worked out. The feint disengage, for him, must be a real one-two or double.

If you've never had a left-handed student, your first will have to be your
guinea pig. You must experiment with all actions until they are reasonably workable.

RIGHT VS. LEFT

The chances are you're a right-hander. The first time you face a lefty (preferably your teacher in a lesson), it will seem to you that his arm is in the way, and
that you can't get to him at all. But his problem is the same as yours except that
he will have had more practice with this unbalanced situation.

One place to hit a left-hander is the pocket under his left collarbone. You
must aim carefully at the foremost surface of the target. You can't afford to make
wide motions of your foil tip in disengaging because you could miss behind his
back or slip by his chest.

If he is slightly open in Sixte, or has a low hand, with his blade at a steep
angle, (point upward), you can possibly glide straight in with slight opposition to
your left. Then if he resists your thrust to his upper body (moves his hand out to
your right), you can disengage.

The best place to hit is the flank, your left-handed opponent's ribs, under his
arm. This can be reached by disengaging from high or by a straight lunge when
you have approached with your hand low.

The one-two is a good type of attack against a left-hander. Try it once in a great while as a change from less complex maneuvers. Either feint below his hand and hit above, or vice versa.

Many left-handers habitually parry by countering Quarte, which to you will appear as counterclockwise circles. This pattern can be "doubled" with practice. Think about it: Your moves would be very similar to doubling against a right-hander countering Sixte, except for a somewhat different placement of the target. Send your point around in *smaller* counterclockwise circles, and pick your time to lunge.

When your left-handed opponent has his hand fairly high, either guarding/inviting or threatening, and you are in Octave, a very good action is to beat Quarte and direct your attack or riposte to his flank.

Also very effective but not so easy to do is the beat of Seconde, upon his low-level blade, unwinding your arm afterward even more than usual so your shot goes to his flank.

Don't worry about hitting foul on head, arm, or hip. You will hit foul plenty of times. But you can't afford wide detours around those areas. You must keep on attacking straight to the front of the target—with ability to continue attacking, parry-riposting, or counterattacking. If you need twenty attacks to win, with fifteen hitting foul, make them. If fouls occur with right-of-way, he can't be scoring on you.

Actions to Avoid. DON'T TURN SIDEWAYS! A lefty will take advantage of the tiniest opportunity to slip around the outside (your guarding/inviting Sixte or Octave) to hit your neck, the top of your shoulder, under your armpit, etc. If anything, you should face a lefty with your hand even farther to the right than usual —make him come to your chest or stomach.

My advice here is similar to that for left-handers against right-handers. Don't lean forward or to the left when lunging, because your right upper chest, neck, and upper back will be exposed. Lean slightly backward—to the *right*. You might also move your front foot somewhat to the right so that in effect you are stepping in *behind* him.

Don't attack deep to his right side: His Quarte-parry will open you up to ripostes to neck, back, and flank. Generally, don't let your hand drift the least bit to your left.

When you guard/invite Sixte, keep your hand fairly high and forward, with your foil tip out to the right, to prevent glides through a weak position. Avoid pulling your arm back. If you adopt Octave for guarding/inviting, make sure you parry Sixte with your arm almost extended, or better still, time thrust.

Instructor: A review of basic actions against a left-hander ought to be given after the first part of a course, including the simple attacks, time thrusting by countering Sixte, and attacking by countering Sixte against a blade in line. Practice against a left-hander should help correct any tendency of a right-hander to be open in Sixte.

The next review would cover beating Quarte, secondary intentions, and countertime against a left-hander. The continuations from beating Seconde are considerably more difficult and should be deferred until much later.

Feinting and disengaging becomes one-two (or double) and perhaps should be withheld for an advanced course.

Actions from and to Octave are workable, but should be well practiced. In particular, time thrusting from Sixte to Octave, and attacking along an extended

54. Right-hander vs. left-hander: time thrusting in Octave

blade in Octave, are very effective. One problem is that tournament judges may not see hits to the flank.

LEFT VS. LEFT

About the worst panic scene in fencing occurs when two novice left-handers meet in competition. It is rare for lefties to have had left-handed coaches or classmates, so they usually are lacking in experience and go wild.

If you are a southpaw facing another one for the first time, you will feel that you are terribly exposed on the chest side. Be brave. You are in the same situation as a right-hander is against another righty. There is no cause for alarm. Your opponent is just as scared as you are, anyway.

Your instructor should give you lessons using his left hand. No matter how clumsy he is with it, you can get some slow and careful practice in the basic actions. By watching right-handers practice and take lessons, you should be able to get an idea of how attacks and counterattacks should go in a balanced situation, and, of course, if there is another lefty in your class, you ought to practice all the routines with him before working against right-handers.

You will be extremely lucky if you do have such a classmate and can get just as much practice with him as with righties. You can become a much better fencer, with the help of your instructor, than most beginning left-handers—IF you work hard on the essentials of form, accuracy, and clean execution of all basic moves. It is *not* good to develop a lot of special tricks (ducking, jumping sideways, jabbing from odd angles, etc.) merely because they happen to work against other beginners. Advanced fencers will cream you.

Don't, when fighting another lefty, allow your foil hand to drift over to the right. This is an instinctive attempt to protect your chest and belly, but in the long run it is a poor solution. Keep your hand and foil tip to the left until the exact moment that you must counter-Sixte, beat Quarte, or whatever, to deflect an attacking blade or remove an obstacle.

Chapter 10

OFFICIATING

INSTRUCTION AND PRACTICE in officiating ought to be given to all beginners in the classroom, whether the class is a regular one for credit in a college or secondary school, or an informal one at a Y, community center, or private club. Understanding of the rules is necessary for full enjoyment of practice bouting and free play, so that partners can agree on who made a touch. Duplication of tournament conditions in class will bring up many illustrative situations that might be overlooked in a lecture or text.

When fencers play without supervision, differences of opinion about right-of-way always come up. Questions can be taken to the instructor or an advanced fencer who has had competitive experience. But very often these questions *cannot* be answered because the answer would depend on the unique sequence of action, its flow and timing, which *cannot* be perfectly described or repeated, and which necessarily is viewed differently by the bouters. The more they know, the more intelligently they can discuss the action. If they can't agree, they might as well forget it and go on playing.

When bouting is first allowed in class, the instructor should remind students of the nature and objectives of foil play and issue warnings about safety, keeping form, trying to use actions as they were taught, etc. A bit later on the class can be divided into groups of four, in order for two bouters to have two judges who will provide outside views of whether touches landed or not. When one pair is finished with a bout the other pair can fence, with the first pair judging; after that, one of the first pair can fence with one of the second pair, and so on. The instructor and any available assistants should observe and comment.

After a week or two of this informal bouting the class should have sessions to demonstrate and practice officiating as similar as possible to tournament formalities. The instructor would act as president of the jury, and students would be picked to judge. It would be preferable to have intermediate or advanced students to fence for these practice sessions, since their actions would more likely be clear and their hits definite, though faster.

JUDGING

The judge's job is to try to see hits and to signal the president immediately when he sees one, fair or foul. The judge signals by raising his hand.

In order to see as well as possible without interfering with the action, a judge keeps position about three feet to the side and behind one of the fencers and looks in the direction of the other fencer. For example, judge JA in the diagram (Fig. 55) looks toward fencer FB. When the fencers move, the judges *must* move also.

When a judge signals that he has seen a hit, the president calls "Halt!" The president then asks the judge what he has seen, and the judge only needs four words in his vocabulary: "Yes" for a valid touch, "No" for a miss, "Foul" for an invalid hit, and "Abstain" to indicate that he doesn't know.

You would only raise your hand to signal a valid or invalid hit, but there might have been several moves in the sequence of action (*phrase d'armes*), and you must be prepared to say something about each. You should not say "Yes" or "Foul" unless you have actually seen the foil tip hit, and you should not say "No" unless you are sure that the thrust missed or fell short. You should *not* say "Yes" even if the direction of the thrust was toward valid target and you saw the blade bend but the foil tip itself was hidden from you by the fencer's arm or body; you should in this case "Abstain." The other judge is usually in a better position to make a positive statement.

REMEMBER—a slap is a *miss*. The most common mistake of inexperienced judges is to call a flat action foul. They seem to think especially that a slap on valid target means something—it doesn't.

(Recently the word "Foul" has been replaced by the phrase, "Yes, but not valid," or "Off target." In your local meets the short word may save time and avoid confusion. If the president is quick, he might hear "Yes" and go on with his analysis before you can say "but not valid." In higher-level competitions the judging is done by an electrical apparatus, and the director (who has the same duties as the president of a non-electrical jury) can say "Off target" if he pleases.

(The only weapon still judged non-electrically all the way through the World Championships is the sabre. In sabre fencing, the valid target is everything above the hips, and judges usually say "Low" to indicate a foul.)

The great problem is to *see* hits (and all the other actions), and a book can't teach you to see. Fencing actions are speedy, and the foil tip often hits and bounces off instantly. This is still a touch or foul. The foil tip doesn't have to stick into the target, and the blade doesn't have to bend. The lightest contact for the shortest moment is enough, provided the blade had forward motion at that moment (or if, being stationary, the other fencer moved forward onto it). A foil tip may hit and then slide, which is a hit. Or a foil tip may slap and then dig in (replacement), in which case you must call two actions, first "No" and then "Yes."

One rather difficult decision for you to make is whether the attacking blade was deflected before it hit. If so, you have to say "No" on that action, and perhaps "Yes" or "Foul" on the continuation. The fencer whose blade has been deflected has lost right-of-way, and his opponent then has an opportunity to strike back.

One piece of advice on seeing is, don't focus on the surface of the valid target. You should gaze along the arm and blade of the fencer beside and behind whom you are standing. In this way you will be more likely to see the actions, if

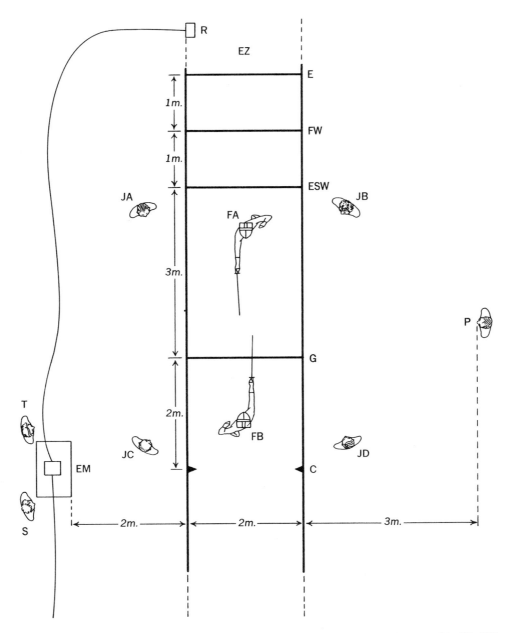

55. *The strip. Non-electric foil or sabre bout in progress. FA, FB, fencers. JA, JB, JC, JD, judges. P, president. T, timekeeper. S, scorekeeper. R, reel of electric apparatus. EZ, end zone. E, end line. FW, foil warning line. ESW, épée and sabre warning line. G, guard line. C, center line*

there are several. Your eye will follow the motion of the hand and arm and thus see when and where the foil tip strikes. If you are looking only at the valid target, you may not see foul hits on the arm or leg, made on the way in. Foul hits nullify any good hits made later, and a fencer who has a touch called against him when he was first fouled suffers an injustice and will be properly annoyed.

Good judging takes practice. Judging practice should be part of your basic training so when you go into your first meet you will be able to do a decent job. Your ability to see fast actions will improve the more you fence and especially if sitting on the side lines, with nothing else to do, you try to see hits in every bout you watch.

A fencer who has had instruction and some practice in judging can judge at least one level above his fencing ability. In his first meet he will probably judge in his own pool, and if he is eliminated, he could judge in the next higher round. This procedure will relieve the fencers in later rounds, especially the final, from judging themselves.

There is a Golden Rule for judges: JUDGE AS YOU WOULD WISH TO BE JUDGED. Keep your attention on the fencing and don't allow yourself to be distracted by friends in the audience, action on other strips, or your own worries. If you can't do this, ask to be excused. Judge as sharply and fairly as you can. Judging is one way to pay for the enjoyment you have when you fence.

Judging *improves* your fencing directly, too. Your eye gets sharper. By listening to the president's descriptions of the action, you gain understanding of the rules. Finally, since your view is at only a slightly different angle from that of one of the fencers, you can observe the opponent's reactions. You can begin to imagine, without having the pressure on you, how you might fence that opponent. This experience in analyzing the possibilities of real bout situations is very valuable.

SCOREKEEPING

The scorekeeper usually sits opposite the center of the strip, on the other side from the president. His duty is to call the fencers who are to bout next and to notify those who are to follow ("on deck"); he marks the touches as the president awards them.

Individual. On the individual score sheet (Fig. 56) the first bout is over, and Fencer No. 1 has lost, beaten by Fencer No. 4 by a score of 3–5. The second bout is under way, and the score is 2 against Fencer No. 2 and 3 against Fencer No. 5. "On deck" are No. 3 and No. 6.

The pool contains six fencers. The elimination method is by "round robin," so every fencer in the pool will meet every other. With six fencers the total number of bouts will be fifteen. The bout sequence is calculated to give each person an approximately equal amount of rest between bouts. The fencers must be called exactly as shown: Inasmuch as the first one called in each pair takes his place on the president's *right*, every fencer should have had equality by the end of the pool as far as lighting, etc., is concerned.

(A left-hander, however, always starts on the president's *left* side. Some presidents cross over to the other side of the strip at the middle of the bout—when one of the fencers has 3 touches against him—making the fencers change also. Others have the judges switch around.)

The pool might have had from four to eight fencers in it according to this score sheet. The total number of bouts is equal to $\frac{n(n-1)}{2}$ where n is the number of fencers in the pool. Thus, an event with eight entries could either be split into two pools of four or run as a single pool of eight. (We assume the two pools would be as nearly as possible equal in strength, with assignment to the pools being made by the Bout Committee.) With two pools of four, two fencers from each pool (50 per cent) would be promoted to a final round robin of four, and the total number of bouts in the two preliminary pools and the final would be 18. This would save time, since the total bouts in a single pool of eight would be 28. Normally, though, the single pool would be used to give every person as much

INDIVIDUAL SCORE SHEET

TOURNAMENT *Utopia H.S. Intramural* DATE 5-7-84

ROUND _1_ POOL _1_ PRESIDENT _____

NAMES	#	1	2	3	4	5	6	7	8	T/A	T/S	W	L	PL.
D. Abrams	1				LHT L									
F. Carter	2				II									
H. Posada	3													
J. Rameau	4	III W												
L. Tamuti	5	III												
N. Volandur	6													
	7													
	8													

BOUT SEQUENCE

4 FENCERS (6 BOUTS)	✗6 FENCERS (15 BOUTS)	7 FENCERS (21 BOUTS)		8 FENCERS (28 BOUTS)	
1-4	1-4 ✔	1-4	3-1	2-3	7-5
2-3	2-5 ✔	2-5	4-6	1-5	3-6
3-1	3-6	3-6	7-2	7-4	2-8
4-2	5-1	7-1	3-5	6-8	5-4
3-4	4-2	5-4	1-6	1-2	6-1
1-2	3-1	2-3	2-4	3-4	3-7
	6-2	6-7	7-3	5-6	4-8
5 FENCERS (10 BOUTS)	5-3	5-1	6-5	8-7	2-6
	6-4	4-3	1-2	4-1	3-5
1-4 2-4	1-2	6-2	4-7	5-2	1-7
2-3 5-1	3-4	5-7		8-3	4-6
4-5 4-3	5-6			6-7	8-5
1-2 5-2	2-3			4-2	7-2
3-5 3-1	1-6			8-1	1-3
	4-5				

56. Individual score sheet

fencing as possible. When there are nine or more entries it is more usual to split the field into smaller pools.

As scorekeeper, you would always be marking in two boxes on the sheet at the same time. For example, the next bout in the sample would involve the box *across* from No. 3 and *under* No. 6, and also the box *across* from No. 6 and *under* No. 3. Touches scored against No. 3 would be marked in the box across from No. 3, and touches scored against No. 6 in the box across from No. 6.

At the end of the pool you would enter in the Win (W) column, across from the fencer's name, the number of victories. In the Loss (L) column you would enter his defeats. When you have done this for all the fencers, you may find that one has the greatest number of victories, and you would mark him as "1" in the Place (PL) column. And so on.

In a final round a tie for first would be played off. The winner of this deciding bout (barrage) would be the winner of the meet, and the loser would be second.

Other tied places would be determined by the count of touches. Add across and put the total in the Touches Against (T/A) column. When this has been done for the tied fencers, the fencer with the *least* touches against him would be given the higher place.

If two people were tied in bouts *and* in touches against, you would have to count touches scored. Add downward under each fencer's number and enter the total in the Touches Scored (T/S) column. Then the one who had scored the most would get the higher place.

In preliminary rounds of important meets, ties for promotion are fenced off rather than determined by count of touches. If, for instance, three are to be promoted from a pool of six and two are clearly qualified by victories while the next two are tied in bouts to be the third qualifier, it is best to have a barrage between those tied for third in the pool. The winner of that extra bout would be promoted. The issue is not as important in beginner, novice, or scholastic tournaments, and may be decided by count of touches to save time.

Team. When two teams have a match, it is arranged so that every member of one team may bout with every member of the other. In large tournaments sometimes three or more teams are pooled, and the pool is usually run as a round robin of team matches, with promotion to later rounds determined by superiority of team victories.

Before the scorekeeper goes to work, the Bout Committee (or the president) may have the team captains flip a coin for choice of A or B position on the score sheet. The A team fences in regular order, No. 1, No. 2, No. 3, etc., while the B team has a shift in order. Team captains have decisions to make about which of their fencers will be No. 1, etc., but this hardly concerns the scorekeeper.

The total maximum number of bouts for teams of three is nine. Therefore, one team will win the match when it has five victories. The match could end at any score from 5–0 to 5–4, in most tournaments—sometimes, for various reasons, all matches are fenced out, even to 9–0.

Again the scorekeeper works in two boxes simultaneously. On the sample team score sheet (Fig. 57) the first bout is over, and A1 lost to B1 by 5–4. In the second bout, A2 has 1 touch against, and B2 has 3 touches against. On deck are A3 and B3; for that bout, touches scored against A3 would be entered in the box *across* from A3 and *under* B3; touches against B3 would be marked in the box *across* from B3 and *under* A3.

TEAM SCORE SHEET

TOURNAMENT *Utopia H.S. vs. Orwell H.S.* DATE 2-30-84

ROUND ___I___ MATCH *I (Men)* PRESIDENT _____

NAMES	#	A1	A2	A3	A4	B1	B2	B3	B4	W	T/W
Carter	A1					⊞⊞ L					
Posada	A2						I				
Volandur	A3										—
	A4										
Abrams	B1	IIII W									
Tamuti	B2		III								
Rameau	B3										—
	B4										

BOUT SEQUENCE

TEAMS OF THREE

A1-B1 ✔	B2-A1	B3-A1
B2-A2 ✔	A2-B3	B1-A2
A3-B3	B1-A3	A3-B2

TEAMS OF FOUR

A3-B4	B2-A3	A1-B2	B1-A1
A4-B2	B4-A1	A3-B1	B2-A2
A1-B3	B1-A4	A2-B4	B3-A3
A2-B1	B3-A2	A4-B3	B4-A4

SUBSTITUTES:

TEAM A _____ FOR _____

TEAM B _____ FOR _____

57. Team score sheet

You can keep track of the match score almost at a glance. If it has been decided that the match will end as soon as one team has five victories, you will be able to advise the president when that time comes. Then you would record the individual victories in the W column and total them for each team in the Team Wins (T/W) column.

Usually substitutes are allowed, but limited to one per match. The captain might decide to lead off with one of his fencers in the No. 3 spot, and then replace that fencer after he has had one bout. The captain will notify the president of this intended substitution in advance. The scorekeeper makes a note of the fact, and continues to fill out the No. 3 string until the match is finished.

Sometimes matches are made between teams of four or five fencers (plus substitutes). We won't go into these situations except to note that a match between teams of four could end in a tie, and the tie may be broken by counting touches against and touches scored. This certainly isn't very satisfactory when, after sixteen bouts, one team may be promoted with a difference of just one touch. The same is true, however, with teams of three or five: the match may run down to the final deciding bout, and that bout may go to *la belle* (4–4 tie), so that the very last touch will decide the match. And it wouldn't be surprising if every bout in the match were a *la belle* bout either. Such matches are pretty exciting to watch—just imagine what it's like to be in one!

Knowing how to keep score will help you as a competing fencer. You will be able to look over the scorekeeper's shoulder and check on your standing and the standings of your opponents in the middle of the pool. You can see how many bouts you have left to fence, whom you will face next, how many bouts you will have for resting while others fence, how many bouts you need to win to be sure of promotion or placing, whether your next opponent has been winning up to that point, etc. Such information has an influence on your tournament strategy.

Everyone is expected to fight all out in every bout, but naturally, smart fencers don't. Imagine that you are in a preliminary pool, are pretty sure of winning enough bouts for promotion, and next have to fence a very strong opponent. The chances are that you might lose anyway, and you don't need the victory. Besides, you will very possibly meet this opponent in a later round, even the final. Without actually throwing the bout away, you can save some energy, you can give him the idea that he can beat you fairly easily, and you can show him a lot of moves that you don't ordinarily use: set him up for later. In the case of meeting a weak opponent when you already have enough victories for promotion, you can simply save energy and practice unusual moves.

What worries us most, I suppose, is the thought that a very close match might be lost through an official's error. As in all other sports, the best thing to do is think about next time. I don't say forget it—you do want to remember the moves so you can repeat the good ones and avoid repeating the bad ones—but blaming the loss on an official's error is a waste of energy. Blaming the loss (if it's not so close) on a teammate doesn't help either.

TIMEKEEPING

The timekeeper has a job so easy that it is hard. He must start the stop watch when the president says "Fence!" and stop it when the president says

"Halt!" The trouble is, the timekeeper may be distracted by the fencing and forget to push the button to start or stop the watch.

You will remember that bouts for five touches have a six-minute limit, with a warning period of one minute. When one minute of fencing time remains the timekeeper must *silently* signal the president, who is supposed to stop the action and warn the fencers. At the end of the full period the timekeeper calls "Time!" (But if the fencers are tied when time runs out, they will continue to fence until one scores another touch.)

PRESIDING

The president of the jury is in charge of everything on the strip. He stands about ten or twelve feet from the side of the strip, halfway between the fencers. He moves along as they go, watching the action of the blades. He issues warnings and imposes penalties for unsafe play, boundary violations, etc. He decides, according to time or right-of-way and the votes of the judges, whether a touch has been scored, and against whom.

(When you are bouting, you cannot win an argument with the president if he says the time or right-of-way was not in your favor. You cannot claim a hit if the jury's vote has been "No" on your action, nor can you claim that your opponent did not hit you if the jury has decided that he did.

(You *can* ask for explanations of the decisions so you will know why the touch was called against you. You can ask for a complete revote of the jury on every action. You might have cause for appeal if the vote was miscounted. You may also appeal penalty decisions. To sum up, you can't deny *factual* statements of the jury, but you can argue about *procedure*. Therefore, you should eventually learn the rules in detail for your own protection.)

At the beginning of the bout the president says "On guard," and the fencers salute and put on their masks. The president then asks, "Ready?" If the fencers say they are, or *do not answer* (if a fencer is not ready, he should say "No" right away), the president gives the command "Fence!" However, the president must not allow fencing to begin if he sees that a fencer's clothing is not properly fastened, mask bib is turned up, etc. That is one of his responsibilities.

The president should be able to see out of the corners of his eyes when any of the judges raises his hand. The president would then shout "Halt!"

At this point if only one judge has a hand up, time can be saved by merely asking that judge what he saw. If the answer is "Yes," the other judge on the same side (looking at the same fencer) *must* be consulted in case his vote is a definite "No" (or "Foul," in which case he should have raised his hand but was negligent).

When there is disagreement the president may break the tie vote, but if *he* abstains, no touch can be awarded. If the judge who did not raise a hand abstains, the touch must be awarded by the single vote of the judge who had a definite call. That judge may nevertheless be overruled by the president, who has one-and-a-half votes to one for each of the judges.

When hands are raised on both sides the president must briefly describe the phrase and take the vote on each move in the sequence. Thus, he says which fencer had the right-of-way (or initiative in time) step by step until a decision can be made. See the tabulation (pp. 136–37) for possible votes on each threatening move.

The president must therefore be able to perceive the actions and identify which (if any) was the right-of-way, instant by instant. He must then be able to talk about the phrase in such a way that the judges can give a vote on each move.

Admittedly, the phrase may be confused or confusing. Inexperienced fencers tend to miss their initial attacks or ripostes and then make jabs. Often it is impossible for the jury to decide whether fencer A's second jab was ahead of fencer B's fourth. It is reasonable to suppose the attacker's first jab has no clear advantage over his opponent's first jab following a riposte that missed, unless judges' hands go up on one side definitely ahead of the other. Often no touch need be awarded—provided both fencers are hit in a flurry of this kind. This is good experience for novices, who may thus be impressed with the value of parry-riposting immediately after missing an attack or riposte, instead of jabbing. Beginners also often start attacks at the same time, neither having right-of-way.

A good president with good judges can unscramble very complicated phrases and arrive at correct decisions, even if the fencers are quite speedy, provided the fencing is clean and sharp. But a good president may have poor judges and may have to give up on confused sequences. The president himself may not be good enough, but he may be the only president available.

(Fencers are well advised to pay some attention to the way a particular jury sees the action. The good fencer is able to adapt himself to the jury. For example, if they tend not to recognize attacks to the flank, other attacks should be used.)

TABULATION: JURY DECISION ON EACH ACTION IN PHRASE

Judges (both looking in same direction)		President	Decision	Further Actions Considered?
A	B			
Yes	Yes	Abstain*	Yes	—
Yes	No	Abstain	No award	+
Yes	Foul	Abstain	No award	—
Yes	Abstain	Abstain	Yes	—
Yes	No	Yes	Yes	—
Yes	Foul	Yes	Yes	—
Yes	Abstain	Yes	Yes	—
Yes	No	No	No	+
Yes	Foul	No	No award†	—
Yes	Abstain	No	No	+
Yes	No	Foul	No award	—
Yes	Foul	Foul	No award	—
Yes	Abstain	Foul	No award	—
No	No	Abstain**	No	+
No	Foul	Abstain	No award	—
No	Abstain	Abstain	No	+
No	Foul	Yes	No award‡	—

* Where judges agree (except in abstaining), the president always abstains because his contrary vote could not prevail, and even to mention his disagreement would shake the confidence of the judges and the fencers, maybe leading to futile arguments about future touches.
† In this case the judges agree that there was a hit, therefore the president's negative cannot prevail.
‡ Here the judges agree, in a sense, saying there was no valid hit, and in fairness to both fencers, no award is made.

Judges (both looking in same direction)		President	Decision	Further Actions Considered?
No	Abstain	Yes	Yes	—
No	Foul	No	No	+
No	Abstain	No	No	+
No	Foul	Foul	No award	—
No	Abstain	Foul	No award	—
Foul	Foul	Abstain**	No award	—
Foul	Abstain	Abstain	No award	—
Foul	Abstain	Yes	Yes	—
Foul	Abstain	No	No	+
Foul	Abstain	Foul	No award	—
Abstain	Abstain	Yes	Yes	—
Abstain	Abstain	No	No	+
Abstain	Abstain	Foul	No award	—
Abstain	Abstain	Abstain	No award	—

** See first footnote on p. 136.

The general conclusions from the tabulation are these:

(1) When the decision is "Yes," a touch is awarded, and the fencers return to the guard lines, unless that is the winning touch, whereupon they unmask, salute, shake hands, and leave the strip.

(2) When the decision is "No," the president may continue the description to the next move in the sequence, if any.

(3) When the decision is "No award" (because of a foul, triple abstention, or whatever), discussion ceases and the fencers are put on guard where they were, with one exception. As shown by the second item in the tabulation, one judge may say "Yes" and the other "No," while the president abstains. In this case, the president should inquire whether there was any hit in the opposite direction. If the vote on that is definitely "No," then the president again may ask for a vote from the judges who disagreed. This is done in case one of them assigns a hit to an earlier move than the other does. If they then agree that there was a good touch sometime (while *nothing* was done in the opposite direction), the touch will be awarded. If they still disagree, there is no award.

Learning to preside is a matter of practice. The best method is to judge in several meets under the supervision of good presidents. You should also keep score, trying to anticipate which way the president will call the right-of-way. At all times when fencing is going on and you are not otherwise busy, it is good practice to watch and pretend that you are the president. If you are at a tournament, you may (silently) agree or disagree with the actual president—sometimes you may be right to disagree. Remember, though, that you aren't in the same position to see the action.

Officials do make mistakes. When you fence you must accept this. Presumably the errors will balance out in the long run. Certainly if you have carried the responsibility yourself a few times, you will understand the officials' problems. Perfection is impossible.

When you are competing, you do have the right to request that any or all of the members of the jury be replaced—BEFORE the bout starts. Whether your request is granted depends on the availability of substitute judges or presidents.

There may be none. The ones you get may, indeed, be worse than the ones you have. Don't jump to the conclusion that they are prejudiced against you, or that they are incompetent. Just assume they have their peculiarities about how they see things. I have said before that you should be able to (or at least try to) change your style and actions to impress or satisfy the jury.

In meets with very few entries, or in class practice of formal bouting procedures, a pool can be carried on with five people. Two will be fencing, two judging —positioned so that they can see the fronts of the fencers—and one presiding. The president can keep score; timekeeping will have to be neglected (the average novice or intermediate bout takes approximately two and a half minutes—much less than the limit). When a lefty and a righty are fencing, the president stands where he can see their backs, the judges stand on the other side of the strip. Under the circumstances, the results can be quite reliable: That is, in a larger pool, these same fencers will place in about the same order.

ELECTRICAL DIRECTING

Until 1955 all foil tournaments were judged by human beings, right through the World Championships or the Olympics. After that the electrical judging apparatus was introduced in the higher levels of competition, and its use has spread gradually downward. We should note, nevertheless, that a considerable number of fencers who were highly ranked before continued to place high afterward.

Most notably, Christian d'Oriola was World Champion in 1947, 1949, 1952, 1953 and 1954, and placed second in 1948 and 1955. Having announced that he hated the electric foil, he won the Melbourne Olympics of 1956 to show that he could do it, regardless of the weapon, which was a quite unbalanced instrument at that stage.

In the United States several competitors who were already well-known before the arrival of the electric apparatus remained near or at the top. The point is that the advantages and disadvantages of the electrical system apply to everybody alike. Novices and intermediates today often cry for the electrical foil, apparently in the belief that their scores would be better just because a machine says so.

Undoubtedly there are disadvantages to human judging, but if judges are well-trained and experienced, the results are reliable over the long run. The trouble is that with the availability of electric apparatus, the training of judges has been neglected—with obvious results.

The apparatus brings its own kind of disadvantages along with the advantages. It is a complex system, and some of the parts are very delicate. For the time that might have been lost previously in jury discussions, we trade time lost in finding and repairing equipment failures. Instead of worrying about whether judges can see, the fencer worries about whether his personal gear is working right. Many touches have certainly been lost because equipment failure has not been detected. Rather than train judges, we have to train technicians to test, adjust, and repair the apparatus.

All of it costs a good deal of money, and I doubt that foilists are any happier with the electric equipment than they were with the judges. The club or organization must spend $1,000 or more for the scoring set, and probably would be wise to get an extra pair of reels for about $250. The individual fencer must invest

$150 to start with if he or she wants the two foils, two body cords, and two metallic vests in perfect condition that are required by the rules. In addition, a broken blade costs about $20 to replace.

Despite the expense, there is no alternative to the electric foil if you are heading for top competition. (Colleges involved in varsity leagues use it as well.) There may be some justification for the argument that lower-level fencers should become accustomed to the electric foil, although I have had a student win his very first electric meet at an intermediate level (after only five minutes to get the feel of the weapon), against opponents experienced with the apparatus.

Though the machine eliminates the judges, there is still somebody in the position of the president: He or she is now called the director. The director has basically the same duties as the president. Instead of awarding touches with the help of the judges, the director must call according to the lights that show up on the central scoring box.

If a person has not had a good deal of experience as a judge, he will probably not make a good president, and if he hasn't practiced presiding, he is not likely to make a good director. For twenty years beginners and novices have been getting less training and experience as judges and presidents, and the results very often show up in directing.

The worst tendency is for the director to watch the lights instead of the fencers. Much of the time the fencers are here and the lights are over there. The director must change the angle of his sight, and comes to prefer looking at the box in order to be able to call a halt the instant a light turns on.

By doing this he often loses track of the action, the sequence of attacks, ripostes, etc. He also may not notice when a fencer reaches the warning line or steps over a side boundary. As we know, a fencer can hit first but not have right-of-way, as in making a swift remise against a parry-riposte, so it is wrong for a director to call a touch simply on the basis of which light went on first.

The director is supposed to move in such a way that he can see the lights while looking *between* the fencers. Unfortunately, this is not always possible. A little exercise in geometry will show that as the fencers move toward one end of the strip or the other, the director must move proportionately farther—and *faster*. He is practically certain to lose sight of either the lights or the action.

Very often when a fencer moves suddenly, his body blocks the director's view of the lights, and when infighting occurs, no view at all may be possible. For this last reason, the rules require that the scoring apparatus have repeater lights up on a "tree" so that the director can see them over the fencers' heads.

On the other hand, if the director concentrates on the action and not the lights, he may stop the bout too soon—when there was no hit at all. Or he may not know which light went on first—that is, there may have been a clear difference in time, but when he looks at the lights, two or more may be on.

We may conclude that the best director in the world will make a mistake once in a while. Others will make more. The electrical-foil judging apparatus is not a foolproof device, by a long shot. Get your training and experience, and do the best you can.

As a fencer, you must adapt to this situation as well as you did to the human-judging situation. Make sure your equipment is in good condition at all times, and that you have spares. If you even suspect—and you should be very suspicious—that you *might* have hit, and your light didn't go on, ask for a test

IMMEDIATELY. Otherwise, fence as well as you can, and as I've told you before, you can expect and plan on having to hit at least seven or eight times to get 5 touches on the score sheet. Remember that the worst director can't call a touch (other than a penalty touch) against you if no light turns on on your side of the box; you might not have an easy time arranging that, but it can be done, for example, by hitting with control of your opponent's blade such as in time thrusting and attacking in Sixte or Octave with opposition.

Chapter 11

TEACHING FOIL

EXPERIENCED FENCERS OCCASIONALLY spend a few minutes giving pointers to beginners. Everyone does this kind of informal spot teaching. It comes naturally when clubmates practice together. What I'd like to encourage you to do is work through a course with a single pupil (your child, younger sister or brother, friend, or whatever) or a class.

You will benefit in several ways. You will help increase participation in our sport. The more fencers there are, the better it will be for you. There will be more opponents (even if you have trained them yourself) for you to practice with. When you teach you will have to think more deeply about rules, principles, and techniques. You will have to observe very sharply to see just what the basic mistakes of your students are, and you will have to figure out how to show and explain the right things to do. This experience will broaden your understanding of the game. Your own technique will get a lot of practice—your hand, especially, will go through many repetitions of fundamental movements.

Or maybe you are a physical education teacher and have been assigned a class because the equipment is there, the time slot is there, you had a fencing course at one time, and the former instructor has left. The course is on the program, and you have the job.

QUALIFICATIONS OF AN INSTRUCTOR

In February 1966, the Junior Olympic Committee of the Metropolitan (New York) Division of the AFLA issued a report on high-school activity. Twenty-eight schools had teams in the Public School Athletic League. The survey uncovered the astounding facts that: (1) 50 per cent of the coaches had never fenced, and (2) 35 per cent had never taken a course in fencing.

New York has always been considered the heart of fencing in the United States. Many national champions have come out of New York high and prep schools. Several colleges in the area have varsity teams recruited from the secondary schools. There are private clubs and a number of masters. Many meets are held at all levels. Yet the situation described existed not too long ago.

The fact that it did exist in one of the strongest centers does not, however, justify complacency in those teaching elsewhere. There are probably hundreds of people conducting fencing classes in Y's, community centers, and schools whose qualifications are not much better, but some minimum standard should be expected. Surely activity without informed direction wastes a lot of energy.

An elementary foil instructor should have had:

1. Study and practice in fencing skills and theory (about six months to one academic year).

2. Competitive experience, including judging, scorekeeping, and presiding. If possible the instructor should be post-novice: that is, he or she should have won a first-, second- or third-place prize in individual extramural (outside of his or her own school or club) competition.

3. Teacher training, such as a clinic, and practice under supervision.

It is not easy in the United States at this time to achieve even the qualifications listed above. There are few masters with whom you might study. There are very few colleges that offer courses beyond the introductory level, and fewer still that have teacher-preparation courses for those who wish to major or minor in physical education. Situations in which you can practice teaching under supervision are rare. Competition is not as difficult to find, provided you reside in or near a fairly large city. As indicated in Chapter 3, an amateur group more or less has to raise itself by its own bootstraps, with a few people serving as instructors in humble recognition of their own deficiencies.

This is something of a warning to students. Highly qualified teachers do not exist everywhere or in abundance. Yet there are honest teachers—people who are interested both in the sport and in teaching and who can provide a sound foundation for the beginner. To some extent this book is offered as a supplement to the face-to-face instruction available.

If you would like to teach, you can render good service. You are probably already convinced of the value of the sport for recreation and physical fitness. Don't be timid if you are lacking some of the listed qualifications. Keeping your shortcomings in mind, go on with your studies, get into meets (your amateur standing is not affected if you do not make instruction your main occupation, nor receive more than a nominal sum for expenses), and consult with better fencers as much as you can.

It is a challenge. Where experts are lacking, you must apply intelligence. You must use an experimental approach, trying to discover for yourself better methods. This can be a fascinating hobby.

FACILITIES AND CONDITIONS

Several factors determine the success and rate of progress of classes. As a student, you might learn faster under better conditions, but you have to accept those that exist. As an instructor, you must plan according to the given situation. Students and instructors can co-operate in different ways to obtain or improve facilities and conditions.

Space, Light, Ventilation, etc. For a small class a full gym is not necessary. A well-lit room twenty feet wide by forty feet long, with a ceiling clearance of at least ten feet, will do. A handball or squash court is suitable. Light from side windows during the day may be bothersome, but usually shades can be drawn. Some people may be dissatisfied if the room is too hot or too cold, but except in the most modern situation there will inevitably be times when the temperature is not ideal. At any rate, a more important factor is ventilation—a group of eight to a dozen people needs plenty of fresh air.

The best floor is a plain wooden one laid on wooden crossbeams. A concrete base, even when covered with linoleum tile or wood, is uncomfortable and possibly damaging to the feet and legs. The floor should be level and without bumps, but not slick. A fencing group with resources might get strips of rubber matting, about four feet wide and the length of the room, to give better traction for bouting.

Equipment. Instructors and students should be outfitted with foils, masks, jackets (or half-jackets), gloves, long trousers, rubber-soled shoes, etc., in good condition. If the special equipment is not provided by a school or community center, the members of the class will have a week or two of conditioning during which they may obtain foils and masks, then another couple of weeks before they need jackets. Thus, the expense can be spread out a bit.

The teacher is usually in the position of advising the institution and the individual pupil about purchase of uniforms and equipment. He or she is also normally stuck with the job of taking care of the equipment that the school or other institution owns. Thus, at this point I'll go into some detail.

The uniform consists of mask, jacket, glove, trousers, stockings, and shoes. The jacket and trousers must be white or off-white. The mask and jacket are manufactured to meet competitive standards, but need care.

For practice, a half-jacket can be used, and the glove can be a fairly cheap unlined leather work glove, to be found in hardware or variety stores. Even for practice, though, the glove should completely overlap the sleeve of the jacket so that a blade can't get inside. For the same reason, the usual fencing knickers or long pants are much better than shorts. Safety! If students must supply their own trousers, they should be advised to get them with room for full leg movement: The best, for the least money, are judo or karate pants.

The competition rules now require all fencers to wear an extra protective plastron inside the jacket. This garment must cover the upper arm as well as provide extra layers of cloth over the forward side of the chest.

Many fencers use ordinary gym shoes. Fencing shoes are a great deal more expensive and, of course, will not make a good fencer out of anybody. But they may give more comfort and support when the student has to fence all day in a big meet.

At school-and-club discount prices, a mask will cost about $14. A practice jacket can be bought for about $17; a regulation three-weapon one for $25 or $30. A half-jacket costs about $15; it is somewhat adjustable in size (for class use or for a student who is still growing) and is a bit cooler for summer practice, but it will not be allowed in regular competition. Some fencers own two or three uniforms, so they can save one for tournaments.

When students get to the bouting stage, I advise them to wear long-sleeved sweat shirts under their jackets. The choice is between heat and the sting of being slapped with a blade. Women's jackets usually have padding, or there is a separate padded vest to go under the jacket.

As for foils, I recommend either the Cetrulo (Hern style) grip, sometimes listed as "Spanish offset," or the French handle with a *short* pommel (Levis style). The former allows almost complete finger relaxation. With the latter, a thin strap or thong around the palm should be used (Figs. 23–25). There are sev-

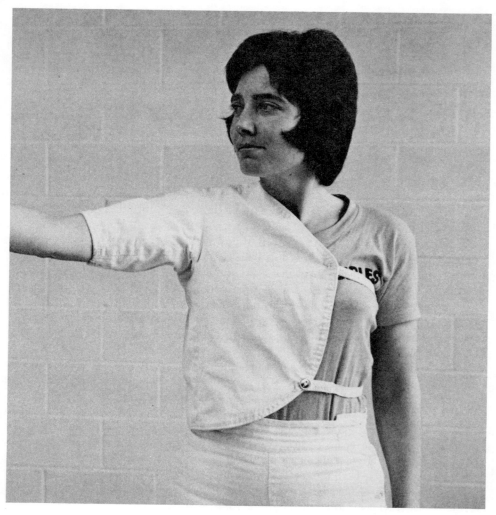

58. Inner plastron required for competition

eral other types of handles, but again I'll say that none will make a good fencer—there is no "wonder weapon" that will solve problems. If a grip doesn't fit your hand, cramps or hurts you, try another. In this respect the French handle is the simplest, and most students start with it. Undoubtedly the Italian is the most difficult grip to use, and should NOT be bought for classes or novice individuals.

Always order an ALUMINUM guard of the largest available size.

A non-electric foil will cost from $10 to $16.

The total cost of a beginning outfit, beyond the exercise clothes everyone might be expected to have, will be between $50 and $75. A school or community center may provide most of the gear, but eventually each fencer should have his own.

Mounting the Foil. A brand-new blade is straight. You (the teacher) may have to take all the weapons in stock apart and remount them, and whenever a blade is broken, you will have to alter the replacement. This is a skill that should be taught to students as soon as convenient.

The part that holds the foil together is called the pommel. On the French foil the pommel is a metal knob that can be unscrewed by hand (pliers may be

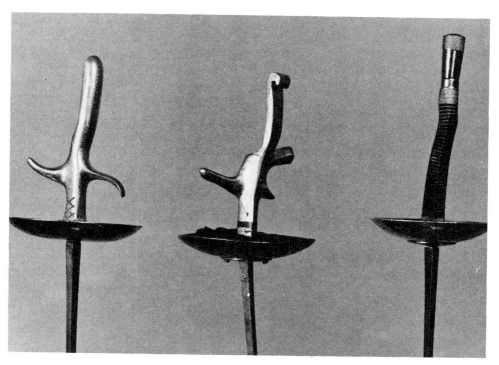

59. *Foil (l. to r.): Cetrulo (Hern style), pistol grip, French*

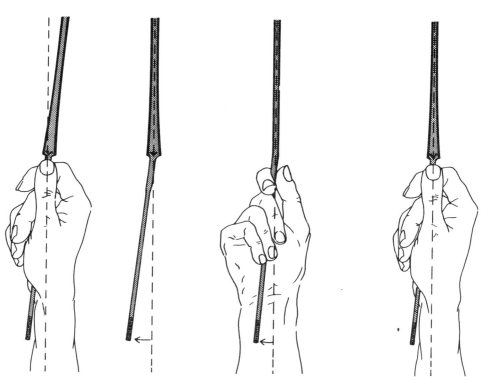

60. *Offsetting tang of French foil*

necessary). On practically all molded-aluminum or plastic grips, the pommel is a cylindrical nut, sunken into a hole in the grip, and must be reached with a screw driver or hexagonal wrench (which has to be the right size).

Once the pommel is off, the foil should come apart, but you might have to tap on the outside of the guard, near the center hole, to drive off the wooden handle of a French foil. The parts are the blade, guard, thumb pad, grip, and pommel. On pistol-grip foils, you should find a lock washer down in the hole—if not, get one.

With the French foil in particular (or any foil that has a long tang and requires a fairly large pommel), you must put a definite bend in the blade at the point where it passes through the guard.

You must choose which blade surface will be the thumb side. The blade is thicker one way than the other. When the foil is assembled, your thumb must be on the same side as one of the broader surfaces (which usually have marks stamped on them, such as the number 5). Let's call the thumb-side "up," even though you would seldom carry the foil with your thumb on top. For right-handers, the bend of the tang should be to the left and also downward (Fig. 60), for left-handers to the right and down. Having bent the tang, reassemble the foil, and when you hold it naturally, the pommel should not dig into your wrist. It should feel better than it did when the tang was straight. If it doesn't, something is wrong: You didn't bend it correctly, you didn't put the handle back on correctly, or you aren't holding it correctly.

The shanks of pistol-grip blades need be bent only slightly, if at all. The grips themselves have off-set butts, to avoid interference with the wrist. The reason for off-setting, either by angling the tang of a French foil or using a special grip of the molded type, is so that the blade can line up with your forearm. That is, imagine a line along the inside of your arm, and your blade should continue that line. You should not have to bend your wrist and strain your fingers to point your blade.

The blade itself must be curved smoothly so that, when you hold the foil with your thumb uppermost, the blade will appear to droop an inch or two toward the tip. This curve is achieved by drawing the blade between your rubber-soled shoe and a piece of rubber matting several times (until the metal is hot to touch), and then by gradually bending the blade with a few long lifting pulls under your foot. At no time should the angle of the blade to the floor be more than about 45°. During this process the blade must be thumb-side down.

The reason for curving the blade this way is so that when it is thrust against a target, it will more likely bend in one direction. A straight blade, striking at slightly different angles, would bend one way one time and another way the next. Just as you can break a paper clip by bending it in different directions, so you would eventually break a foil blade. It will break some day, anyhow, but the useful life of the blade can be prolonged by precurving it. The proper curve will help insure that the blade will bend most often to the right for a right-hander, and thus *away* from the opponent; should it snap when it hits, the jagged end will tend to spring off to the side, giving an additional margin of safety.

A replacement blade costs about $6.00. You can save yourself a bit of money over the years by bending the tangs and precurving the blades and, certainly, by learning to fence with a light hand.

With reasonable care, most of the equipment items will last from three to five years. The cost of keeping equipped is quite low compared, say, to skiing, for which the costs are about $50 a day if you have to rent all the gear.

Time. Ordinarily a class is allotted one hour or less for each session by the institution providing the space. An hour and a half would be better. At best, time is lost if students come from other classes, or have to leave promptly, because they have to change clothes. More practice time is lost in calling the roll, making announcements and so forth.

Very often classes meet only once a week. Twice would be better. Three sessions a week is rare. In most cases students will have to do homework in order to make satisfactory progress, and that means they must learn in class how to practice alone.

The instructor is usually given a certain number of weeks for a course, and must plan accordingly. In a course of eight weeks with one class of one hour each week, treatment of the material must be greatly simplified, especially for the introductory course. Naturally, an instructor anticipates that there will be follow-up courses and that he will be able to fill in, refine, and continue.

Number of Students. About the maximum number of students that can be handled by one instructor—for a good rate of progress—is fifteen. Ten or twelve would be better. Model courses below are designed to accommodate a maximum of fifteen students. Larger classes waste quite a bit of time and accomplish little.

You might be lucky and start your teaching career with one student alone, or a tiny class. Problems in keeping them busy and satisfied are fewer by far. Nevertheless, start slowly—you can easily build up to a rapid pace after the initial conditioning period.

After taking attendance and going through the warm-up and drills, and allowing time for practice in couples (or bouting) and cool-off, the teacher can only spend two or three minutes with each student. With larger classes progress will be slow—and thus disappointing to those students who could learn much faster. Large classes *do* become smaller—but the dropouts are often the most promising students.

The rate of progress can be increased very nicely when there is just one advanced (or intermediate) student to help as a demonstrator. The teacher then does not need to describe every move, or every part of a move, but merely needs to say, "Do this." A good rule is, *talk less and demonstrate more.* Beginners can observe the maneuver, which can be repeated for them a half-dozen times from several different angles. The assistant can also circulate among drilling or practicing beginners and make basic corrections.

Better still is teaching in teams of two or three. For one thing, the students get individual attention from teachers who vary in height, speed, style, etc., and thus become more adaptable.

FORM OF A CLASS LESSON

Each session of a course, be it three quarters of an hour or an hour and a half, would go something like this:

1. Warm-up.
2. Drills (footwork). Repetition of basic moves and combinations (exclusive of fingerwork), with or without weapons.
3. Lesson (new material or review). Demonstration, explanation, individual teacher-student work.

4. Practice in couples. Routine repetition, against a partner, of actions related to the current lesson or previous lesson. (Students must always seek different partners.)

5. Bouting (when students are ready: in addition to, or substituting for, practice in couples). Fencing for a specified number of touches. (Again, students must always seek different partners.)

6. Cool-off. Jogging and walking backward around the gym, etc.

PRIMER COURSES

The objectives are to get students to understand competitive foil play and to participate as competitors and officials as soon as possible. Skill is required, but the student does *not* need to be able to perform many different combinations near perfectly before he begins to play. He can get by with two or three simple attacks and two or three ways of responding to his opponent's attacks.

Heavy emphasis on complications has driven away thousands of potential fencers. To say that those who are "truly" interested will stick with it despite these difficulties, until they learn it well, is negative. It is the teacher's job to stimulate and promote interest, and this can only be done by preparing the student to play the game quickly and easily. The character of fencing is *not* that it is complex and difficult, but that it is a combat sport. Human beings instinctively know about fighting. The means of winning—within the rules—can be presented without frills.

The majority of fencing courses offered by colleges and secondary schools in the United States are limited to one quarter or one semester. By tracing out complications, most of these courses do not produce fencers. But I believe a semester is quite enough to cover the essentials with some thoroughness. Students will not be champions at the end of the course, but they will be able to play the game intelligently. They will not have great skill, but they should have fairly good control and speed in the fundamental actions. Once they get into bouting—especially if they have to face the teacher and more advanced students once in a while—they will improve much faster than if the teacher picks at details.

The model lesson plans below may be expanded or simplified according to the time allowed for each session and the number of sessions in the course. A numbered lesson (as listed) might consume from one to three class periods, or some of the review sessions may be omitted.

BEGINNER TWELVE-LESSON COURSE

Courses of fewer than twelve lessons are usually offered by Y's and community centers, without requiring exams or grading. Twelve lessons (one per week) will consume approximately one school quarter or semester, or two lessons per week will extend the course to the usual mid-term grading period. You can construct your detailed lesson plan on these blocks:

1. Warm-up exercises and footwork drills.

2. Three simple attacks: direct (with sub-variations from Sixte, Octave and low invitations), indirect (deceiving or releasing), and by countering Sixte against a blade in line. Review against left-hander. Several footwork variations.

3. Three responses to attack: retreating (to attack as opponent recovers), time thrusting by countering Sixte, and beating/extending Quarte (parry-ripost-

ing). Review against left-hander. A few footwork variations. Possibly response-beating Quarte.

4. Introduction to tournament situation: supervised bouting, judging, score-keeping, outline of rules, and theory.

5. Possible real tournament experience.

INTERMEDIATE TWELVE-LESSON COURSE

The beginning amateur teacher, or one of those on a coaching team, should have more experience before taking on this job. A helper is even more useful than ever.

1. Beating Seconde in parry-riposting and in attacking on an available low blade. Review against left-hander.

2. Exchanging: response-beating Quarte, countering Sixte against a beat from the inside, and response opposition in Sixte against action on outside of blade. Review against left-hander.

3. Secondary intentions, using the exchanges above: easiest variations, with advance lunge or retreat lunge, exchanging done in lunge. Review against left-hander.

4. Countertime, using countering Sixte, beating Quarte and beating Seconde: advance, take, and go. Also same handwork used after inviting opponent to attack. Review against left-hander.

5. Bouting and judging practice. Tournament experience should definitely have been obtained, preferably earlier in this course, if not before the end of the previous one.

"ADVANCED" TWELVE-LESSON COURSE I

By now some of the students might be giving some of the coaches a bad time in bouting practice—if the coaches dare to face it. The teaching team should work out demonstrations of all complex sequences well beforehand.

1. Composite attacking: feint disengaging against parries of Quarte and counter-Sixte. Review against left-hander.

2. Secondary intentions: advanced variations, such as beat advance, beat lunge. Review against left-hander.

3. Countertime: false hand preparation (e.g. countering Sixte) accompanying advance to invite stop thrust. Also same handwork combinations used when opponent attacks on the invitation. Review against left-hander.

4. Octave, actions from and to: simple attacking on blade in line, time thrusting, beating Quarte. Review against left-hander.

5. Judging and presiding practice. Bouting. More tournament experience.

"ADVANCED" TWELVE-LESSON COURSE II

If classes have been meeting twice a week, the fourth twelve-lesson course will end the academic year. If classes have been held only once a week, this course may take place in the spring of the second year. Since the semesters are longer than the courses, extra time will have been used for review, bouting, and free play.

Nothing new is offered here. The difference is not in complexity of combinations, but in the sharpness of students who now have combat experience and good control over preparatory footwork maneuvering. The freshness of the class-work will be found more in time variations than in hand patterns. Students will be more concerned with fencing psychology, discovering their opponents' habits, "setting up" for attacks, and the like. They can do this because they are no longer so preoccupied with their own physical problems.

Nevertheless, if the group is much involved in outside competition, such as varsity team matches with other schools, they should have intensified training. A good proportion of class time can be taken up with tougher, longer, faster and more intricate mobility drills: multiple advancing and retreating (mixed up), multiple lunging, etc.

The class has already made one turn of the spiral, having been introduced to all the examples given in earlier chapters, and can very well do it all over on a higher level. The simplest and yet the most difficult type of attack is the simple/direct: The great problem is getting the exact time/distance. Likewise, the most difficult response to an attack is to retreat and lunge just when the opponent recovers. Practically every complex action or sequence is based on these simple patterns.

You might draw the students into doing repeated attacks (the same or different) with a series of three lunges after preliminary footwork, or with a series of advance lunges. The attacks can be simple or composite. Fairly often you should break the pattern with a parry-riposte or a stop thrust.

You might continue the study of composite attacking by introducing and polishing the one-two and the double.

PRACTICE IN COUPLES

The following methods of routine practice which strengthen fundamental movements, have been mentioned previously in this text:

Drop-the-glove. For guarding/inviting and extending the foil arm quickly, fully, and accurately.

"Timing In." For extending/lunging, guided by perception and anticipation of an opening.

Countering Sixte. Done in two ways, depending on whether "dummy" is lunging or not.

Beating Quarte from Sixte. Done in two ways, as a parry-riposte of a thrust and as a parry-riposte response to a beat attack.

Advanced students will continue to use the beginner routines from time to time, as well as those below:

Beating Seconde. After some practice in beating Seconde the student will probably show an improvement in beating Quarte and in lunging.

Beating Quarte from Octave. Further practice in beating Quarte, which is one of the most useful moves.

Taking in Octave from Sixte. An alternative to countering Sixte or beating Seconde when opponent's blade comes in low.

Taking in Sixte from Octave. Depending on whether the "dummy" lunges or not, the active partner time thrusts or takes and lunges.

Countering Octave. This action is about the most subtle and most difficult, whether used in time thrusting or in attacking on a stationary blade in line.

Advanced students will still devote time to practicing the more fundamental actions, so that those actions can be used almost automatically in combat. As ease is gained by practice, all actions should become faster, more accurate, and more direct.

Free Play. Bouting for a specified number of touches is preferable for beginners and intermediates so that their tendency to wildness will be curbed by their desire to win (or avoid losing). Inefficient actions tend to disappear.

Advanced students may be allowed to indulge in free play (without time limit and without counting touches), which affords an opportunity for experimentation. Dedicated competitors will ordinarily avoid actions in which they are not extremely confident. While they may be able to execute such actions quite well in lessons, the best way to expand the useful repertoire is through free play. Classroom bouting does not have the intensity of real tournament performance, but free play is even more casual. Quite often a pair of fencers will end a period of free play with a bout, in order to shift the emphasis back again to winning.

EXAMINATIONS

I very much dislike teaching where students must be graded, and especially where the course is required (or where some P.E. is required and students pick fencing just because it is available on the right day at the right hour to fit their schedules). I believe that anybody with at least one eye, one hand, two feet (even if one is artificial), and sense enough to find his way to the classroom at the right time can fence if he wants to and will keep at it. A problem is imposed by the system of formal education that sets a time limit and an external standard.

An exam is a teaching device. The only real purpose of exams is to discover the student's deficiencies in *verbal* knowledge, in order to fill in the gaps. Grades can just as well be given on the basis of classwork, the best measure being the student's progress related to his own original condition or ability. The very apt student might be graded high by performance or skill compared with his classmates, but for him the work is easy, and he may coast along, not developing his potential. The student who finds fencing difficult may progress relatively further by devotion to practice, careful self-control in drills and lessons, sensible bouting, etc.

The experienced teacher is usually able to estimate quite closely the degree of a student's knowledge, especially when officiating is included in the course and everybody judges, keeps score, etc. Very few students would complain about this kind of grading, but if written exams are required by the administration, they might include the following topics.

Rules. Every student should be able to summarize the principal rules by the end of the beginner course. Intermediate and advanced students can be questioned more closely about details (e.g., exact dimensions of the strip), basing their answers on experience in tournament situations. Knowledge of concepts becomes apparent when students officiate.

A scorekeeping quiz can be given to beginners. The procedures are simple, and the scorekeeper actually needs no knowledge of the sport.

Terminology, Description. It is undoubtedly more important for the student to show that he wears the protective uniform properly, can care for his weapon, and can fence with some skill and intelligence, than for him to know the *names* of movements and pieces of equipment. But such items are usually included in exams. Questions should have some wider application: e.g., "What is the most important piece of protective equipment?" rather than "What do you wear on your head?"

By frequent repetition the names of actions become recognizable to students, but the spelling of terms only heard is often hilarious. If no text is assigned, students should at least have a guide sheet of some kind that lists the most common terms.

Bouting Situations. Class practice of bouting under tournament conditions gives the instructor a chance to spot errors in comprehension of rules and theory. On a written exam, bout situations must be described very carefully to get clear answers.

Questions would be of two types. The first, suitable even for beginners, would test knowledge of the rules by outlining a sequence of action and asking which fencer, if either, was legally touched. The second would ask the student to give his reactions, as a fencer involved, to a particular maneuver of his opponent: At least two alternatives should be traced.

Historical, etc. The history of fencing has nothing whatever to do with appreciation or performance of the modern sport. Maybe the instructor ought to know something about it, because he is likely to be quizzed by students. You can easily sidestep such questions by saying that we can't be sure; the articles in different encyclopedias and other reference books disagree with each other on many points. Evidently the sport developed during the nineteenth century, becoming more and more remote from training for dueling or war.

Fencing events were included in the first Olympic Games of the modern series in 1896 and have been on the program ever since. Similarly, fencing has been part of the Pan American Games since 1951. In other than Olympic years, World Championships are held.

The best effect of an exam comes from an immediate review and discussion. Preferably, the exam should be short enough so that students can exchange papers, grade each other's work as answers are given, get the papers back to their owners, and then discuss. The teacher can find out why wrong answers were given (what misconceptions led the students astray) and re-explain on the spot.

Sometimes the fault will be found in the question, or in the teacher's original presentation—that is, the test often tests the teacher, who should be quite ready to learn from this and to improve.

GUIDE SHEET

You should have a guide sheet duplicated. This, with plenty of space for marginal notes, might include a digest of rules and theory, a list of common terms, and the lesson plan for the course.

INTRAMURALS

The best stimulus for students is the extramural meet, where they bout with strange opponents and are governed by unfamiliar officials. A low-pressure alternative is a meeting of classes from two or more schools or clubs. But these opportunities may not come so often, and when they do, novices will derive much more benefit if there have been previous intramural meets.

A class can be divided into pools of four or five, women only against women and men against men. In regular fashion, 50 per cent or so would be promoted from the preliminary pools to higher rounds. Try to plan for a small final, since a pool of six usually takes over an hour to run. Eliminated fencers should still be active as judges, scorekeepers, and timekeepers.

The intramural can lead up to a school or community center championship if more than one class section is involved in the program. An arrangement must be made to bring the finalists from all classes together at a mutually convenient time and place. When this is done, prizes should be obtained for at least the first three places.

If there are advanced fencers in the area, a leading official could be brought in for the intramural finals. This will give the coach a chance to sit on the side lines and see how his students conduct themselves, an experience that often arouses mixed emotions.

For learning purposes there should be a discussion and workout at the earliest moment after a meet. Well-prepared students are highly stimulated and very receptive at such a time. By my own fuzzy subjective standards, I'd say beginners are 25 per cent better (whatever that means) in class practice, taking lessons, etc., after their first meet.

MORE REFLECTIONS ON LEARNING

I remarked in Chapter 1 that learning seems to proceed in steps, with periods of slow progress alternating with periods of rapid progress. You should try not to fight this—on the plateau, go along with practice, drills, reviews, and refinements; on the climb, pour on the new material. Of course you can't expect to catch it perfectly, partly because every student is a unique individual and the class as a whole can't *be* a whole—they can't all be on the same curve. But don't make your lesson plan so tight that you can't adapt by staying with the same topic one more hour if you think most of the group is still on the flat slope, or by jumping into a fresh development if you think the group is receptive. Perhaps you will notice that the students seem particularly energetic and yet in very good form during the footwork drill that follows the warm-up. That might indicate readiness for a different move or combination.

Certain interesting phenomena crop up. Fencing habits, good or bad, seem to be retained almost indefinitely. I've had people come to me for lessons, or seen them bout, after lapses of as much as twenty years. It's apparent that they do the moves they were taught, or got into doing, in that long-ago time, despite the fact that they have not practiced or played since.

In a considerable number of cases, I have been the teacher both before and after shorter layoffs, ranging from the summer vacation to about two years. It is very strange, but practically always these students are *better* when they come back than before they left! Certainly they are out of condition, they have lost flexibility and endurance to some degree, and their timing is a bit off, but technically they have improved—without practice. How can this be?

Very often the returning student goes immediately into a period of rapid progress. The teacher should take advantage of the gift. Good times to work intensively are after school vacations, the usual one-week breaks in fall and spring, the two weeks of Christmas holidays, and so forth. The fencer will probably overdo and be very sore for a few days, but the receptiveness to learning is very high.

There is a feature of all kinds of school courses that is so common and obvious that apparently nobody sees it. Suppose we have found out that most of the people in a fencing class can progress so far in such-and-such a period of time; for instance, the beginner course in six weeks at the rate of two one-hour sessions a week. That makes a total of twelve hours. Now think: Could you take one student, or a small class of apt students, and teach them all that in *two days* in succession, working six hours a day, assuming they were in condition to stand it physically? I'm sure you would answer "No." How about three hours a day for four days in a row? Very probably not. How about two hours a day, Wednesday through Friday, and resuming the following Monday through Wednesday? Doubtful. How about an hour a day, exclusive of weekends, until the twelve hours were completed? Maybe.

What would be the best schedule? I might guess at one hour Monday, Wednesday, Friday for four weeks, or an hour and a half on the same days for about two and a half weeks. These are class periods in which the students spend time warming up, taking footwork drills, taking an individual lesson from the coach, practicing together on set routines, and bouting.

As some readers may know, there are dedicated competitive fencers who take four to six individual lessons of thirty minutes or more every week, along with free play and other related activities. This is the kind of program that most international fencers follow, and in the period before the World Championships the team that will represent the nation goes into camp for a few weeks of very intensive training.

But I don't think that these fencers *learn* anything, in the sense of acquiring new knowledge and skill, as the beginner does. They are sharpening themselves to a razor edge, striving for the last possible millimeter of reach, trying to cut a millisecond off the time of a lunge, building more endurance in order to be able to fight through just one more bout at the end of a long tournament day. They are preparing for the highest kind of competition, but they already know the moves and the stratagems.

A question for researchers in education is, what happens between lessons? We are pretty sure that lessons cannot be crowded too closely together—whatever the limit is—and still produce a satisfactory end result. We must suspect that there is some value to the periods when the student is not practicing or even *thinking* about the subject. Moreover, we must suspect that some process goes on within the student that produces better results when he is allowed time away from the subject than when he undergoes long, uninterrupted periods of concentrated study.

This applies to academic courses as well. Students commonly take a mixed program, such as English, history, math, foreign language, and so on. Perhaps they "rest" from studying one subject by studying another, and rest from all work by sleeping, playing, watching TV, or just fooling around. We may blithely say that it takes time to "absorb" the material, but that is hardly a good description —a human is not a sponge, and information is not water.

As another example of this kind of event, most of us have had the experience of going to bed with a nagging problem and waking up with the answer.

For background, we might consider that what we call mind and body are not separate things, or even parts of a whole, but aspects of an integrated organism. When a person is supposedly at rest, brain activity (as measured by electroencephalograph) is accompanied by muscular activity, at a very low level. Other functions of the organism continue as well, but we might wonder whether the rates of digestion, glandular secretion, metabolism, and so forth, differ under various circumstances, such as the events and experiences of the preceding hours. By analogy with a computer, the mind/body seems to work on problems and deliver solutions, whether the person is conscious of the problems or not. This functioning shows up, in the case of fencing, as more skillful performance.

With regard to the often uttered opinion that hard work produces more results, we must be more particular, I think, about the kind of work, how it is done, and on what schedule. The law of diminishing returns must apply. Running is prescribed as part of most training programs, but beyond a point, twice as much running will not give you a proportional amount of improvement. A person learns running skills, but they do not transfer to fencing skills—the movements are quite different. Running on a regular progressive program supposedly improves cardiovascular efficiency, which shows in endurance or stamina, but, after all, a fencer does not bout for more than a few minutes at a stretch. The kind of stamina a fencer must have differs from that of a marathon runner.

Thus far, my argument rests merely on indications from common experience and practice. There have been studies of "fatigue" in learning, with measurements of the decrease in rate of progress. There have also been experiments on the influence of "just thinking about it," instead of actual physical repetition of the given task, with positive results—"mental" review or rehearsal is followed by improved performance. But I know of no study or theory about the apparent process of learning or problem solving during rest. We simply take it into account and make use of it. If we knew more about this phenomenon, we might be able to choose much better schedules for lessons and practice periods, and thus save time and effort.

ELABORATIONS

The reader with a few years of fencing background will have noticed that I haven't dealt with a number of actions in the traditional repertoire. My intent was to describe ideas and movements that would, in general, take care of the situations that might arise in foil play. I hope that I have given what is both necessary and sufficient. There are, of course, alternative movements and theories that are ordinarily dwelt upon at considerable length in "classic" presentations of foil technique. My intent has been to be as basic as possible, and the implication is that the time spent on alternatives should rather be spent on refining the simpler techniques until they solve almost all possible variations.

I have said very little about attacks with preparations on the blade such as pressures, binds, transportations, envelopments, *froissements*, etc. These seem to be unnecessary. Very few modern competitors try such actions in initiating attacks, probably because they are too often deceived; they may appear later in an exchange, and even fencers who have not been trained to do these actions may improvise them to suit the situation. I have presented two beats, Quarte and Seconde, and the slender takings in Sixte and Octave as examples of such actions on the blade: Chiefly these are to be done when the opponent has been induced to extend, and they are to be done with emphasis on forward motion, rather than with a strong lateral component. The fencer must perform these moves with consideration for time and distance factors.

I haven't gone deeply into composite attacks such as the one-two. Very frequently, I've found, students "invent" such combinations spontaneously, before the topic ever comes up in a course—provided they are allowed to bout as soon as they have been introduced to the three simple attacks and the three basic responses to attack. Certainly after learning about feint disengaging, students will see the possibilities. The one-two and the double can be polished up in advanced lessons.

The coupé has been entirely ignored. Its value is dubious. It is very easy to do incorrectly, leaving the attacker vulnerable to a stop thrust. The time required to learn to do it reliably could be much better spent on other techniques. A fencer could very well become champion of the world without ever using a coupé.

There are a number of parry-ripostes that I have not mentioned. Countering Quarte has subsidiary value because the fencer need not ever invite in Quarte. In practice, a genuine invitation in Quarte (in reasonable distance, not as a fake when out of reach) can lead to too many troublesome following moves—parrying too wide in Sixte or Octave, etc. To students who have very good skill in the responses to attack described in the preceding chapters, I teach a beat by countering Sixte, response beating in Sixte, and beating Prime, but these are not necessary for effective foil play.

The worst of all actions in the traditional system is the parry of Septime: It makes an extremely complex demand on the fencer's anatomy (many muscles in the arm must work against each other) and so may be too slow, too heavy, or otherwise ineffective in deflecting the attack. Without a great amount of practice, the riposte from Septime will be too slow or inaccurate. The fencer has several better alternatives to parrying Septime, such as an evasion (retreating) stop thrust to the upper front chest (since the area of target supposedly protected by Septime is farther from the opponent), a low parry Quarte (traditional Quinte), and beating Prime.

Closely related to the actions of binding, transporting, or enveloping the blade are the "yielding" or "ceding" parries. Yielding is supposed to be the answer to strong takings. I haven't gone into this topic because: (1) Takings with a strong lateral component are seldom tried in today's foil play; (2) the student can better spend his time on refining his deceiving techniques; and (3) the fencer with a soft hand will often yield automatically, without being taught. Yielding is a case of the best thing to do is nothing at all. Go limp—the opponent expects to meet blade resistance and overpower it, but meeting none, he throws his point out of line with the target. By playing a long-distance game and by not offering his blade except at the crucial moment of attacking, the fencer can avoid most situations in which yielding would be an alternative answer.

A fencer is not made by the teacher. A fencer develops out of (1) his or her own unique capabilities, (2) the coaching available, and (3) the fencing of the other people in the locality. Whatever "talent" may be, the most talented person could probably not be developed into an excellent fencer by the best of coaches without the presence of other fencers against whom he can fight all along the way. A fencer learns many, if not most, of his best moves by himself, often apparently without being aware of it, while fencing with a variety of opponents.

From the beginning, if at all possible, he should play against people who are better than he is, and he should continue to seek superior opponents by daring to enter meets that are "over his head." Inevitably, there is a gap between even the speediest or most complex lesson and the real, ever-changing situation of bouting. For these reasons, the teacher should not try to force a student into a "perfect" framework of stances, poses, and movements.

Part Three

THE ADVANCED WEAPONS

Chapter 12

TRAINING FOR ÉPÉE AND SABRE

As WE HAVE seen in Chapter 1, the épée and sabre in modern sport fencing are thought of as advanced weapons. A grounding in foil is still advisable, though methods of play have become specialized and most people fence with only one weapon, or limit themselves to either the point weapons or the sabre. A few start with an advanced weapon and stick with it throughout their careers. In itself, the foil is worth a lifetime of study.

If you are a beginner, you should get three to six months of foil training. You will acquire flexibility and toughness in those parts of the body that are used much more in fencing than in other sports. You will pick up some of the basic ideas. I am assuming in what follows that you have had that groundwork. (Refer to Chapter 1 for a general discussion of the characteristics of the épée and sabre as opposed to the foil.)

Fencing masters have written long books on épée and sabre. My purpose is not to tell you everything (which is impossible), but to help you play with good basic technique and understanding. The methods described here are greatly simplified so you can get into bouting as quickly as possible. Knowing a comparatively few movements should be enough, and you will be able to devote your time to more thorough practice of these movements.

It is better to do a few things well than many things poorly. Fencing, after all, does not consist of complications, but rather of the efficient and intelligent use of what you know and can do.

At a later stage you can study more technique. This depends on the availability of a master who can demonstrate these refinements, particularly in sabre. Still, one of the principal characteristics of modern fencing is its simplicity: The fencer attempts to use the most direct action at exactly the right time.

I certainly don't mean to say that fencing now is easier than "in the good old days." On the contrary, today's competitor must work harder. Footwork is dominant. You must strive for perfection in your movements, and you must try to achieve your maximum possible speed. You must have endurance so that you can keep up this rapid, variable footwork throughout a tournament day.

STANCES

The guarding/inviting stances for épée and sabre are not the same as far as arm positioning is concerned. The carriage of the head and trunk, and the arrangement of the feet and legs, are similar. Starting from the ground up: Place your feet at right angles, the front foot (the right, if you are right-handed) aimed toward your opponent and the rear heel in line with the front foot. Your feet should be separated about 15–18 inches, depending on your height and length of leg. Your knees should be only slightly bent, and your front knee should be directed toward your opponent.

Your weight should be distributed equally between your feet. You will move more on the balls of your feet than you did in foil.

Your torso should be erect. Your head should be held high and a little back (the head is fair target in both épée and sabre). Your shoulders should be as loose as possible; your hips and shoulders level.

For épée, your rear arm (the left, if you are right-handed) may be carried pretty much as it is in foil—slightly bent, with the hand about shoulder-high and relaxed. Your fighting arm will be almost straight, slanting somewhat downward. Your fighting hand will usually be palm upward (Fig. 68).

The majority of sabreurs now let their rear arms hang at ease, but your rear shoulder must not come too far forward. The elbow of your fighting arm points downward, about five inches ahead of the ribs. Your forearm slants very slightly downward. Normally your sabre hand is carried thumb up. (Fig. 85).

Understand: These postures are merely basic. There are no rules about how you must stand. Almost all fencers change the spacing of the feet, the placing of weight, the positioning of the arms. At a safe distance—far away from your opponent—you can abandon these stances. It is good to do so, in order (1) to rest and (2) to confuse your opponent. Naturally, you will make other changes to adapt to various situations, for purposes of attacking and counterattacking.

FUNDAMENTAL FOOTWORK

Your foil training should have included several basic moves and combinations of them: advancing, retreating, lunging/recovering, and hopping forward and backward; advance-lunging, retreat-lunging, appel-lunging and hop-lunging. You should have reached the stage of lunging about 50 times a day, each time with a preliminary move (advance, retreat, appel, or hop).

These moves will be about the same for épée and sabre, except that you will be a *little* more on the balls of your feet much of the time, and you will lunge quite a bit shorter than the "all-out" attack in foil. Rather than recover forward from lunging, as most foilists do, you will recover backward.

The sabreur, especially, recovers instantly from lunging, without waiting to find out what his opponent intends to do, and without trying to parry at the extreme of his lunge. But not always.

In recovering backward from lunging, be sure your rear knee bends first. You do this to avoid standing up. Your front leg will then push you directly back at about the same level.

A most important point is that you must not lean forward, but rather keep your head well back. During the lunge and recovery, your opponent might well make an attack to your head, which is a bigger target than your fighting arm.

61. *Lunging practice, arms behind back: early phase*

62. *Lunging practice, arms behind back: maximum length for épée and sabre*

63. *Recovering backward, arms behind back: rear knee bends first*

64. Recovering backward, arms behind back: later phase

EXTRA FOOTWORK TRAINING

Sabreurs and épéeists hardly ever attack without a good deal of preparatory footwork, which is necessary to get the exact range and timing. Often, too, these fighters must escape from explosive attacks. In addition to the basic footwork reviewed above, you will want to slide, brake, jump back, run back, etc.

Sliding. Since you will stand with knees less bent than in foil and your weight a little more on your toes, you can move forward, backward, and sometimes to the side by sliding your feet lightly over the floor. This kind of movement is sneakier than other foot actions. It gives you a way of changing your timing. With your feet actually in contact with the floor all the time, you can easily shorten movements when necessary, stopping or even reversing your direction.

Sliding can be done in the same manner as advancing, by moving the front foot forward and then bringing the rear foot along about the same amount. Or, you may choose to slide the rear foot up close to the front foot and put the front foot out afterward.

Braking. You probably have habits of advancing and retreating about the same number of inches each time. You should practice changing this by starting a fairly long advance and quickly cutting it off in the middle. As your front foot skims over the floor, dig in your toes.

A good exercise is to move the same foot twice: the rear foot backward, as though retreating, but returning it to your normal stance without moving the front foot; or the front foot forward and then back.

Advance Check. To advance and then hop forward is a rather clumsy combination. Instead, most fencers do what is called an advance check. This is similar to the braked advance, except that you do want to continue forward, but with a change of rhythm. Step out as usual with your front foot; just as you are about to move the rear foot forward, skid *both* feet farther forward, setting both heels into the floor. The front foot makes contact with the floor in the advance, but you can't afford to put weight on it—you must move it again before it is pinned down.

Since the advance check is a substitute for an advance followed by a hop forward, you could make up a longer combination by adding a hop back or a retreat.

Retreat and Hop Back. This move is carried out on the balls of your feet. As usual you reach back with your rear toes to retreat, but instead of planting the front foot flat as you finish the retreat, prepare your front toes to hop back immediately. For a right-hander: left-right-both together, very quickly. As you land, you must be able to balance on your toes. For later co-ordinations, you should be able to continue with another retreat, a jump back, an advance, or a lunge, at least. Longer combinations should be tried out in order to improve your mobility.

Jumping Back. A nearly instinctive reaction to an unexpected attack is to lean back away from it. Novice fencers get caught off-balance this way, with their weight on the rear foot. Their shoulders and arms stiffen so they can hardly execute a counteroffensive action.

Through training, the natural response can be turned into an effective means of escape—actually not an escape, but a retirement to a better location from which to deal with the attack. Your head jerks back and your front leg shoves. Instead of getting stuck on your rear leg, continue the motion into a big jump backward.

It is essential that when you jump, you should get your rear foot well behind you. Thus, your movement will be stopped. You must land *softly*—on your toes, letting your knee give—and immediately get solid to parry-riposte or counterattack. Your opponent, having failed with his original surprise action, may very well continue, but you should have gained a little more time in which he might go off-balance. If you practice jumping back so as to come down guarding, you can take advantage of his faults.

Running Back. Some fencers, instead of jumping back, convert the reaction of swaying away from an attack into a run back of a few steps. To run back, cross your front foot behind your rear foot, then move the rear foot back and repeat as often as you like.

Again, it is a good idea to stop suddenly after a certain number of steps, with your rear foot well behind you. You should be prepared to stand firm in the new location and deal with your opponent's continuation.

The Test. No matter which of these footwork combinations—or any others of a similar kind—you may use, the great test is whether you can lunge at the end of a chosen pattern. This means that no matter how fast you're going forward or backward, you should have such control of your balance that when you put on the brakes and stop, you should be able to lunge (and recover) without falling over or even wobbling.

In competition you might get so excited that you can't be perfectly smooth, but the more you practice a variety of combinations, ending with lunging/recovering, the less trouble you will have in a real bout. After you have worked out some of these suggested combinations, you could get a lot of benefit out of making up different and more difficult ones for yourself.

Instructor: These moves should be included in drills as soon as the fundamentals are well established. Repeat blind drill with arms folded behind the back, blind drill with arms in their regular attitudes but without weapons, blind drill with weapons, and silent drills without and with weapons.

For the silent drills, students will have to discriminate between a number of visual cues. It should already have been established that the student will advance when you retreat (and by the same amount), hop forward when you hop back, etc. The student will now have to perceive a sliding advancement, for example, and do a sliding retreat. Alternatively, you may face in the same direction as the student, in which case he will imitate your movements instead of responding to a theoretical opponent, but this is a less effective teaching device. Naturally, in combat the student would not necessarily match a sliding advance with a sliding retreat, or whatever, but would choose other movements for his advantage.

Your problem is to make unexpected aggressive moves, sprinting forward without warning, etc., and you will find this more and more difficult as time goes on. Students are challenged by the game, and they become very alert and clever. They will begin to react at the slightest "telegraph" move.

Test your students by requiring a lunge at any moment. In a blind drill you may say, for instance, "Slide forward, lunge!" or "Run back, lunge!" In the latter case, the student must lunge the very next time his rear foot grabs the floor. In silent drills, you must give the lunging signal (dropping your weapon hand or moving it far to one side) irregularly. Students will get so good that eventually you will have to cue them for a lunge almost simultaneously with the preparatory footwork signal.

65. *Jumping back: take-off*

66. *Running back: start*

INTENSIFIED CONDITIONING

You will need explosiveness, variability, and stamina to fence well with the épée or sabre. Class drills, individual lessons, and all footwork described should be supplemented by trackwork, and other sports activity may be helpful. Get warmed up thoroughly before you start on the harder work.

Falling. Fencers do, sometimes, lose balance. Once in a while a wrinkle in the mat, a button popped off a fencing jacket, or some other unforeseen obstacle will make a fencer trip and fall. It is extremely worthwhile to know how to fall with the least chance of injury—an ability that is valuable in everyday activities, too.

Rule No. 1: NEVER try to stop a fall with a stiff arm.

Whether you are falling forward or backward, it is better to tuck in your head and go right into it (not trying to hold back) and roll or spin. Begin by practicing forward and backward somersaults on a wrestling mat or other padded surface. Then find somebody who can show you the falling techniques of judo or aikido.

Once you have discovered for yourself that you can roll out of a fall without getting hurt, you will probably be more relaxed, which is essential. Stiffness, caused by panic, often leads to more pain.

Sprinting. Indoors or outdoors, mark off distances of 10 or 15 yards. Starting from a standing position or a slight crouch, right foot forward if you are right-handed, sprint as fast as you can. You should stop suddenly, as close to the line as possible, without preparatory slowing down. The shorter distance is more difficult, but the goal in both cases is to get a fast start and a fast stop. You should be able to keep this up for a half hour or so.

Hurdling. Cardboard cartons of different sizes (maximum of 18 inches high) make good hurdles. They should be placed at irregular intervals around the border of the gym or along the track. The gym is better, requiring sharper turns at the corners. Two laps around the gym, one clockwise and one counterclockwise, will fit nicely into a class period.

Hopping. With your feet together, hop forward 10 or 15 yards. Hop the same distance backward. Hop sideways, right and left. Hop in a zigzag forward, then backward. This could be strenuous for you at first, and you might build up to it over a period of a week or two.

When you have advanced your conditioning, do the hopping sequence on one foot. If you are right-handed, use only your left foot. Usually the right-handed fencer overworks his right leg, mostly by recovering backward from lunging, and this kind of exercise will help equalize the development of the legs. The added toughness and power of the rear leg may give you a split-second advantage in some situations. You should work up to about 100 bounces a day.

Half-Squatting, Rear Leg. With the hopping described above, you can also do half squats on your left leg (or right, if you are left-handed). Reach down behind you and hold your right toe with your left hand. Squat as far as possible with your foot flat on the floor. You should work up to fifty a day. You can do this in sets of 20 bounces and 10 half squats, perhaps only one set the first day but adding sets until you have reached the total.

Ordinarily it is up to the fencer himself to do this kind of training. Most classes are not designed to produce advanced competitors—or even varsity teams for the college or high school. These are recreational courses. If you're a novice, you have to take my word at this stage that the better you are, and the better your opponents, the more fun it is, and that it's worth impoving your conditioning. But you probably have many good years ahead of you, and you needn't rush. Build up carefully.

FLÈCHING

One of the most obvious features of épée and sabre competition is that instead of lunging the fencers seem to dash forward a lot. The spectator who keeps his ears open hears the word "flèche" (pronounced *flesh*) applied to this method of attacking.

I must make clear that flèching is NOT a running attack. The hit is NOT made by running at the opponent. Sometimes the flèche doesn't reach, and the fencer continues by running. The idea, though, is to launch yourself and hit on the very *first* motion.

Running is then merely a way of recovering your balance after the hit has been made. If you don't hit on the initial spring, your flèche has failed. In such a case, you run off the strip at an angle, and this may help you avoid your opponent's counteraction.

Some fencing masters have stated that flèching should not be taught to a student with less than a year, or even two, of thorough preparation. Furthermore, children who are not full-grown (under about fourteen) should not do it. I must emphasize as strongly as possible that every other foot action should be practiced a great deal first.

Students with less than about a year of training will probably not have developed the toughness of muscle and tendon to take the strain. Flèching demands a very quick and powerful action of the front leg. Two undesirable results may come if the student is not prepared: a joint injury and/or a slow and ineffective flèche. Those who have not attained full growth, especially, may not have the bones, the strength, and the co-ordination to do a flèche correctly. And just as with other things, it does no good to repeat mistakes.

Use of the various conditioning exercises already mentioned will ready students for flèching. After a few weeks, while other footwork is being polished, this technique can be gradually introduced into the program.

We must note that *the* flèche is not the same for both épée and sabre. The difference is that in épée the fighting arm is usually already extended. If you go from foil into épée, this extended-arm attitude will require a few slight adjustments in many of your actions. But if you go on from épée to sabre, you will have to change again, and more. This is one of the reasons most fencers specialize in a single weapon.

To flèche, you suddenly extend your whole body from your toes to the tip of your weapon, exploding toward the target. The same purpose might be achieved by lunging, but ordinarily you can reach farther and more quickly with a flèche. Both legs drive you rather than just one.

Some preliminary action is *always* necessary. You have to assume your opponent knows about flèching, and he won't deliberately come within easy reach. Also, and perhaps more importantly, you must get your center of gravity ahead of your feet. One problem is to get close enough, even with this tremendous spring, and the other is to hide the preparatory shift or make it so quickly that your opponent can't react soon enough.

A good example of a preliminary maneuver for the flèche is the "rocking start": If your weight is a little on your rear foot, sway forward smoothly onto your front foot. While ordinarily you don't allow your weight to become unevenly distributed, in this case you swing on until your center of gravity (in your lower belly) passes over your front foot. The rear leg gives some drive, but the sharpest impulse then comes from a snap of the front leg. (This puts a very sudden and extraordinary strain on the foot and ankle.) You are totally committed, off-balance, springing forward, your body at a slant, feet close together—this is the instant at which you should hit.

Practice rocking forward and back a few times before going smoothly into a slow flèche. As soon as you are stretched out for the hit, your rear leg will swing over, and you can trot on away. After you have the sequence going smoothly, you can gradually increase speed.

You may prepare to flèche by advancing. Instead of checking your weight behind your front foot, as you normally would, continue the motion into the flèche. Your forward movement is suddenly accelerated the instant your left foot (assuming you're right-handed) grabs the floor. Your opponent will see you advance, but should expect you to stop momentarily as usual.

The flèche may be started by hopping forward into a slight crouch. Here again your weight is allowed to continue over your front foot, and you kick off from there. At this stage of your practice, you might work on a combination of advance, hop forward, flèche, which gives you a longer preparation, more time to build up the top-speed drive. Some experienced competitors, even after three or four very rapid advances, can break into a flèche—which means that the weapon tip speeds up amazingly to catch an opponent who is retreating as fast as he can or running backward.

Another way is to begin as though you were going to retreat. Don't let your weight go as far back as usual, but withdraw your front foot right under you. This works when your opponent follows you immediately—you should attack while he is still in the midst of advancing.

Next, practice flèching from a hop backward or jump backward. Instead of landing on balance, throw both feet slightly *behind* you and bounce instantly into the flèche. The combination beyond this is retreat, hop back, flèche.

The most difficult way is to start from a standstill. Sometimes, after a series of foot maneuvers, you will actually pause in place for a noticeable period. From a guarding/inviting posture, you must simultaneously pull back your front foot— that is, pull one of your props out from under yourself—and drive with your rear leg. The front leg immediately takes over, kicking back, speeding the action to maximum.

Now you know what the running is all about. The fencer who flèches is completely off-balance, and he either falls flat or recovers by running.

WARNING: The rules specify penalties against a fencer who collides with his opponent, or even looks as though he might ("dangerous play"). Flèching is certainly risky in this respect. Therefore, as soon as the single attacking motion has been made, you must swerve and run at an angle past your opponent. A right-hander usually goes to the right so his opponent is not behind him as they pass. This requires a tricky little hip twist as the rear foot crosses over on the first step of the recovery (running). Finally, to avoid counteractions, the fencer who flèches sprints as fast as he can and ordinarily ends up off the strip.

If the hit is not made on the flèche (as defined), the fencer who has tried it is extremely vulnerable. A hit made against you immediately after you cross the strip boundary is allowable.

If no hits are made, you will be penalized two meters of ground for going off the strip; that is, your opponent will be advanced two meters from where he was standing when you made the action. These are excellent reasons for not overusing the flèche and for practicing long and hard to do it very well indeed.

The practice for sabre may be introduced in an easier way (Figs. 82–84). You may take a position like a runner's standing start, but with your front foot (in fencing terms) forward. From this crouch, spring, shooting the tip of your weapon at an imaginary target no higher than your own eyes and usually no lower than your chest. You must lead with and emphasize the extension of your arm. Run off to one side of your original line.

Advanced sabreurs often get to the stage of being able to check the running recovery on the sixth, or even the fourth, stride (third or second step with the front foot). Staying on the strip, they "put on the brakes," guarding/inviting again, and fight it out with the opponent who has retreated too fast to be reached by the flèche. This kind of thing takes even more co-ordination, control, and strength than the flèche itself. Getting the body going at top speed (in auto-racing terms, from zero to 15 mph in about ⅕th of a second or less) is difficult, and certainly the prime objective is to hit immediately, not to get involved in any riskier complications. Stopping dead is much harder. It is *not* advisable for heavier-than-average people—the strain is too great. Even if you are small and light, this should be a low-priority technique to practice.

TO INSTRUCTORS

An instructor should, of course, have had more training and experience than his students (although some great teachers of champions have not been champions themselves). I assume you will have had at least a year of training, foil plus the weapon in question, when you begin to lead students who have had no épée or sabre experience, and that you have had some competitive experience, including service as an official.

The more background you have, the better. But the essential thing is that you should want to teach, and teach well, so that you will study up on rules, theory, and technique, and will try continually to improve.

One objective of this book is to get more young people *started* in play with the advanced weapons. Students don't need to know everything. They need fundamental skills and a framework of ideas. Good basics can be refined and elaborated later. There are not enough masters to start everybody from scratch, but if a much larger number of students get the essentials, plus some competitive experience, a general rise in quality ought to follow. Elementary instruction can very well be given by teachers who have not had many years of study and practice.

WOMEN'S PARTICIPATION

Can women compete and coach in épée and sabre? In a great number of American high schools and colleges the teachers are women because in this country fencing is more likely to be part of the program for women physical education majors. Women thus far have competed mostly in foil. Hence when they become teachers they usually teach only foil. But with the growth of the sport there may be a demand for follow-up courses in the so-called advanced weapons.

In the past few years there have been more épée and sabre meets for women, and soon these may be regular events in the national championships and perhaps on higher levels. There is no longer any question about whether women are capable of handling these weapons. The sabre, in particular, is lighter in weight than most foils. Teachers do need the competitive background, and now women have more chances to get it.

The principal benefits to the woman competitor are improvement of mobility and accuracy, greater power and endurance, and wider variety of actions that will be effective in foil play, which is still the main area of women's activity. The rules do prohibit women from fencing against men (with any weapon) in official competitions of the Amateur Fencers League of America or the Fédération Internationale d'Escrime (the world organization). Wherever there are enough women in a given locality to make up a competitive pool—at least four—then official meets could be held. Further, trained women could direct épée, and judge and preside at sabre, even if the competitors are men.

Since she can't ordinarily get as much tournament experience, the woman who wishes to teach épée or sabre must get proportionately more training. She may very easily turn out to be better technically than a man in the same length of time. She can get bouting practice at least with her coach and with male épéeists and sabreurs in the classroom. She can, to some extent, make up for lack of competitive participation by attending meets and observing play, preferably at fairly advanced levels. She can watch men take lessons and practice.

When bouting or teaching, a woman should be dressed for maximum protection. In addition to the fencing outfit, which for women includes a padded jacket and breast shields, she ought to wear at least one thick long-sleeved sweat shirt under the jacket. Over the jacket she should wear a plastron when teaching. For sabre she should have an elbow cup (like everyone else) and a very well-padded glove: The risk is that her (presumably) lighter bones might be cracked or chipped. These same risks exist for men, too. (*Machismo* in fencing is sillier than usual—I don't like having welts and bruises, I wear all the protection I can without being immobilized when teaching épée or sabre, and I take plenty of Vitamin C.)

Very possibly the male students of a woman might become better fencers than those studying under a man. Men, in their conventional masculine role, tend to "go easy" on a woman, and therefore should develop lighter, better-controlled actions, especially hand and arm actions, through practicing with a woman teacher (or partner). Sure, guys, you might be able to win with your superior power and speed, but can you really outsmart her? Experts agree that more refined thrusts, cuts, parries, etc. contribute to fencing success.

In the past men have had the opportunity to try all three weapons, and very often a man makes a choice of one as his favorite. Women now have that same opportunity.

Chapter 13

ÉPÉE RULES, THEORY, AND OFFICIATING

AT FIRST GLANCE, épée fencing seems the easiest or simplest branch of the sport. There are fewer rules about how you should play, although more attention is paid to technical matters such as the dimensions of the weapon, how far the tip button must be depressed before the circuit is closed, etc.

SAFETY

Safety in épée, as in all aspects of fencing, is supremely important. We don't want anyone injured, and if we can't fence with the utmost safety, we shouldn't fence. The épée is the heaviest of the three weapons, and has the stiffest blade. When driven at top speed, as in a flèche, it can cause damage.

Uniform and Equipment. Fencers not properly dressed are disqualified from competitions. The same or higher standards should be maintained in practice.

The mask should be of a stronger type than for foil, with heavier-gauge wire mesh; many of them have reinforcing bars inside, plus a forehead shade. It should be examined regularly for weaknesses caused by rust or previous hits. The bib should be larger than for foil, with deeper overlap of the jacket collar. The jacket and trousers should be of heavier material than the foil uniform; the jacket is supposed to overlap the waistband of the trousers by about four inches in any position, which means that the trousers must be high-waisted and held up by suspenders (i.e., "braces," in the British Commonwealth).

Be sure to wear the short-sleeved inner plastron (Fig. 58) at all times. I've seen a broken blade punch through three layers of canvas.

Many épéemen wear a "cup jock," although this would seem to interfere with running. I would recommend some kind of tough inner pants, such as mid-thigh-length tennis shorts. Such a garment is not required by the rules, but if the triple-layered jacket and extra plastron are specified to prevent wounds in the chest, why not be just as cautious about wounds through the groin? The attacking blade may miss the *cuissard* (belly apron) of the jacket.

A kneepad for the front leg is also a good idea. An épée shot to the kneecap can be rather uncomfortable, to say the least.

Suppliers offer an extra outer sleeve. This is for practice, to keep the jacket sleeve undamaged, so that it will continue to give maximum protection in tournaments. It is particularly good for teachers.

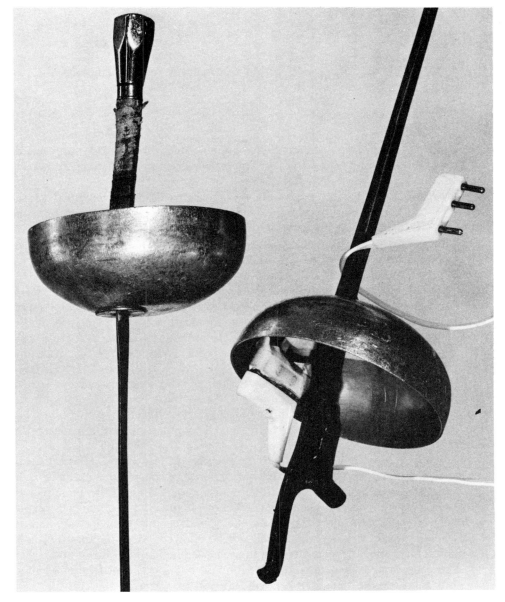

67. Épées: French (left) and pistol grip

Manner of Play. The rules set penalties for collisions or any body contact; "unsportsmanlike conduct"; unnecessary roughness, without regard to whether it is intentional; brutality, such as hard hitting with the side of the blade, or with the guard or pommel; "dangerous play"—any behavior that appears to the director to threaten collisions and the like. Penalties range from award of a touch against the offender, or annulment of a touch he has made, through dismissal from the tournament in progress, to suspension from all tournaments for various periods of time.

Leaving aside the question of whether a violation was intentional, these penalties force all fencers to play as safely as possible with, ideally, no body contact. The implication is that if a fencer's poor control is a potential danger, if he can't gain control after a warning, he will be sent "back to school."

In case you're scared—good. Fencing is one of the safest of all sports. Injuries are extremely rare. The safety record results from keen vigilance on the part of teachers, officials, and competitors.

LIMITATIONS

You should begin immediately to try to figure out what you can and can't do according to the limitations. As explained in Chapter 1, they apply to the weapon, the target, the ground, and the time for a standard bout.

Weapon. "If you don't poke him, it won't go off." For theoretical consideration, we are most interested in the fact that the épée can only score by a forward motion of the point. Sideways movements of the blade have very little use, and you're wasting your time and energy if you slash and hack. With the electric scoring apparatus, the light simply won't go on unless you push the tip button directly against solid target.

Epées are tested to make sure that at least 750 grams (about 1.65 pounds) of pressure is needed to close the switch at the tip. If the spring is too weak, it must be replaced. The blade is tested before a tournament to make sure it is neither too stiff nor too flexible. There is a limit on the amount of curve. You are responsible for changes that take place through use, such as bending of the blade and weakening of the tip spring.

Target. Unlike the foil and the sabre, the épée can score against *any* part of the body. There are *no* target restrictions. Officials must be alert for hits on the floor (unless the strip is metallic and neutralized by connection with the apparatus), or by the fencer on his own body, which would register the same as hits against the opponent.

Ground. We are concerned, for theory, with the fact that a fencer may be penalized for leaving the field of play while action is going on. For example, if he steps off the side with both feet (as might occur in flèching), the bout will be halted and his opponent will gain two meters of ground. If the offender is hit immediately after he goes off, the hit may be scored against him, but any hit he makes while outside the boundaries will not be allowed. Most importantly, if he retreats too far, a touch is scored against him whether he has been hit or not.

The épée strip is 14 meters long, as for foil, but the épéeist is allowed more retreating room by the rules. He may go back all the way past the end line with both feet before a halt is called. Then he is placed with his rear foot on a warning line, which is 2 meters from the end (as compared to 1 meter for foil). If he again retreats until both feet are past the end line, he automatically loses a point.

You should note that if he already has both feet behind the warning line, and has been properly warned by the director, and then goes out of bounds *sideways,* a 2-meter ground penalty puts him past the end line. He is, therefore, penalized by 1 touch.

Time. As in foil and sabre, fencers in épée have 6 minutes of total playing time to complete a bout for 5 touches. But épée bouts do not go into overtime, because if the score is tied at the end of 6 minutes, *both* fencers are considered to have *lost* at 5-all. However, see below.

SCORING

Foil and sabre are called "conventional" weapons: There are rules about "right-of-way," or precedence when both fencers are hit "simultaneously" (as nearly as the director can tell). Épée has *no* conventions. The sole determining factor is who hits first. This is gauged by the machine, which discriminates at $\frac{1}{25}$th of a second: if fencer A hits $\frac{1}{25}$th of a second before fencer B, then B's circuit is automatically switched off, and any later hit B may make will not register.

Often enough both hit within $\frac{1}{25}$th of a second. Unlike the situation in foil and sabre, this double hit will be scored *against both* (unless one of them is off the strip at that instant). Therefore, if the score is 3–2 and a double hit occurs, the score becomes 4–3. It may happen when the score is 4-all, and the score becomes 5-all. In such a case the competitors must continue to fence for a deciding hit, and if one is made (all later doubles being disregarded), the score is entered as a loss for the fencer who was hit and a victory for the other, but with 5 touches against each. If the score is still tied when time expires, it is recorded as a *double loss* at 5-all.

THOUGHTS ABOUT ÉPÉE

Since it is a thrusting weapon, the épée offers a natural continuation to foil. Basic training received with the foil contributes to skill with the épée. Épée experience, conversely, is worthwhile if you expect to go into electrical foil competition.

Foilists should benefit from the emphasis on point accuracy and timing, the need for careful judgment of distance and practice in playing at greater distances, the use of more positive (forward) actions, the increase of arm strength from carrying a heavier weapon, etc. To a much lesser extent, people who become sabreurs may also profit from épée training.

But épée fencing is a very special field in itself. You might think that it is much simpler than play with either of the other weapons because there are no rules about right-of-way and no target limitations, but it has its own subtle complications. For example, although the hand and wrist are legitimate targets you must know the risks of shooting at them: The area is small and capable of fast evasive action; the hand is pretty well hidden by the bell guard. Again, although you might be tempted to attack the foot or lower leg, these targets may escape from you, and they are much farther away—your opponent could hit your chest or head $\frac{1}{25}$th of a second before you could reach his foot (besides, attacks to the foot are often wasted when there is no neutralized metallic floor).

You may prefer, after thinking it over, to make the great majority of your attacks to more reliable targets: from your opponent's forearm toward his shoulder, chest and head, and (much less often) from his knee upward. Your point will stick more solidly in these places. In the long run more of your attacks will be likely to register. Later, of course, you may develop such accuracy that it will be feasible to go for smaller, faster-moving targets which, being closer, give you a little better chance of being $\frac{1}{25}$th of a second ahead.

Épée actions should be POSITIVE. In other words, you should not use *defensive* hand movements (sideways or backward) but devote yourself to attacking and counterattacking. There is a special "feel" about this, since you don't want to act recklessly and overcommit yourself, thus undertaking undue risks. Exact control of balance and footwork is necessary so that you will be ready to attack or respond to your opponent's attack at the best time and distance.

There is an old and often-repeated saying that goes something like, "The art of fencing is to hit without being hit." This is very misleading if you think defensively. The game today, in foil and sabre as well as épée, is to *hit first*. If you do, according to the rules, you will not be hit because your opponent's later actions don't count. In electric foil some confusion arises because the machine continues to register after the first hit has been made, and you have to hit *enough* ahead to impress the director. Looking at it another way, you can only "turn off" your opponent by hitting him quicker and more often than he hits you: If you give much attention to defense, he will still get through eventually. No prizes are given for pretty parries.

One thought-worthy aspect of épée strategy is the use of the touch differential. Supposing that you had a lead of 2 touches at 3–1, you could take the risk of increasing your aggressiveness, on the chance that doubles would occur, raising the score to 4–2 and then 5–3. Even the loss of one touch would leave you with a lead and the chance of stalling until time ran out or regaining a wider lead. If you are behind, you can expect such strategies to be used by your opponent, and you should conduct yourself accordingly. Think over what you might do at all the different score combinations.

Another approach would be to play very aggressively (but not stupidly) throughout. This scheme often results in a string of double hits. At 4-all the situation is scary—the bout has become a 1-touch affair, or "sudden death." But, having attacked strongly all the time, you may have a psychological advantage. Of course, against any reasonably good épéeist, your attacks must start without warning (without telegraphing), even in order to get double hits, because your opponent will simply back off and pick at your arm.

You must be able to play the careful game as well as the explosive one. You must be able to fit your strategy to the situation and to your opponent. Your technique must include more than just one kind of action.

To become "strip wise" you must do a lot of competing, that's all. Your experience will fill in the above outlines of rules and theory, and no book or coach can tell you all about it beforehand.

OFFICIATING

With the machine, épée officiating is comparatively easy. The director, as the referee is called, usually watches the floor more than anything else.

If there is no metallic strip connected to the apparatus, a couple of judges are employed just to watch for floor hits. A double, with one hitting the floor, would be scored against the man who hit the floor. However, if the official or officials are in doubt, both hits should be disregarded.

One main job of the director is to watch for boundary violations. A fencer who goes off the strip sideways must be penalized. The fencer's use of the ground is very important. In cases where hits are made while one fencer is off the strip, or going off, the director has to decide whether or not to allow the score. This is particularly important when one man is going past the end line the first time back: Theoretically the strip is much longer and does not end there, so the question may arise of allowing a hit made by the man going off, a hit made against him, or possibly a double. These are about all the sources of arguments in épée, since the machine solves practically every other question, assuming that all the parts of the apparatus are working right.

The director must see that the weapons are tested at the beginning of each bout. He must watch out for violation of safety rules, must give warnings, and impose penalties. He ought to be alert for blades that have been bent more than the allowable amount by the shock of hitting. These are only a few of his duties. In general, his job is to help the fencers have a fair and safe contest.

Chapter 14

ÉPÉE ATTACKING

HOOKING UP AND TESTING

WHEN YOU DRESS for épée practice or competition, you will put one end of your body cord down inside your sleeve as you get into your jacket. The cord should, however, be outside your special protective plastron.

After plugging the cord into the reel connection and the weapon, you should test with the 750-gram weight and a feeler gauge. You could practice without these tests, or without using the apparatus at all, but it is best to get as close to tournament conditions as possible. At a competition the director will make the weight and feeler tests before each bout, even though all weapons should have been examined by a technician before the meet. Sometimes, at minor events when the proper equipment is not available, tests of weight and point travel are omitted, but it is unfair to the fencer whose weapons are up to specifications if his opponent's épées have weak springs, etc. Finally, each fencer presses his tip against his opponent's bell guard, to make sure it doesn't register.

The fencers then salute one another and the officials, as they would in foil, put on their masks, and await the director's command to begin.

Hold the épée in the same way you would the foil, with your fingers as loose as possible most of the time. Your thumb will be on the grooved side of the blade. Be sure, if you are left-handed, that you have a left-handed bell guard and handle.

Épéeists guard/invite with the fighting arm almost fully extended and palm up (most of the time). The positions of the hand cannot be described in quite the same terms as in foil, but if the épée tip is slightly above the horizontal, we say the fencer is guarding/inviting Sixte. More commonly, the tip is just below the horizontal, and this stance is called guarding/inviting Octave. The difference is only a very few inches in tip elevation in contrast to a very distinct difference in foil. Somewhere in between, the blade is "in line" (but very seldom is it NOT aimed at *some* part of the opponent).

68. Épée stance: guarding/inviting Octave

SIMPLE ATTACKING

Simple attacks are made in a single motion: by fully stretching the arm, by extending/lunging, by extending/advancing, by extending/flèching, etc. Attacks in two or more motions are called composite or compound, but épéeists often make a rapid series of simple attacks, or little jabs, without doing what would theoretically be classified as a composite attack. The simple attacks may be divided into three types: direct, indirect, and taking.

Direct attacks go practically straight. For instance, if you were guarding/inviting Sixte, you could thrust over the top of your opponent's bell guard. For an indirect attack, you shift your aim to another "line." If you were guarding/inviting Sixte, a thrust to the underside of your opponent's arm would be indirect. "Taking" attacks are intended to deflect your opponent's blade while you try to hit; these may also be thought of as indirect.

All attacks must be made on a favorable change of ground. You can't afford to wait until you are already within your opponent's reach before you start.

Whether your opponent steps toward you or you step toward him, whether you advance a little farther than he retreats or he advances a little farther than you retreat, you really start your attack right then, as the step is made. So even though you use a simple attack, which takes one hand move, there is almost always preliminary foot action (by you or your opponent). Very rarely can you launch an attack from a standstill—you can't take the preparatory step and then hesitate for more than a split second.

One of the best times to attack is when your opponent is recovering, as from lunging or even in the tiny instant after he has made a short jab. Almost everybody will pull back slightly, or pause, after an effort, and the épéeist who develops a knack for striking at this time will often succeed.

Direct Attacking. Your opponent is always open somewhere. But all targets are not at the same depth (equally near). Ordinarily his blade is aimed at some part of your body, too. We may say that the only time your opponent is not open is when his arm is fully extended and aimed at the closest target, your hand. Your target choice is determined by: (1) your original attitude (guarding/inviting), and (2) the target that is available to you at a closer range than *his* target.

Suppose you are guarding/inviting Sixte, with your blade pointed toward his chest, and your opponent is guarding/inviting Octave, his blade aimed at your waist. His épée tip would have to travel farther in a straight line to strike your body than yours would to strike his forearm. Your direct attack, then, would be right over his bell guard, first toward his wrist but lined up along his arm so as to catch, perhaps, his biceps or the hollow of his elbow. If your attack is more than merely an extension of your arm, say by lunging, recover with your feet but leave your arm stretched out (except when flèching). Possibly, if your opponent escapes from your attack and tries to attack as you recover, your point will catch him. If you recover with a bent arm, he is more likely to hit you.

Instructor: In the individual lesson, give the opportunity for this attack about three times for these footwork combinations (students attacking as you advance from pretty far away): extending/advancing, lunging, balestra,* or, later, flèching. The student should stretch his arm fully without locking the elbow or hunching the shoulder, extending palm up as though he expected to slide his blade through the forearm at a slight angle to it. Make sure the student recovers from lunging with a straight arm.

Target practice: You can rig up hanging targets, about the size of a golf ball, for your students to thrust at. These should be free to swing a couple of feet in any direction, the strings should be three or four feet long, and the targets should be about four feet above the floor. The student should approach to extending distance, thrust at the ball, and retire with a stretched arm. He should not stand at the given range for more than a half second. At first his thrust can be made when the ball is still, but after some experience he may try to hit it when it is swinging from side to side or forward and back. Next, he should try to hit it by lunging, from progressively greater distances with various footwork combinations. This will keep other students busy while you work with one.

Practice in couples. The object of practice between beginner students is to set up the easiest possible situation for repetition of a fundamental move. We suppose that if you have trouble hitting an immobile target at a fixed range, you will have even more difficulty hitting one that is in motion. Agree with your part-

---

* *Balestra* means hop lunge, the hop being forward.

69. Lunging over the guard, opponent in Octave

ner about who is to be the dummy. The dummy will then stand still, guarding/inviting Octave, and the active partner will approach to whatever range he likes and make a simple direct attack from guarding/inviting Sixte toward the upper surface of the forearm. If the active partner lunges, he must immediately recover whether he has hit or not, and if he has attacked by extending/advancing, he must retreat—at this stage he must NOT stay in close and make additional jabs. Each kind of footwork should be repeated at least three times, but the flèche should not be used by students against each other. At the end of the sequence, the fencers change roles.

If your opponent's blade happens to point away from any part of your body, but his bell guard covers his hand and wrist, you could make the same kind of direct attack from guarding/inviting Sixte toward the deeper targets of upper arm, shoulder, upper chest, or head. The closest target would be your primary aiming point. You need to try to play at the longest possible range in order to overcome your foil training.

Instructor: Go through the footwork schedule again, calling for hits to the deeper targets by lunging or, after the recommended conditioning, by flèching. The student must make at least one advance from out of range before the attack proper begins.

70. *Lunging under the guard, opponent in Sixte*

Another possibility is that your opponent's blade will be directed to one side, exposing his wrist. Usually, if both you and he are right-handed, his fingers will show when his épée tip drifts to your left. You may then try a direct attack along the *inside* of his arm instead of along the top. Practice in couples can be done methodically as before, the dummy in either Sixte or Octave with the wrist exposed. Be sure to work at long range, and concentrate on smooth balanced movement rather than speed.

Instructor: Again, the student should extend along the forearm at a slight angle, "following through" so that if he misses your wrist there is a chance of hitting as deep as the elbow—but no farther. The beginner should be discouraged from jabbing with too great an angle sideways at the wrist, although this technique is useful later on. The beginner needs plenty of practice in smooth, long thrusting.

When you are guarding/inviting Octave, your direct targets would be, strictly speaking, low ones. They are farther away. But your opponent may make the mistake of guarding/inviting Sixte as a foilist does, bending his elbow too much. The undersurface of his forearm will be exposed, and you can try a direct attack right under the rim of his bell guard with a slight rise of your point, thrusting along from his wrist to his elbow.

Instructor: With the student guarding/inviting Octave, offer the underforearm target. As usual, attacks should be made upon closing the range, with each of a few exemplary footwork patterns repeated three times. Practice in couples is not recommended, as the dummy would be repeating a serious mistake; the foil-like habits must be superseded. Later on, students will learn to thrust from under-

71. Recovering backward with straight arm

neath even when they can't see any target, tilting their blades to get beyond the bell guard.

If you are not guarding/inviting, but have your blade level (your hand just a little below shoulder height), simple direct attacks may be made to close targets as they are offered. Your point path may drop or rise or otherwise swerve very slightly, but you want to thrust toward and *through* your opponent's elbow or the crook of his arm.

("Thrusting through" does not mean that you make a hard action, nor should you "choke" or "peck." The target may be moving away, and you need the "follow-through" to assure that your tip button will be depressed enough to register. Or you may miss the closest target, and it is better to continue forward somewhat, instead of pulling away too soon. Moreover, you should *leave* your arm stretched out in most cases and get away with your feet if you wish. Advanced fencers do seem to peck and jab, but they really extend fully without locking, while beginners are more likely to choke up and withdaw before they have made a good shot.)

During all this practice in Sixte and Octave, or for direct attacking in general, you should keep your hand palm up—if necessary, twist your arm and shoulder (clockwise, for right-handers) to counteract the tendency of your hand to turn thumb upward.

Instructor: Students might be allowed to bout as early as this—on the machine—with only footwork (retreating) as response to attack. No doubt some of their foil training will show, but those who make wide parries and deep attacks will soon find that they are losing touches or, at best, getting "doubles." You (or another student) can act as the director and should intervene when the fighters get closer than long lunging range, even in situations that would be allowed to continue in formal competition, Ordinarily it is necessary to keep saying, "You're too close, you're too close, you're too close."

Indirect Attacking. When both épéeists are in Octave (engaged or not) and one attacks to the top of the other's forearm, the action is indirect. When both are in Sixte and one attacks to the undersurface of the other's forearm, the action is indirect. These are the most common instances of an indirect attack: Your point loops *forward* from low to high, or from high to low. You could go from Octave to head or from Sixte to knee, but the odds are that a good fencer would catch you with countershots to the arm—practice thrusting at the *closest* targets.

Instructor: Since this type of attack is most frequently used, lots of practice should be given with a variety of footwork. The attack from Octave to top arm is the most common and easiest and should be worked out very thoroughly. By this time the students should be accustomed to the weapon and should be more relaxed. They should not "freeze" as much but should move in to attack and move out again with greater smoothness and freedom. Flèching may be tried out.

Attacks from Sixte to underarm, keeping the hand palm up, are much more risky and difficult to execute, and there will probably be fewer opportunities for this maneuver in combat. Flèching is not recommended. The student may be introduced to this variation and then coached in competition to look for opponents who offer the underarm, but a great expenditure of lesson time is not indicated.

Practice in couples. Both you and your partner will now guard/invite Octave. At the various ranges the active partner will repeat attacks with appropriate footwork, shooting at the top of the forearm. Don't flèche. At this stage the dummy should also use some footwork so that his opponent can't take too much time to get set.

In foil your indirect attacks were usually launched when your opponent tried to take your blade. That is, when he tried to beat, press, or bind, he made a sideways hand action—one that did not go forward—and you had an opportunity to deceive or to release from pressure, extending. Épéeists more rarely try to take the blade in those ways, so the chances are fewer, the openings are smaller, and the targets are exposed very briefly, if at all—the main targets are, however, closer, and can be reached more quickly. Should you happen to meet an opponent who is primarily a foilist, you can take advantage. You have developed your feel for thrusting in lessons, practice in couples, and practice with the hanging target. Remember, you can't wait to see which way your opponent is trying to take your blade, you must simply try to extend with a loose hand at the very first sign of his motion—and don't pull back too soon.

Instructor: Give a lesson or two on counteractions against comparatively wide attempts to take the blade. The student who has had foil training should be able to

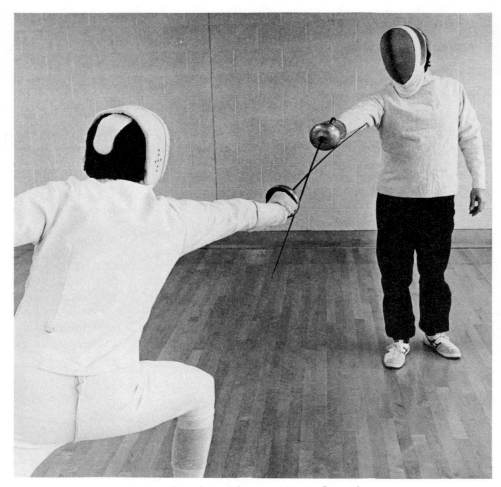

72. *Lunging with opposition in Seconde*

deceive-attack against a lateral beat, half-circle sweep (from Sixte to Octave, or vice versa), counter-Sixte or counter-Octave, and to release from pressure whenever contact is made. The principal value of this exercise is to train the student not to resist. His hold on his weapon should be very light, practically limp. In later lessons he will make similar hand actions, retreating, against large advancements: deceiving/stop thrusting. Practice in couples is not recommended, for the usual reason: The dummy would be practicing mistakes as much as the active partner would be practicing good moves.

The idea behind these simple direct and indirect attacks is that your opponent cannot cover his entire target all at once (and neither can you, remember). If he guards faultily for the given situation—including the distance factor—your attack may be made directly. Otherwise you may attack indirectly to any target that is convenient.

Simple Taking Attacks. You would naturally feel a lot better if you could get your opponent's blade under your control, making it point beyond you when you attack. There's a great temptation to take it for security's sake. But there's a great risk also, because your opponent may deceive. He merely needs to hit $\frac{1}{25}$th of a second before you do—or perhaps all he wants at that stage of the bout is a double. Consequently, you shouldn't try to take very often, you mustn't take with a wide movement, and as you take, your tip should *always* be moving forward.

By definition, a simple attack is made in a single motion. A simple taking attack must be just as fast as a direct or indirect attack. Therefore, it can't be done with a beat or *froissement*, because two moves would be used. Simple taking attacks are, more or less, binding actions with the arm extending, co-ordinated with footwork such as advancing, lunging, or flèching. These could be summarized as follows:

    a. From guarding/inviting Sixte: by countering Sixte or by changing to Octave or Seconde.

    b. From Octave: by countering Octave or by changing to Sixte.

Your opponent's blade must be in line, or nearly so—but it often is, anyway. Your épée tip makes a spiral (or part of a spiral) forward, gathering the blade and keeping it in opposition as you attack (Figs. 72, 75). You can't hesitate, or your opponent will release or counterattack with responsive opposition. In all cases, *your* opposition must be to the outside (to the right, for right-handers). This does NOT mean that you push your opponent's blade sideways—the forward movement of your bell guard will do that.

Attacks by countering Sixte or from Octave to Sixte would of course be aimed along the top of your opponent's arm, following through toward shoulder, chest, or head. By countering Octave or going from Sixte to Octave or Seconde, you would strike at deeper targets such as the knee, the hip, or the waist.

Instructor: Give opportunities for repetition of these attacks, particularly those ending high (in Sixte), with the usual preliminary shift of ground and co-ordinated footwork. The student's tip must not describe a circle, or part of one, and then proceed, but must "funnel in" toward one spot. Unless he has flèched, there must be immediate foot recovery—a retreat, if he has attacked merely with advance—with his arm remaining straight.

Practice in couples. The dummy stands with blade in line. The active partner must repeat all the kinds of hand actions: (1) countering Octave, (2) Octave to Sixte, (3) Sixte to Octave, (4) countering Sixte, and (5) Sixte to Seconde, together with all the most useful footwork patterns, lunging, advance lunging, and *balestra*. Don't flèche. Recovering from lunging should be automatic by this time.

These are the simple attacks. You may do very well by mixing them in the course of a bout—one direct, one by taking, one indirect; one short, one long—without ever needing to use any composite actions as such. A rapid *series* of simple attacks can win for you, provided you practice for accuracy (not speed, at first), make a good preparatory change of ground, and go at the right time and range. After some training you should be able to move around continually so that your opponent can't be too sure where you're going to be in the next instant, and you should be able to make shots from various positions.

REMEMBER: No attack is IT: Always figure that you might miss and that you might have to get away and try again. You may have to make *ten* shots to get one touch marked on the score sheet.

Instructor: In the suggested lesson plan we go from simple attacking to counterattacking. Most of the counterattacks are simple also, and the work amounts to a review of the above section, but with the opponent on the initiative.

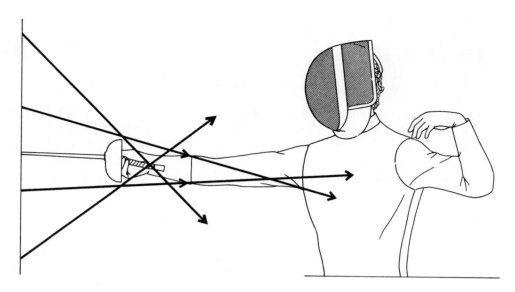

73. *Angles for striking through arm to deeper targets, side view*

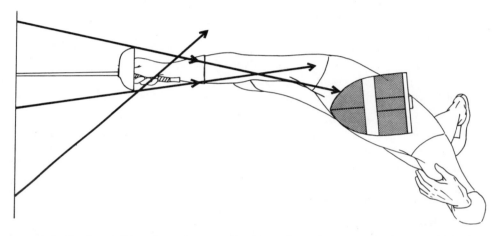

74. *Angles for striking through arm, view from above: larger angle is a poorer risk*

COMBINATIONS

The épée student who has had a good deal of foil training already knows about more composite attacks than he needs or should try in this branch of the sport. What the beginner must do is *eliminate* most of these habits.

You should not try beat attacks, other types of taking-disengaging attacks, feint disengagements, one-twos, etc. These are two-count actions (you may even know some three-count attacks), and your risk multiplies every split second that you stay within your opponent's range and don't really try to hit. But when you get into trouble, or are surprised, you will probably use foil actions (parry-riposting and the like) to save yourself.

Your best combinations are the ones you have already tried involving footwork. By sliding, braking, jumping back, side-stepping (seldom), etc., as well as advancing, retreating, hopping, lunging, appel lunging, and flèching, you can keep moving, avoiding regular rhythm, in and out of your opponent's range (and/or your own), to confuse him. In essence you use *foot feints* to cause him to react. You use footwork to sneak in closer or to lure him into your reach.

75. Flèching with opposition in Sixte

Mixed into these foot actions would be your simple attacks—and counterattacks, as you will see in the next chapter.

By this time you should have been practicing hooked up to the electrical apparatus. You will have discovered for yourself that negative or non-positive moves (those which do not go forward) often result in touches against you. You are better off in the long run if all your hand actions are positive. About the only backward moves you should make are with your feet.

Continuations. It's important to get away after making a shot. However, a person will almost instinctively flinch, freeze, lean back, or otherwise recoil from an unexpected attack, even if very slightly and for just an instant. This may indeed save him from your initial attack. Thus, it is very often worthwhile to follow up. There are names for these continuations, such as remise, redoublement, and reprise; the unsophisticated spectator might call some of them jabs.

The *remise* is defined as a straight continuation in the same line. Since your opponent may try to block but at the same time may be afraid to go too far with it, you just go on. The word "insistance" is often used to refer to a remise. In épée deeper targets are frequently available. Having tried for the wrist, you may stretch on toward the elbow and then to the upper arm, torso, or head—a series of three rapid attempts (or nearly one long action) which you should study formally first and then work out in class bouting and free play.

In the case where your opponent is backing up, you are following him with this kind of series. Distance is always relative: If he withdraws his hand and/or retreats in the face of your attack, your remises may be repeated shots at the wrist.

For a *redoublement*, you must have an opponent who parries but does not riposte immediately. Instead of continuing in the same line, which is blocked, you have to disengage to make your follow-up toward another target area, after his blade or guard contacts your blade. Sometimes this continuation comes about unintentionally or automatically just because you have trained to release from contact and to follow through, or to try another shot instantly when your opponent hesitates. A soft hand is very valuable.

The *reprise* is a more distinct second attack. The term means "retake." When your opponent reacts only by moving away (neither blocking nor counterattacking) you may carry on with another attack. This doesn't necessarily mean that you take his blade either time, but that you might, for instance, recover forward from lunging and lunge again.

It is very hard to say whether any épée action is an attack or a counterattack. A continuation or a series might be described by some observers as a composite. The movements are usually narrow and fast, the timing very subtle.

My separation of the subject into two chapters, one called "Attacking" and the other "Counterattacking," is rather arbitrary. I would advise you to work through the next chapter and then come back and rework the material of this one.

In practice it makes very little difference what the names of the actions are: in competition the fencers try to make hits, the electrical apparatus shows which hit was first, and the director doesn't bother to describe how the hits were achieved. It is only in theoretical discussions, in teaching, etc., that we need to name movements for purposes of analysis.

INFIGHTING

Despite the ideal of a long-distance game in which the great majority of attacks do not go deeper than the front of the opponent's body and most are directed at the arm (from midway along the forearm to the shoulder), infighting does occur in épée. The general advice would be the same as for foil: Keep the front foot in place, neither backing out nor crowding in; get low and stay low; keep your hand fairly high and your elbow pointing down; if appropriate, move your rear foot to pivot your body; keep head and torso up straight, etc. The main difference between foil infighting and épée infighting would be that in épée you should do nothing but try to hit. Any kind of parrying or blocking move would mean time spent without producing a hit—make repeated jabs as rapidly as possible, like a machine gun, until the director calls a halt.

Your blade or guard might meet the opponent's blade, which may be all to the good—but incidental. If you do find that you have control (opposition), you could take a split-second longer to place your next jab and finish off the exchange. What very often happens is that the original attack misses everything, and as you pull your arm back, elbow down, fist coming to about the level of your throat, you automatically block the line of your opponent's response (parry-riposte, time thrust, or whatever you wish to call it). Your real purpose, however, is to get your point back between you and him in order to jab. You would not hesitate an instant on the contact of blades, you would pull back and jab as fast as you can.

This is quite a different thing from remising, which you should certainly do if you have missed the forward-most target and a deeper target is still available.

In that case there would be no pulling back. There might be angulation—going around a corner—to get your blade to dig into the target; if it merely skims, the light won't turn on.

LEFT-HANDERS

A left-hander against a right-hander should, and almost instinctively will, thrust along the outside (the right-hander's right) of his opponent's arm. He should ordinarily follow up to the biceps, the bulge of the shoulder, the neck, and the mask. If his right-handed opponent tries to block by parrying Sixte, and makes the awful mistake of pulling back his arm, raising his fist and slanting his blade upward, the lefty has a good chance of continuing to flank or hip.

The right-hander against the left-hander would reverse the procedure.

As usual, the primary advice for both is to stay at long range, be patient, and keep making thrusts at closer targets. Do not adopt a guarding/inviting attitude that is too wide to the outside (the lefty's left, the righty's right). Change timing, distance, and invitation (Sixte, Octave, etc.) frequently.

Having set in your mind that the best plan is to stay out of reach except when you choose to shoot—and don't always go in for one shot and back out again, rather go in sometimes for a double or triple shot—if your opponent does attack first, attack him anyway. This method will be analyzed in the next chapter.

There is more about the left-hander in the chapter on teaching épée. Your coach should sometimes use his left hand in lessons so that you won't be so befuddled when you have to bout with a lefty (even if you are one yourself) for the first time.

Chapter 15

ÉPÉE COUNTERATTACKING

EVEN MORE THAN in foil and sabre, you must not think defensively in épée. You might look at it this way: If your opponent attacks, you must *respond*, but your response should not be a defense because—although you might prevent him from hitting initially—you could be touched by his follow-up attacks or continuations. The best way to keep him from scoring is to score before he does.

The first response to a threat is *evasion*. That is, you may run away, side-step, dodge, or duck. At the speed and depth with which modern fencing attacks can be made, though, some of these methods are not often successful.

The odds are that you can't run backward as fast as your opponent can run forward, assuming he gains the first step and you are responding to the sight of his move. There's a small but significant lag in reaction. Besides, there's a limit to how far you can retreat. The greatest care must be taken not to let the enemy get too close in the first place.

It's not easy to move your whole body out of the way, especially when your opponent starts and you have to see his action and tell your muscles to get going. A human being needs about $\frac{1}{10}$th of a second to respond, and that is when he is "set": looking for a certain signal and ready to act in a certain way. In that time your opponent can travel two or three feet. (But he also has to respond to what he recognizes as an opportunity, and if you are continually in motion, his reactivity is somewhat dulled.)

Consequently, the usual trick is to move only the part that is being attacked —most often, a part that is more forward, such as your hand or knee. Your hand can be shifted up, down, or sideways—causing your opponent to miss—or pulled back—causing him to fall short. Ordinarily your foot or knee should be drawn to the rear instead of being moved sideways.

Please keep in mind that evasion alone can't keep your opponent from scoring. But *every other method of responding to attack is usually co-ordinated with evasion*. These effective responses are categorized as: (1) counterattacks, and (2) parry-ripostes. The counterattacks are subdivided into stop thrusts and time thrusts.

Stop Thrusting. When your opponent attacks or prepares to attack, you may simply try to hit him before he hits you, and this would be called a stop thrust. Most often your shot would be at his forearm, so if he did reach you on a part of

76. *Stop to top of arm, withdrawing leg: evasion as opponent attacks knee*

your body farther back than your own forearm, the chances are that you would be $\frac{1}{25}$th of a second ahead.* (If you miss, you have a chance for a double.) At the same time you would evade.

If he attacks your wrist from the inside, move your hand *forward*, stretching your arm and putting your point over his guard at his elbow region. Your hand rises, and his point may pass beneath it. Hop back or retreat speedily in case you miss and he continues: Your back foot should be starting to the rear as your arm shoots forward. Leave your arm extended to the utmost, and he may run into your point. Or if your opponent is one who does not continue but withdraws, you might follow up with a deeper attack.

If your opponent attacks your knee or foot, he will probably expose his upper arm. Thrust solidly, drawing your front foot back. You will naturally stand up and lean forward slightly (Fig. 76). Sometimes a fencer will duck when trying this sort of attack, so you might hit him in the mask—if he is really going for your foot, and not just faking, his head may be closer than his arm. To get away from a continuation you can hop back or let your front foot swing on past your rear foot, then take two or three running steps. If he pulls back, go after him.

Your most common posture will be that of guarding/inviting Octave. Your

* In $\frac{1}{25}$th of a second, a fencer's point can travel 7 to 15 inches, from a standstill, farther if speed has already been built up.

77. *Stop to underside of arm: in Tierce, beginning retreat, opponent aiming at head or upper body*

opponent will see a tempting target along the top of your forearm. Many fencers try to throw shots over the rim of the bell guard. Given this opportunity, you can twist your hand into Tierce, palm down, while thrusting forward and upward. Thus, your wrist is taken out of the line of his attack, and you strike at a good angle toward his elbow (Fig. 77). The instant you make this attempt, retreat or hop back, turning your hand up into Sixte: your bell guard will then hide your shoulder better. Once in a while, however, you should turn your hand palm up and lunge or perhaps flèche.

Instructor: Each of the stop-thrusting situations must be repeated a number of times, both with immediate getaway and with attacking continuation. The three methods described are the most typical and are worth a good deal of class time. Practice in couples is recommended, but only with the active partner retreating or jumping back after the attempted stop thrust. No doubt your novice épéeists will invent their own maneuvers in formal bouting or free play. For extra practice, students could profitably spend a lot of time at the hanging targets: (a) thrusting/backing up, or (b) thrusting and chasing. In instance (b), a student could pretend that his first shot, hitting the ball, had hit the bell guard, and as the ball bounces away he could lunge or flèche.

Time Thrusting. Another way of dealing with an attack is to extend (trying to hit) and simultaneously deflect the incoming blade. This type of action is called time thrusting. You should have learned about it in your basic foil course, and it is similar to the taking attacks discussed in Chapter 14.

One difference between the foil and the épée is that the latter has a much

78. *Time thrusting in Octave*

larger bell guard, *a bigger shield*. In foil you often have to sweep the opponent's blade with your own, but in épée it's possible to time thrust with just a slight shift of your guard—up, down, or sideways as required. (Sometimes a stop thrust turns out to be a time thrust because the bell unintentionally blocks the opponent's point.)

Assuming your opponent is attacking the closest target available to him, you can shoot and block in one motion. He will have to continue to a deeper target—which will take more time—or quit. The trouble with blocking with the guard is that you will probably not have close targets open to you either, because his arm will be stretched out behind *his* bell guard. Double touches may result from continuation by either fencer, but maybe that will be desirable under certain circumstances (review Chapter 13).

You can control your opponent's blade more effectively by taking it with your own, extending at the same time. The ways are: by countering Sixte or Octave; half-countering from Sixte to Octave or from Octave to Sixte, and, from Sixte, substituting a change to Seconde for the half counter to Octave. For the last-named maneuver, twist your hand palm down as your point goes forward and down; you may prefer this for strength. The hand/arm co-ordinations are similar to those for taking attacks.

Remember that your time thrust must be co-ordinated with footwork. In one split second you will make your counterattack by a finger/arm movement. In the next split second you must get away or, possibly, follow up. The usual move is to retreat. If your time thrust redirects your opponent's blade toward your lower body, added insurance against his hitting would be given by leg evasion.

Parry-riposting. The third method of responding to attack—other than by evasion alone—is parry-riposting. You are familiar with the idea from your foil training, but you must have gathered from earlier remarks that parrying in épée involves greater risks and loss of time. Épée parrying is therefore considerably modified compared to any foil system. Time thrusting, if you must deflect a blade, is considered a much better choice. Parry-riposting theoretically takes two moves instead of one, the riposte thrust following a deflecting action. Still there will be situations in which parry-riposting is more secure, especially when the initial moves by you and your opponent have not hit. In other words, you should usually attack or stop thrust or time thrust first, and go into parry-riposting afterward.

The preferred way is to block with your bell guard. Your opponent's blade should either be obstructed (his point hitting your guard) or bumped out of line momentarily. By moving your hand only an inch up or down, right or left, you should be able to prevent his initial stroke from hitting. Then your riposte would be made by the most direct route to the closest available target.

You might couple your parry with evasion. For example, if your opponent attacks the undersurface of your forearm, you could bump his blade downward, and as you make your riposte to the top of his arm you could pull your front foot back and straighten the knee, to delay any continuation he might make to deeper low target (Fig. 79).

Blade-against-blade parrying in épée is similar to the comparable foil maneuvers. From Octave, your most usual guarding/inviting position, you can parry Sixte by flicking your point upward in a half circle (clockwise for right-handers). Do this without pulling your hand back. Assuming you both fence with the same hand, your direct riposte will be to the crook of your opponent's arm, with a possible continuation to the shoulder.

This action, by the way, is likely to provoke a wide parry of Sixte. Take the opportunity of disengaging to the inside surface of his arm, and from there onward to his chest.

From Sixte you can parry by beating Octave or Seconde (palm up or palm down, respectively), deflecting your opponent's blade so that it points past your lower back. Most épéeists riposte indirectly from these beat parries, bouncing the point up and over to the top of the arm.

The ideal is to make the two-count parry-riposte nearly one action. Beat lightly. Think, "One!"

You should never (or hardly ever) parry to the inside (left, if you're right-handed). These parries lead your opponent toward deeper targets. Parries or time thrusts of Sixte, Octave, or Seconde make your opponent's blade point past your back. At closer ranges, once he passes your profile he can't hit without pulling back his arm.

Instructor: Considerable practice in these parry-ripostes may be necessary, especially for classically trained students, to reduce the size of the deflecting movement. Counterattacking is preferable, but the former foilist will tend to use previously learned or natural responses—which are normally too large—and has to substitute new responses. He must come to realize very clearly that his forearm is the primary target of his opponents, and that he need only deflect attacks very slightly—provided he makes instantaneous ripostes—at épée distances.

79. Parry downward with guard, riposting to shoulder, with leg evasion

The student should be drilled to retreat before the parry-riposte, and then again afterward. Ordinarily, the fencer should not retreat with the riposte, because that would negate the force of the stroke and also, possibly, spoil accuracy. At top speed, hopping may be necessary to keep the footwork in time with the hand. On occasion, the fencer would want to make an attack following up the parry-riposte, or even riposte with lunge, therefore retreat lunging and hop-back lunging should be brought into the lesson. Advanced students might parry and flèche, having first retreated.

You should do some formal repetition with classmates on these moves. Then, as always, you should consciously use parry-riposting in formal class bouting and free play. In this way you will discover at first hand what works best for you. Stop thrusting and time thrusting are usually better than parry-riposting, which is why this chapter concentrates mostly on counterattacking. Parry-riposting would be worthwhile if you could set up your opponent so that he commits himself pretty strongly. When he goes off balance his ability to block decreases, and one way to set him up would be to attack or counterattack, ready to parry-riposte against his reaction.

Chapter 16

TEACHING ÉPÉE

MY CONVICTION IS that épéeists are born, not made. The "natural" has a peculiar feel for the right time to move, along with great point accuracy and sense of distance, seen especially in simple attacking and stop thrusting. The knack can't be taught but can be cultivated. The student who doesn't have this intuitive capability might reach a good level of competence through training and practice, but beyond a certain stage no amount of study will make him into a champion. The one who has it shows it early and doesn't need a great deal of technical instruction. I have had students who have won their first competitions, topping more experienced, higher-rated épéeists; others have done well with hardly any special training, although they were already pretty good at foil.

Many beginners have a tendency to stop thrust almost instinctively. This is a fault in foil fencing, and it's a fault in épée if it is a panic reaction accompanied by a locking or freezing so that a follow-up is delayed. Often the student stands up and throws his hips backward at the same time, or crouches down defensively and is immobilized. The habit should have been trained out of him in foil class. You have a lot of work to do in such cases. The tendency must be guided into effective patterns.

A common misconception is that épéeists must be tall, but there is no particular advantage in height or reach. The closest target is at the same distance for everyone: exactly a blade's length. The smaller man may be superior in fleetness of foot, which may be worth more than length of arm and leg. One physical characteristic that seems valuable is a large hand to manipulate the weapon easily. Another asset is a skinny arm which can be completely hidden behind the épée guard.

The teacher who has conducted a class through a foil course may be able to predict rather closely which students will excel at épée. The épée course will develop and confirm those capabilities for special accuracy, the precise estimation of the range, and the sense of time.

Those students who are not born épéeists will benefit from this kind of discipline, and may pass on to success with the electrical foil. Some will become two-weapon "point fencers" with the foil as their favorite. Nor is this additional work wasted on the future sabreur, inasmuch as the body posture and leg exercise are similar in sabre, the range is very much the same, and many attacks are made to the hand, wrist, arm, and head.

There isn't much sense in offering an épée course when a machine is not available. Lessons can be given without hooking up, and students can go through paired practice of formal moves, but very soon bouting and free play must be done with the apparatus. Students should fence under conditions as near as possible to those of a tournament. A class of any size might need two machines; the capacity can be doubled by having two sets of reels for each, so that fencers "on deck" can be plugging in while the preceding couple is bouting. Free play could be excluded altogether, in order to limit time and demand more concentration. But essentially the machine will do a great deal of the teaching. To put it another way, the students will learn most by using it: In psychological theory, unsuccessful behavior tends to disappear.

You must "accentuate the positive." That is, all hand actions must be preeminently forward rather than sideways or backward (i.e. bending the elbow more than slightly). It would be best not to demonstrate any non-positive moves. Footwork will include retreating actions, but they are calculated to insure proper distance, to invite and to mislead. The épée repertoire should consist almost entirely of attacking and counterattacking, repeated and continuing attacks.

COMPETITION

There is no better way for an épéeist to develop—after an introduction to the most basic actions—than through competition. I assume a foilist may have had a taste of tournament play even within his first one-semester course (twelve weeks or so), and certainly within his second course. The épée beginner, then, should have been in a fencing meet before. Aside from the early practice on the machine in class, he or she should go into a meet at the earliest opportunity.

This will match him or her against strangers and probably against fencers of higher quality. As a teacher I have found that students who were inexperienced return to class greatly improved after their first competition. They have been strongly stimulated, and during this post-tournament period they usually concentrate much better and absorb faster than before. You may take advantage of this enthusiasm, for students are then impressed with the need for careful and thorough practice.

In some parts of the United States competition is hard to find. The sport at present is well-established in relatively few centers, usually around large cities. A trip of a hundred miles may be necessary to get students into any kind of extramural competition. It is worth it. The meet may be sponsored by the AFLA and open to the highest-class fencers in the area. Beginners may get horribly clobbered—but they will have the experience of fencing with some of these experts. They will be able to watch a number of bouts. Ordinarily, experienced fencers will comment on the novice's performance, give pointers and advice. All this comes back into the class for re-examination and experimentation.

THE LEFTY

The left-handed opponent in épée does not present as many problems as in foil. The fighting arm, which receives many fouls in foil, is no longer an obstacle but an available target. The right-handed pupil only needs to be shown one or two attacks, mainly to the outside of the southpaw's arm, and further adaptation will occur naturally, providing there are opportunities to practice.

If there are no left-handers in the class, you (I assume you are not left-

80. Beating Quarte against a left-hander, who could do the same in reverse

handed) must give that practice yourself. A left-handed teacher would certainly help produce competitors who will be quite successful against left-handed opponents, and his students will get enough practice with right-handers among themselves.

The right-handed student must become sensitive to the danger of being hit on the outside of his arm by a left-hander. He will ordinarily have to carry his hand *slightly* more to the right, with the thumb turned well outward so that his hand is definitely palm up. Guarding/inviting Octave should be employed almost exclusively.

The same warning should be given to the left-handed student. He must be careful about exposing his elbow and not move his hand to his right. Any actions he makes to deflect an attacking point should cause that blade to go to the left—that is, more than usual the student needs to be drilled in Octave to Sixte and counter-Octave takings.

On *rare* occasions, the right-hander may use a beat of Quarte against the left-hander, and vice versa. This action is very tempting, as it may open up good targets along the top and outside of the arm, to continue to shoulder and head. It should not, however, be relied on too heavily. Many left-handers develop a habit of ducking—down, forward, and to their right—if given too much warning, and

81. *Outside angulation against a left-hander, who could do the same in reverse*

shots may go past their shoulders and heads, leaving the right-hander in bad trouble.

LESSON PLAN

The form of a class session is: (1) Warm-up calisthenics; (2) blind and silent drills, or extra conditioning work; (3) lesson, new material, or review; (4) practice in couples, or bouting; and (5) cool-off, usually by jogging and walking backward.

Your lesson plan may follow the text. Starting with enough conditioning sessions to make sure the class can do all the footwork required, you can follow with simple attacking against both right- and left-handed opponents. The emphasis should be on direct and indirect attacks from long range, recovering backward from lunging, and keeping a straight arm during the recovery. This can take up several sessions, but students could almost immediately begin practice in couples and should very soon get on the machine with each other.

Attacking by taking the blade would be next, with less emphasis. The primary idea is to go around, over, or under a blade in line, provided the opponent's target, the wrist, can be displaced a little. That is, the opponent's blade should be aimed close to the rim of the student's guard somewhere, but in attacking the student should be able to evade that point. When taking is done, it should be very slim (and include a great deal of forward motion), otherwise the opponent might deceive or release from a sideways push.

The student should become sensitive to his own inviting attitudes, with regard both to distance and opening. Mirrors are very useful, as students can get an idea of which arm targets are visible to opponents (especially left-handers) above, below, or beside the guard. Then the student should work on the stop thrusts (with evasion) that can be done against direct or indirect attacks to the several inviting target areas.

Generally, counterattacks should be made by time thrusting or parry-riposting when the opponent is more fully committed. Otherwise, the student should stop thrust or actually take over the attack, with or without the blade. Whether an outside observer would identify the actions as attacks or counterattacks, the épée fencer would commonly make multiple thrusts, and very probably the first in any sequence would be direct or indirect, with any taking done later. This is not an invariable course, for if a fencer finds that his opponent reacts to a taking by blocking wide, the obvious trick would be to take and immediately release.

You can do a good deal of your teaching by commenting on the actions done while students are bouting on the machine. Keep the comments relevant to the topic currently being studied. There are always a number of alternatives, and, of course, you should constantly remind the students about keeping a long distance.

You could post a "ladder" from the time bouting is first allowed. That is, bouts would go on record. Everybody should eventually fence everybody else, and there would be jockeying for position on the ladder. Alternatively, a regular individual score sheet could be kept, to insure the completion of a round robin, because in a ladder situation some people may consistently avoid certain others, while some people repeatedly challenge and re-challenge.

If you have an apparatus with two sets of reels so that one pair of fencers can be hooking up while another is bouting, these practice bouts can be set for a reduced number of touches, three or even two. This puts on the pressure by allowing less leeway for getting even again after losing a point: Students must concentrate on not taking risks, on not giving opponents any free gifts. The time is practically unlimited, and students can learn to play a very cautious game. On occasion they should play for just *one* touch, which raises the pressure to the maximum. The value of this kind of practice will be seen in extramural tournaments.

Although prizes could be given for this type of class competition, it is not really fair to give a grade bonus for high placement in the meet. Some people are naturals in épée. Others develop more slowly but may actually prove superior later. Even those who could never become champions may eventually contribute a great deal to the sport by teaching or in other ways. Technical understanding, at this stage, is most important.

The course is adaptable, depending on whether students are high-schoolers or older. In the high-school course, the flèche would be assigned only to seniors with at least a year of fencing background—naturally, lower-class students will see and imitate, and you will have to keep warning them against it. For high-school seniors, collegiates, and others with presumably full growth, the flèche could be introduced at the third or fourth week and covered, in its variations, through the remainder of the course. This would ensure that students have plenty of conditioning by way of calisthenics, other footwork practice, and running of sprints and hurdles, etc. Nevertheless, the basic advice from a strategic view is not to flèche very often, because of the risks.

A guide sheet should be duplicated and distributed. This fixes what students are supposed to be doing for practice at each session along the way. Things are getting serious now, and each student should be busy at the hanging-ball targets, repeating routines with a variety of partners, or bouting on the machine—*not* indulging in loose play.

A BIT OF HISTORY

The electric épée was developed a few years before World War II. In the non-electric era judgment about which hit was first rested with the president of a jury, as it does in sabre and non-electric foil today. The materiality of hits was determined by judges. At that time a bout was for one touch only—the encounter was supposed to be a replica of a duel for first blood. You may well imagine that the fencers were *extremely* careful.

The electric apparatus immediately made judgments about time and materiality perfectly simple. One transient effect was that a number of well-known competitors retired: Quite naturally, the presidents had tended to be unconsciously prejudiced, believing that a known champion would most often hit first in a bout with an unknown contender. Since then it has been very rare for any champion to successfully defend his title.

The bout was next expanded to three touches, and eventually to five, as in other events. You will recall that we considered, in Chapter 13, the strategy involved at various score differentials. You can now understand how the change in the number of touches for a bout has changed the style of épée fencing. The game today requires much more vigor and stamina. Ultimately, however, any bout may be decided by one touch, so coolness and precision are as valuable as ever.

Old épéeists deplored the appearance of the modern style because to them it seems wild, desperate, undisciplined. Often the competitors, especially collegiates, do run, dive, and jab frantically. Their impetuous attacks get them into tough situations from which the only ways out seem to be violent stabbing and panic flight.

As an example of the effectiveness of the old style, the famous Peter Meijer continued to qualify for the finals of the U. S. Nationals when over seventy years of age, looking small, scrawny, and almost incapable of movement. By extremely clever and accurate counterattacking he could consistently hold off the powerful actions of men less than a third of his age.

Épée is now the easiest branch of fencing for the uninformed spectator to understand, and if your group wishes to interest the public, and has a machine, one of the best ways is to put on an épée demonstration. The main ideas of the game can be explained in a few words. A person who has never seen fencing will immediately favor one of the fighters and will try to keep track of the hits and the bouts won and lost. Extension lights for the apparatus, with a bank of score lights, and a large scoreboard will improve the show for the audience at a real tournament. Promotional material, obtainable from the AFLA, can be distributed. Whether to get new members for your group, or to get support from the community in other forms, an event of this kind can be very helpful.

Chapter 17

SABRE RULES, THEORY, AND OFFICIATING

For details of the rules of sabre fencing and their uses in officiating, you should study the AFLA manual. The following summary should be helpful as a guide through the tortuous maze of legalistic syntax and vocabulary that you will find in "The Book."

Summary of Rules

SAFETY

The safety warnings are very like those for foil and épée regarding equipment condition, environment, and avoidance of body contact, dangerous manner of play, unsportsmanlike conduct, etc.

I would recommend that your jacket have a padded front (and a sweat shirt under it), and that you have a stout mask with a bib that hangs lower than for foil. Leather trim is not really needed on the mask. Most fencers use an elbow guard in class as well as in competition. An extra inner plastron (with half sleeve) is now required. Some sabreurs wear a cup in the athletic supporter, but this is not essential since sabre attacks are mainly directed at the head and upper torso, and the extra protection may interfere with movement.

LIMITATIONS

Weapon. The sabre might seem to be an unlimited weapon. It has, theoretically, a sharp point, a sharp main edge (opposite the fencer's thumb), and a sharp back edge on a third of the blade measured from the tip back. In effect almost any flick with the end of the blade is considered to be damaging: The blade is so narrow, officials say, that a cut would be inflicted whenever the tip snaps against a target. In other words, officials admit that they can't tell whether most cuts are flat or not—the action is too fast.

There are some restrictions, however. You can't score by hitting with the

82. Sabreuse guarding/inviting Tierce (note elbow protector)

guard or pommel, and any such blows are penalizable. An attempt to thrust with the point, which does not stick but grazes, is not allowed as a slice. A *cut* that is blocked but lands by whipping over is not considered to have sufficient force to do any damage. On the other hand, a cut that is blocked and then continues to a point hit becomes a touch, but in two tempos. An immediate riposte would have precedence.

Questions arise fairly often about whether the parry was adequate and the cut whipped over, or whether the parry was too narrow (*malparé*). In a few cases the blade will be "laid on" (i.e., pressed against the target), but almost any sabreur with good training will avoid stiffening his hand so as to give this effect, which does not achieve a touch.

Target. Every part of the body, front and back, above a horizontal line drawn where the tops of the thighs join the trunk is valid target. Cuts and thrusts to the hands, arms, and head may therefore be scored. An invalid hit, or "foul," is one landing below the specified line. If an attack has been deflected low by a parry or has glanced downward off the shell (guard), an immediate riposte by the defender is allowed. That is, the attack is said to have been parried, and the foul hit is a remise. Of course, if the parry is held, the remise will hit before the riposte begins, and the riposte will be nullified.

Ground. The boundary rules for sabre are similar to those for épée. The strip is 2 meters by 14 meters, but the warning lines are 2 meters ahead of the end lines (compared to 1 meter for foil)—that is, 3 meters behind the guard lines. As in épée, a retreating fencer is allowed more room. He can go all the way back over the end line once, at which time a halt is called, and he is placed with his rear foot on the warning line. If he goes past the end line with both feet a second time, having been properly warned by the director, he will be penalized by 1 touch.

The penalty for going off the side is a loss of 2 meters (or the opponent, who stays on, gains). A fencer who steps outside the boundary is also vulnerable to an immediate attack or riposte, but cannot score with any such action that he makes when he is off the strip. Finally, you should remember that if a fencer has retreated past the end line once and has been placed on the warning line, and if he retreats so that both feet are behind the warning line and *then* goes out of bounds sideways, the 2-meter ground penalty would put him past the end line. Therefore, he would automatically lose a touch.

Time. The standard bout is for 5 touches, and may finally be scored as high as 5–4. There can be no tie. Six minutes of fencing time are allowed, with a warning announcement one minute before the end, and at the expiration of that period, the fencer with the fewest touches against him is declared the winner. The score, as in foil, is adjusted. For example, if it is 3–0 when time expires, it becomes 5–2, the same number being added to each side. If the score is tied when time expires, it is brought to 4–all (if it isn't at that stage already), and unlimited overtime is allowed for the deciding touch. The rules in this respect are exactly like those for foil.

THE CONVENTIONS

Time. A hit that lands clearly earlier than one in the opposite direction has precedence. A foul hit that lands first nullifies any later good hit—even if both are made in the same direction. It is the prerogative of the president of the jury to determine whether there was any difference in time between two opposing hits, and a fencer may not contradict him.

The puzzling feature is the definition of a tempo, or one unit of "fencing time." The rules say this is "the time required to perform one simple fencing action." There is, however, no very clear definition of what a simple fencing action is. Presumably a lunge is one, and so is a stop cut, the former often taking much more time than the latter, but you aren't allowed to stop against a lunge. A flèche is considered one action from the instant the arm starts to extend until the rear foot reaches the ground (having crossed over).

So—a unit of fencing time (*temps d'escrime* or *tempo*) is a VARIABLE: you can't define it as $\frac{1}{25}$th of a second, which the machine does for you in épée, or two seconds, or anything, exactly. This is one of those things that everybody knows and can argue about, futilely, without end. A tempo is whatever the president says it is, and you, as a competitor, must try to make your actions hit well ahead of those of your opponent.

Right-of-way. The sabre, like the foil, is called a conventional weapon because the notion of right-of-way is used. This means that an attack must be parried or evaded: The attack has right-of-way. The attack is a movement of point or edge toward target, a movement that will hit (essentially in one tempo) *unless it IS* blocked or evaded.

The question of right-of-way arises *only* if hits are made in both directions, *and* if there is no clear time difference between them. If one fencer misses, there's no problem. If one fencer hits a tempo ahead of the other, there's no problem. But with opposing hits that are practically simultaneous, right-of-way is a matter of who *started* first, who took the initiative in attacking—if anybody.

The fencer who is attacked is not allowed to score by sticking his point out (stop thrusting) or making a stop-cut so that both he and his opponent are hit at the same time. He could even hit first (in real, honest-to-God time) by making a short action while his opponent was making a long one, but that would be wrong. When he is at fault for causing a double hit, the score is against him. You might say if a fencer has time to parry or evade, he should, rather than cause such a double. And if the attack hits foul, it nullifies the opposing hit, even if that is on valid target.

When an attack has been parried, for an instant *neither* fencer has the right-of-way. The original attacker might continue, or his opponent might seize the opportunity to make a return attack (riposte). When an attack has been avoided, a counterattack (stop) made at the same instant as the evasion is ahead of the remise, but with any delay, the whole phrase may be canceled.

Often enough today, the speed of sabre fencing is such that true double hits are made. Neither fencer hits ahead in time and neither has the initiative—they both decide to attack at once. The president, in such a case, annuls the action. The problem became chronic: there were occasions when twenty or more simultaneous attacks were made in a row—strategically the fencers are correct to do this—and the rules were rewritten or amended to emphasize the conventions. Now after three such double hits, a coin is flipped to determine award of a touch.

Compared to foil fencing, sabre play includes many more frequent attempts to stop hit. The fighting hand and arm, being ahead of the rest of the target, are tempting objects of counterattack. But officials are very strict about stops, which must be executed clearly ahead of the "final" of any composite attack. In other words, a stop (commonly a cut) will not be allowed against any simple attack whatever (assuming the attack hits).

OFFICIATING

A few of the problems of officiating are hinted at above. Inasmuch as the modern sabre is very light (lighter than many types of foils) and cuts are employed, the blade disappears from the perception of the president and judges. A cut may flick the target so quickly that contact can't be seen.

Consequently, a judge is allowed to call a touch on a combination of sight and sound, the "pop" of the blade against target, and the direction of arm movement. So important is sound in judging that a cut will rarely be called good if it doesn't make a noise. A "laid-on" blade is one example.

At different times a judge may hear the blade strike the guard (shell of the hilt), which indicates a proper block; the sound of a blow on cloth and metal together, which might be called an inadequate parry; or the sound of a cut followed by metal, which is also a touch. A block made with the guard or the thicker half of the blade nearest the guard (those parts of the weapon considered stout enough to break the force of a cut) is required for a legitimate parry, so a judge has to try to distinguish between those sounds and that of a beat (thinner part of one blade striking the other). To further complicate matters, the sound of a head cut may resemble one of the other steel-to-steel contacts.

With training and experience, level by level, juries do their work in sabre all the way up through the World Championships. The fencers are usually satisfied (they hate losing, but acknowledge the correctness of the officiating). The results are consistent, with the same assemblies of fencers ending up in relatively the same order. This reflects on the situation in foil, where fencers at mediocre levels tend to believe that they must have electric apparatus to get a fair deal. They ignore the fact that there is still a human element, the director, who might not call the "time" to a particular fencer's delight. Sabre presiding and judging is obviously more difficult, but the sport survives without electricity.

Properly, there will be four judges (in class you can get along with two), one pair watching and listening for hits against one fencer and one pair watching and listening for hits against the other. The president stands back three or four meters in order to see the whole scene. Upon sensing a hit, fair or foul, a judge is required by the rules to throw up his hand. The president then calls "Halt!" and describes the immediately preceding actions so as to clarify the time and right-of-way situation.

As in non-electric foil, a judge can serve very well with just four words: "Yes," "No," "Foul," and "Abstain," meaning respectively a valid hit, no hit (miss or adequately parried), an invalid hit, and "I don't know." The judge must be prepared to explain his vote, since his "Yes" may refer to an attack going through an inadequate parry, and his "Abstain" may indicate that he heard a hit but wasn't sure of where it landed, etc.

Some may object to my preference for the word "Foul" to designate a hit on invalid surface. This word was always used in the United States until a few years ago. "Foul" is short, and distinct from the other words needed. There is some feeling that "Foul" implies unsportsmanlike conduct, but a foul is about as intentional as putting the foot over the foul line in bowling—the player would always much rather make a good hit.

Quite a few international sabre judges merely point to the leg, indicating a hit below the valid target. Other gestures are used and accepted for other judgments.

Beginners and their instructors should know most importantly that a foul is a *hit*, with point or edge, on a part of the body not designated as valid target.

A judge must follow the fencer whose hits he is supposed to see, maintaining a position to one side and behind (Fig. 55). If the fencer moves forward, the judge must go along, and if the fencer retreats, no matter how fast, the judge must try to stay in the rear.

Sometimes when the opposing fencer flèches a judge may have to leave his position to keep from being run over—a fencer is not supposed to collide with his opponent, but there is no rule about preserving judges. Under the circumstances, a judge may not honestly be able to say anything but "Abstain," because his view of the target becomes obscured.

The duties of the president are: (1) to start and stop the action; (2) to decide about time and right-of-way, briefly describing the parts of a phrase or sequence; (3) to take the votes of the jury on each action and award touches; (4) to impose penalties; (5) to watch out for all unsafe conditions—although this doesn't relieve anyone else of the duty to guard against accidents, and (6) in general to control the entire conduct of the bout to which he has been assigned. His decisions on time and right-of-way are not subject to appeal. He is the only official to whom a fencer or a judge should speak—a fencer may be penalized for starting an argument with a judge, and a judge should not answer. Discussions must be carried on through the president. Recapitulation of the action, and a recount of the jury's vote, are given by the president on a fencer's request.

It may seem that a fencer has no chance at all in arguments with officials. Not so. First of all, he may ask to have any member of a jury, or all of them, including the president, *replaced before the bout begins*. He need not state any reason, such as that the jury is overloaded with members of his opponent's club, or that he believes an official to be incompetent (he shouldn't say things like this, anyway). If he exercises this right, he should be able to obtain an impartial jury. Next, he is entitled to hear a clear description of a sequence, with the votes of the judges, and he may point out an error in the process of arriving at decision. Finally, he may appeal to the Bout Committee against any penalties. Honest errors of judgment are to be expected, and most fencers don't argue—they figure that in the long run their opponents will suffer from about the same number of errors, so it all evens out.

When you compete you will be expected to help officiate. After considerable service as a judge, you can try presiding. There is no doubt that this experience will improve your own competing ability, because the knowledge gained by watching closely, initially working under older presidents, must add to your understanding of the game. Your viewpoint, as a judge, is nearly that of one of the fencers: Almost standing in his shoes, you can get a feeling of how he deals with his opponent, what attacks and counteractions are used, successfully and unsuccessfully, etc.

Class practice in judging and presiding is included even in beginner courses. Thus, you should be able to assist with fair competence in your first sabre tournament. The Golden Rule is, "Judge as you would be judged"—that is, with keen attention and fairness. Nobody can be perfect, nor can he satisfy all the fencers all the time. Your ability in this will grow with practice.

In spirit, the president and jury have an overall *duty* to help the fencers. When bouting, a fencer is too involved with what *he* intends to do—he can't know what his opponent intends to do, and he doesn't notice everything his opponent actually does after a fast phrase begins. Officials furnish outside views, presumably objective, fair, and impartial, for the benefit of the fencers. Officials are not the stars of the tournament drama.

THOUGHTS ABOUT SABRE

Sabre theory—how to act to win, within the rules—somewhat resembles that of foil because of the convention of right-of-way. An attack must be an immediate threat to the target with edge or point. If it is, it must be blocked or evaded. Stop hits can be made only against preparations of attacks—or before the final motions of broken or composite attacks—in order to be awarded.

We might decide that good policies are: (1) not to try to stop hit very often, and (2) not to use many composite attacks. But, as in épée, the opponent's hand and arm are the closest targets, and should be important objects of attacks, counterattacks (stop hits and time hits) and parry-ripostes. As you will see, training includes practice in *attempted* stop hits immediately followed by parries—that is, the stop hit may be "wrong" (lacking right-of-way), but if the attack can be parried (and/or evaded) and the stop has *already* been successful, the stop will count. When the attempted stop misses, the parry-riposte should be effective.

The part of the target that receives the most hits is the head (mask). A survey made by Maestro Nicholas Toth* of the final round of the 1965 U. S. Championship revealed that, out of 202 successful actions, at least 101 (50 per cent) of the touches were made on the head (remises and stop and time thrusts are not included in this figure, since the landing places of those actions were not specified). Of these 101 hits, 57 per cent were direct (simple) attacks, and 38 per cent were simple ripostes (these simple one-count actions totalling 47 per cent of all touches scored), only 5 per cent of the touches to the head were by composite actions. We might conclude that a lot of actions are made to the head and that even the best fencers have trouble blocking or evading such actions. The explanation may be that, in order to block a vertical cut to the head, a sabreur must raise his hand and expose his arm, thus fear may inhibit him from parrying fully and quickly enough.

While half the successful actions were made to the head, a mere 8.4 per cent or so were by chest cut. This might be explained by the fact that the Quarte parry, which protects the chest, is one of the quickest and easiest actions.

Maestro Toth, fencing master at the U. S. Air Force Academy, also remarked (with disfavor) that the finalists fenced at close distance. The normal range in sabre is considered to be longer than that in foil and more comparable to that of épée. The hand is usually kept well back until the instant of attack since the forearm can be more easily hit by a cut in sabre than by a thrust in épée. In consequence, sabreurs are expected to be more mobile than foilists or épéeists. Much thought and practice can be devoted to ways of covering the distance gap in order to attack the head and torso, to leading the opponent to approach so that an attack can be made against him, and to speedy retreat from his attacks.

This statistical analysis of top-level American sabre play is now several years old, and changes may have occurred. (My own observations indicate an improvement in mobility.) By no means was Maestro Toth, with whom I have had correspondence, happy with the situation: Just because this is the way things *are* does not mean that this is the way they *should* be. Maestro Toth would like to see better sabre fencing in America.

Beginners, however, can learn a great deal from the data surveyed above. In the first place, it would seem worthwhile to concentrate on a few very basic actions that are demonstrably workable. From what I saw at the 1967 World Championships (and from the tapes I saw of the 1976 Olympics)—and my views seem to be in line with those of other commentators—international sabre play is

---

* Printed in the AFLA magazine, *American Fencing*, Vol. 17, No. 2, January 1966.

comparatively simple (not a synonym for *easy*) in handwork and very arduous and complex in footwork. I will stress here that we *do* want to play "the big distance." Beginners must immediately get their legs in shape.

One of the principal strategies is to attack so fast that your opponent can't react soon enough. Another is deception. In either case, your handwork need not be intricate, but must be accurate, exactly timed, and efficient (without wasted motion). The speed attack depends on footwork, maneuvering to get to exactly the right place, and the developed ability to take off in the least time. To a great extent deceptive attacks depend on confusing your opponent with irregular shifts of location on the ground, change of pace, and change of rhythm, almost all by legwork.

A couple of years ago I started a sabre class at Reed College, and as an experiment, we had a crash program to put the students into competition after just five hours of classwork. Half the students had had foil, one had studied karate, and the rest had had no training in combat sports. The students co-operated by doing a good deal of work outside of class. These students didn't do badly in the competition against some more experienced men. They also did their part in judging. Naturally there was much left to study afterward before any of them could make it to the finals of even the state championships, but the cold-plunge treatment seemed to have some value. Here's an outline of the course:

1. Conditioning footwork.

2. From Tierce, point attack (just to get started) and head cut, lunging and recovering to Tierce; parrying Tierce, riposting with head cut.

3. Review head-cut attacking; parrying Tierce to Quarte, riposting with head cut; mobility drills.

4. Review head-cut attacking; parrying Tierce to Quinte, riposting with head cut; mobility drills.

5. Bouting and judging; general review.

Chapter 18

SIMPLE ATTACKING IN SABRE

FOR THE FIRST three or four hours of your beginning course, you could concentrate on footwork and armwork—*without* the sabre. Much of the footwork will be new to you unless you have previously taken épée, and the armwork is different from either foil or épée.

Every kind of conditioning calisthenics, sprints, hurdles, and drills should be started. Review Chapter 12. You must continue many exercises on your own, since you will not have time in class to go over them as much as you will need for good competitive performance. Therefore, you should be sure you understand, in these first few hours, how to do these moves. All class periods should begin with warm-up and drill, and end with a cool-off, usually jogging backward twice around the gym.

After building up with all kinds of exercise and footwork patterns, you may begin flèching practice. Ease into a flèche from rocking, advancing, retreating, and so forth. Try to float out into the flèche, extending your arm and rear leg smoothly until you are just about to fall over your front toes. You can get the proper sequence at a slow pace, swinging the rear leg over as the front leg straightens, and just walking away, bringing your fighting hand back after the moment of full stretch. Keep this up, gradually increasing your spring, timing your hand to *lead* the push of your front leg, leaning into it more, reaching farther, and taking a longer step with your rear leg until you have to trot and later run to keep from falling down. Take a good long runoff: don't try to stop yourself too soon at this point.

Smoothness is the best—the only—way. Flèching is a total commitment to attack, and you won't be able to stop, back up, change direction, or do very much about protecting yourself. You can't compromise, you can't do it halfway. On the other hand, if you have to make too much effort to get started, you will signal to your opponent too soon. A smooth action is often well on the way before he notices it. Practice now without the sabre, and later, when you have learned to strike by extending with an advance or a lunge, you will be able to think about setting up attacks with a flèche.

83. Flèching practice for sabre: crouch

84. *Flèching practice for sabre: spring. Hit should occur now*

85. *Flèching practice for sabre: run. This action is to get away, angling off the strip, and to recover balance*

86. *Holding sabre, blade vertical: guarding/inviting Tierce*

87. *Holding sabre, blade "horizontal" low invitation*

HOLDING THE SABRE

You should hold the sabre very loosely, your thumb barely in contact with the pad inside the shell, opposing the main edge. Your first finger will also touch the pad in the normal grip, and will be curled part-way around the handle. There should be a small space between your first and middle fingers. The handle should sit in the crook of your last three fingers, along the front margin of your palm. In the most common attitude, called guarding/inviting Tierce (or just Tierce, as long as you remember that you are simultaneously guarding and inviting), your thumb will be up. The blade will be nearly vertical if seen from the back or front, and the point will be only a bit farther forward than the hilt.

If you own a sabre, play around with it. Flip the point forward, back, left, right, in good-sized ovals (major axis vertical) clockwise, counterclockwise, and free arcs. You could even do this while sitting down reading or watching TV, so as to become familiar with your weapon. Lacking a sabre of your own, use a stick, dowel, or umbrella.

Rolling. Hold the sabre straight up and roll the handle between your thumb and fingers. One way, the knuckle bow (the distinctive part of the sabre guard, see Figs. 87 and 88) should swing around to the back of your hand. The other way, it goes opposite your palm. This rolling action is a part of a number of hand movements in sabre. Usually the turn is not as extreme as you can make it in your practice exercise, but cuts and parries are often made with the hand turned a little one way or the other.

You will sometimes make actions with your palm more or less down, facing the floor. The location of your fingers will be approximately the same, but the handle should be rolled more toward the fingertips. You will have to squeeze a

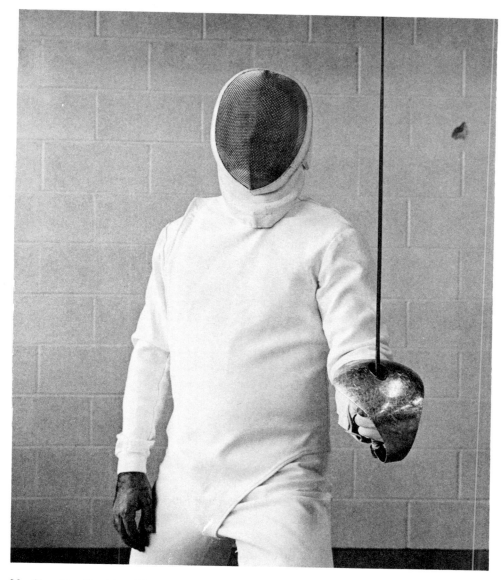

88. *Guarding/inviting Tierce: front view of a left-hander, or what a right-hander should see in a mirror*

little with your thumb and first finger to keep the sabre from dropping out of your hand, but you should use the loosest possible grip.

To become used to the feel of the weapon, since this manner of holding and manipulating is different from the fingerwork for foil and épée, move your blade from vertical (Tierce) to "horizontal" (palm down) and back again by rotating your wrist no more than $75°$ (i.e., in the "horizontal" position, the sabre tip is still higher than the guard). Don't displace your hand sideways. Don't let your elbow stick out. Later try extending as your hand turns palm down, and withdrawing your arm as your thumb turns up. Reverse, extending as the blade turns to the vertical and pulling back with the blade turning to the "horizontal." Repeat these exercises smoothly and easily about 50 times. Speed and force will come later.

89. Low invitation: similar to position for beginning a flank cut or feint of a flank cut

You should, most of all at this stage, practice extending and recovering your arm with your thumb up, in Tierce. Make sure your hand doesn't rise: You may feel that your hand is bent upward, with your arm slanting down from your shoulder. Thus, the blade will not tilt forward any more than in the starting position.

SALUTING

Saluting with the sabre should be done in a simple and dignified manner, without flourishes. From first position, heels together, and fighting arm straight, palm down, weapon tip just off the floor, raise your arm to point at your instructor, partner, or opponent. Next bend your elbow downward, bringing the shell to your chin as you turn your palm toward yourself. Then snap your arm down to first position.

TWO INVITATIONS

Guarding/inviting Tierce is most important. Your hips and shoulders must be level, head and trunk upright, feet at a right angle and about 15 inches apart, front foot and knee pointed at the opponent, knees slightly bent. Your weight should be a little on the balls of your feet (heels light). Your rear hand may be on your hip or hanging in a natural way. The elbow of your fighting arm should be about a hand's breadth forward of your waist, and your fighting hand should be about hip high. If you glance down, you should be able to see your leading thigh, as your sabre hand will be carried to the outside (right, for right-handers). Your wrist will ordinarily be straight forward in order to direct the main edge of your sabre toward your opponent, but bent down to keep your hand low. It is a good practice to go on guard from first position (attention) by moving your rear foot backward.

I recommend only one other position, called low invitation or just "low." From guarding/inviting Tierce rotate your hand palm down, and you will be in low invitation. You may carry your hand a bit lower than in Tierce, or even let your arm hang, to relax it, but only when you are out of range. This is strictly an invitation, but if your opponent doesn't accept, you may attack.

Traditionally, there are invitations of Quarte, Quinte, Prime, and Seconde, but I think they are too risky. You may show them to your opponent when you are out of his reach. Things will get complicated enough with two invitations, as you shall see.

Simple Direct Attacking

ATTACKING WITH POINT

Point attacks aren't used very much, and when they are, they don't often succeed. Maestro Toth's survey, mentioned in Chapter 17, listed only one touch scored with the point by lunging, and eight stop or time thrusts (counterattacks). Still, in 1968 Alex Orban won a decisive bout in an international competition with four stop thrusts and one stop cut—and topped the tournament, the first such victory for the United States in modern fencing history.

Be that as it may, the important thing is that ALL hand actions with the sabre should start with the point (and that means the fingers), whether they are attacks, parries, ripostes or counterattacks, cuts or thrusts. The rule is, LEAD WITH YOUR POINT! Fingerwork is essential. Later you will see that cuts are *not* made by swinging the arm.

Now I assume you have had from three to six months of foil training and possibly an épée course, so you should be familiar with directing the point. But you hold the sabre differently, and thrusts are made so as to finish with your hand *down*. The aiming spot, at first, is on the forwardmost surface of your opponent's chest, halfway down from chin to waist. In combat you may, of course, try to hit anywhere on valid surface, including the fighting hand, keeping in mind that judges may not see these épée-type shots.

Begin from Tierce by dipping your point forward with finger action, rolling the handle until you are palm down, and extending, in one smooth motion. Your hand must not be displaced inward (to the left for a right-hander), but must extend outside of your hip. Thus, your blade will be at an angle to your arm, slanting inward to the target. Never jerk your elbow or lock it. Keep your hand as soft as possible. Return to Tierce and repeat a dozen times or so against your instructor, a partner (who must be fully uniformed), a fixed target on the wall, or a hanging-ball target.

90. Lunging with point: note angle of blade to arm

You will rarely hit merely by extending. After practice in co-ordinating your fingers, wrist, and arm to thrust smoothly and accurately, you must add footwork. Extending may be done before, with, or after a preliminary* foot movement. Much time must be expended in combining different foot patterns with different ways of timing the hand action. But your labor will pay off eventually: If you can't do these simple things well, how can you expect to do anything complicated?

However, since the point attack is not the most important method of scoring, you can economize a bit by trying just two foot patterns: advancing/retreating and lunging/recovering. Differences in timing will give you five variations. Do each one at least six times.

First, extend a split second before your front foot moves in the advance. Next extend just after the front foot starts. Finally, extend on the movement of the rear foot. Inasmuch as your advancement is quite small and rapid, the co-ordination is not so easy. As soon as you have extended/advanced, retreat and PULL your hand sharply back as fast as you can. Your elbow should go back to your waist, your hand should turn so the blade whips up to vertical, and your wrist should bend slightly so your palm is forward. (This arm-hand action is called Tierce parry, a firm block to the outside.)

* Not lunging or flèching.

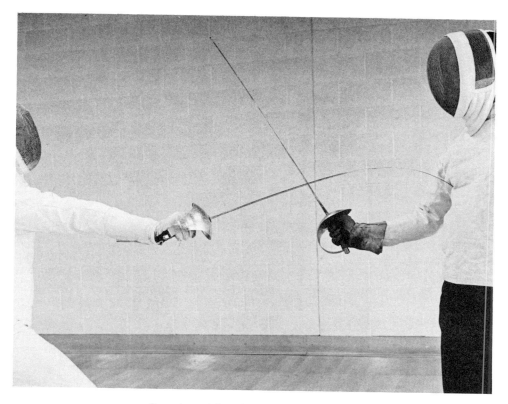

91. Lunging with point: note wrist kept down

When thrusting, your hand will rise somewhat, from hip level to lower chest level. Remember to bring it back low for the Tierce parry.

In lunging you may extend your point very, very slightly before your front foot starts, or at the same time. Don't wait until your arm is completely extended before you move your foot. You must try, nevertheless, to make the point hit the target before your front foot *lands,* or at least your point should reach its forwardmost position ahead of your foot (that is when you don't hit because your opponent has retreated or perhaps parried). Since your opponent might take a cut at your wrist, you don't want to put it out too early, and certainly there should be no hesitation once your point starts forward. Complete the lunge but recover immediately: don't stay there, bounce right back to Tierce parry. Doing a complete lunge (though a short one compared to the foil lunge) and then recovering is not as easy as it sounds. Practice for smoothness and let speed come later.

Instructor: The earliest lesson deals with the direct point attack upon closing of range. At first you should stand still, asking the student to approach to hit by extending/advancing and by lunging. Next, from longer range, he should attack as you advance, so that both you and he are contributing to the reduction of distance. Each pattern should be repeated three or more times.

In every case, the student should recover to Tierce parry immediately—with retreating, if he has advanced. The instructor should lightly cut the student's shell or the forte of his blade on the outside, to confirm this recovery. And the student should extend again with point (riposte). Thus, the very first blade exercise consists of attack, recovery to parry-riposte (plus a final recovery to Tierce). For realism, the instructor should not allow the student to hit every time on the attack,

*and not always on the riposte. The physical manifestations that reveal an inten-
tion to hit must be eliminated—the student should not lean on the target, and
yet he should stretch his arm, following through on the stroke.*

Further uses of the point will be explained later in this chapter, in the sections on indirect attacking and on counterattacking.

VERTICAL CUTTING

Most sabre touches are scored by cutting. But again remind yourself, THE
POINT MOVES FIRST! Your arm should never swing to deliver a cut, but should
simply extend. Your fist should move directly toward the center of your opponent's upper torso. Only a very light action is needed to score, just enough to
reach the target and make a small sound. Therefore, fingerwork is very important.
Sometimes you may cut *not* by snapping your hand shut, but, on the contrary, by
letting the tip of your blade *drop* on the target.

Pair off with another student—completely uniformed, of course. Salute and
put on your masks. Without going on guard or using any footwork, put your
hand more or less in its usual Tierce position. Suppose you wish to cut the head:
directing your point at the upper-right-front of the mask, extend your arm, and at
the end of the extension let your point fall forward to hit. Instantly pick up your
point on the rebound and withdraw your hand to Tierce parry. You should have
tapped your partner's mask very lightly above his left eyebrow (assuming you're
right-handed). Repeat about six times, then let your classmate use you for a target (Figs. 92, 93).

Continuing this exercise, reach and tap *twice*, withdrawing your hand
immediately on the second tap. Do not strain or push. Eventually the two hits
will sound very close together but distinctly separate. Finally, try three taps on
each extension. Use the bounce from the last to carry your hand back. You
shouldn't poke your partner in the front of the mask, but it's better to do that
than to reach too high and too far so that you hit him on top.

Another way is to stand farther apart and have your partner extend his arm,
blade vertical. Extend and bounce the tip edge of your blade off the top of his
wrist. We'll refer to this target as "top cuff" from here on. In order to make the
cut without hitting his guard, and since you must keep your own hand to the outside, you will have to lay your blade at an angle of about 30° across his wrist.
Repeat until the action is smooth for a single cut. Next, practice a double cut,
and finally a triple cut.

After this exercise, which will help you gain lightness and accuracy of
finger control, you may go into your lessons. Once again you will have to adjust
the range with footwork, deliver the cut to the head, and RECOVER. Furthermore,
at longer range you should go through the whole routine with the top cuff as
your objective. As previously mentioned, you will normally extend as you lunge,
but not too soon. You can see now that early homework on foot actions is valuable. If you have done it, you can concentrate on fingerwork in lessons and class
drill.

*Instructor: The preparatory finger exercises can be done by students in couples
after a demonstration. The lesson can then begin with a head cut delivered by extension only, followed in succession by a head cut at the end of a balestra, a hop-*

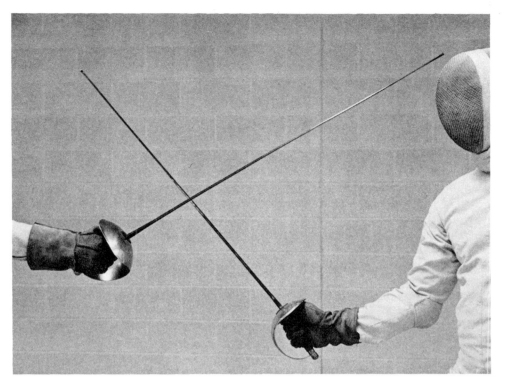

92. *Vertical cutting: just before and after striking—fingers loose*

93. *Vertical cutting: edge nearest point strikes front curve of mask on nearest side*

back lunge, and possibly a flèche, with several repetitions apiece. Smoothness and lightness are not to be expected at once, but the student should make them his goals.

As before, recovery should be immediate (except when flèching). The student, without neglecting the lunge, should bounce back to Tierce parry. Cut into this block, requiring a head cut and a second Tierce parry. Speed is not of the utmost importance: The student should perform the entire sequence lightly, smoothly, on balance.

He must also be made acutely aware of the range. Although you will cooperate by standing still (for the first round), he must not be allowed to start from too close in, and neither should he take such large steps that he hits with anything but the first inch or two of his blade. The actual cue to attack is the closing to proper distance, *whether this comes about through his own footwork, yours, or both.*

In all probability the first cutting lesson can only include a very few repetitions of the given combinations. The class can be directed to pair off, one partner being an absolute dummy—actually standing in first position—so that the other can go over these fundamental actions slowly and thoroughly under the simplest conditions. Then have partners switch roles. At later sessions you can have the student attack on your approach, and eventually he can be led to attack in pursuit.

A further round of lessons and practice in couples can be devoted to attacking the top cuff from various ranges, with you or the dummy standing still, advancing, or retreating. Not too much time should be spent on this, however, since the more forward target is too easily removed or blocked. The best target is the head.

The point thrust and the vertical cut from Tierce are called simple (one-count) *direct* attacks. Most of your work should be devoted to perfecting the vertical cut. However, there is one simple action, almost direct, very similar to it: cutting the upper chest. There's also a simple direct cut from low invitation, attacking the flank or outside cuff.

CUTTING CHEST

Supposing you and your opponent both fight with the right hand, it would seem fairly easy to cut his chest by turning your hand a few degrees clockwise as you extend. This can be done pretty much in the same manner as a head cut.

We have noted that chest cuts aren't supposed to work very often. But your opponent may mistake your motion for a head cut—then you may succeed by cutting in at an angle under his Quinte parry. You will also see in a later chapter how the chest cut can be used in an effective combination.

HORIZONTAL CUTTING

From low invitation the only simple direct attack is by what we call a horizontal cut. This cut doesn't actually swing in a level plane, but it strikes the side of the body (flank) or arm, so we distinguish it from the vertical cut or the slightly angled chest cut.

Your opponent usually can't be hit from his outside when he is in Tierce. Sometimes, though, you may meet someone who gives you the low invitation, or guards/invites Quarte, or otherwise exposes his elbow. Your action, called "flank cut" for convenience, should hit either just below his shoulder or somewhere along his arm. At long range you might strike the outside of his wrist.

Line this up for yourself with a partner, and you will see that your blade wouldn't be horizontal, but slanted 30° or more upward from fist to point. In a genuinely horizontal cut, you would probably raise your hand too high and hit the guard or even cut foul surface (leg). You must keep your hand at about waist height to protect yourself as much as possible against cuff cuts. On occasion a horizontal cut, when the opponent is in low or Quarte, might strike his right cheek.

By this time you should be able to invent some exercises for practice in couples. Be sure to include long-range cuts to outside cuff. Don't flèche. Recover to Tierce parry.

Instructor: The lesson plan suggests that from this point you should jump to the material in Chapter 19, parry-riposting. Simple indirect attacking will be useful a bit later on. We can consider counterattacking as a refined version of attacking, and in order to get students into play as quickly as possible, we should offer them a parry-riposte system now.

GAMES

Targets. Hanging targets can be made from rubber balls or golf balls, strung up at various heights from 3–6 feet above the floor. Try thrusting, head cutting, chest cutting, and flank cutting—always returning to Tierce—from a standstill, then advancing to range, then lunging, then advance lunging, etc.

A similar target, but one that will behave differently, is a ball mounted on a wand—bamboo stick or thin metal rod—with a floor base. When this is put in motion by you or a partner, it sways. With a 3-foot wand you would get a quicker movement than with a 6-foot wand, so the opponent's hand usually moves faster than his head (and is smaller).

Tag.

(1) Unarmed, the partners stand facing each other, about 10 feet apart. Behind one of them is a line about 15 or 20 feet away. The other partner starts running forward, trying to tag anywhere on the upper body. This is good practice for both, in running forward and backward. If the partner running backward gets over the line, he is safe. It would be well if both have had practice in falling, for the game gets frantic. Better still, a third person could be ready to catch the player running backward.

(2) With weapons, masks, and jackets, a similar race can be run. The chasing partner must score with a headcut within the set distance. The target partner should not parry.

(3) With weapons, masks, and jackets, the partners guard/invite Tierce at a fairly easy lunging distance for the attacker, who must score with a head cut by lunging. (The other partner must watch keenly and try to retreat out of range.) The attacker is expected to win, provided he doesn't telegraph his move.

Simple Indirect Attacking

CUTTING HEAD FROM LOW

When you approach your opponent and you are guarding/inviting Tierce, he will probably be most ready to cover against a head cut or chest cut. Your footwork would have to be exceptionally tricky to give you success if all your attacks started from the same invitation. Try low invitation, and he might shift his hand wider, lower, and farther back. A direct attack to the outside forearm might be needed to convince him. Then make an indirect head cut from low.

All at once, extend, twist your hand thumb up, and lunge. Need I say that you must somehow get the range first?

With a bit more rotation of the fist, you could make a chest cut. Your opponent will probably assume, when you start a motion from low invitation, that you're going to cut at his head, and a chest cut might work.

CUTTING FLANK FROM TIERCE

As was mentioned above, your opponent may anticipate that you will cut head or chest when you Guard/Invite Tierce. If this danger worries him enough —and you should certainly make plenty of attacks to convince him—he may begin to carry his hand higher, or more to the left, or both, thus exposing his outside forearm, elbow, and flank. It is a bare possibility that he will guard/invite Quarte, blocking any possible chest cut, or even Quinte, covering his head (this is almost too good to be true).

Extend, twisting your hand palm down, and lunge. Remember that your blade will not be cutting in a horizontal plane, but will be slanted so as to intersect wrist, elbow, shoulder, or cheek, depending on the distance. That is, your hand should not rise, but your point should be no lower than armpit level.

This type of attack will probably not get you as many touches as the vertical-cutting attacks, but the technique will be useful later on, when you are building combinations.

INDIRECT POINT ATTACKING

Although it is fairly rare in sabre today, your opponent might try to make blade contact. If you let your blade slant forward too much, he might apply beats or pressures. You can avoid contact, or release from contact, by sending your point in clockwise or counterclockwise arcs, as required. So why not attack at the same time?

Without such a lead from your opponent, you could still make an indirect point attack from Tierce, by flipping your point in a counterclockwise spiral. He may think this is a flank cut, at first, and parry Tierce. Your point would, however, continue under his guard and end in line with his chest.

From low, a smaller arc of the same kind would pass under the shell of his weapon. Sometimes, when you give the low invitation, your opponent may change his attitude to Seconde (palm down, blade tip lower than fist), hoping to block or possibly to beat your blade. This, of course, opens his flank for cuts or thrusts by a small clockwise movement of your point.

Instructor: Emphasis remains on the vertical cut, direct or indirect. Depending

94. Cutting flank

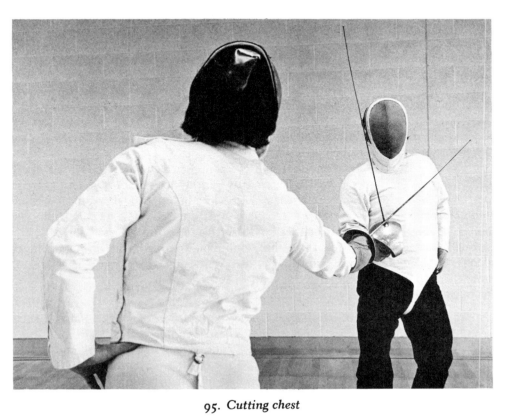

95. Cutting chest

on the time available, you can schedule some practice on the indirect attacks, with priority for the head cut from low, or merely demonstrate the possibilities and let the class work them out in routine exercises, bouting, and free play.

COUNTERATTACKING (STOP CUTTING)

Counterattacks include stop thrusts, stop cuts, time thrusts, and time cuts. You are already prepared to do counterattacks—stop cuts in particular. Actions of this kind can succeed against poorly executed attacks (sometimes against simple attacks that are made with wide, swinging slashes) and against the preparatory moves of all attacks.

Theoretically your opponent must make a mistake for your counterattack to succeed: telegraphing, moving too slowly, attacking with too many complications that really don't keep up a continuous threat. In actual practice, the boldness of your counterattacks sometimes cause him to flinch—you steal the right-of-way from him. Once in a while you should lunge all out, or flèche, when you think he's about to start, or even after he has begun: perhaps only 25 per cent of the time will you be "right" when you take off, but if he hesitates, he forfeits his precedence, and you will be right when you finish. Successful or not, your aggression will tend to make him doubtful.

Very, very often a counterattack is coupled with evasion. For example, if you're in low and your opponent raises his hand as he comes in for a head cut, you might flick your blade tip at his outside cuff, at the same time pulling your head back and starting to retreat (Fig. 126). The move to the the rear must be completed quickly, and further steps may be necessary. Your fist should then assume Quinte parry. Naturally, if your cut lands and his falls short because of your retreat, the touch is yours, as a tempo has passed.

When you are guarding/inviting Tierce the best stop cut to try is the vertical one to top cuff (or maybe to the head if your opponent is wide enough and close enough). This may work against an attempted point attack, head cut, or chest cut (Fig. 124). The same kind of vertical stop cut can take the head as its target when your opponent tries to cut your outside cuff: His blade may swing under your arm as you extend if you raise your hand slightly—you shouldn't let him get close enough to reach your flank.

The stop thrust is the least useful of the counterattacks that you should use, partly because the target is farther away. It would be necessary for you to extend your blade in line with your opponent's chest while he was still preparing (with a preliminary advance, for instance) and *before* his attack began. Theoretically he should be able to see this and either take your blade or not attack. Many beginners will, however, fail to recognize the point-in-line or will come ahead without taking the blade and will run right onto your point. You must have great confidence (perhaps acquired in foil and épée) that your move is correct, and you must stand firm while your opponent attacks.

Instructor: Concentrate on the two best stop cuts (those described above) and emphasize co-ordination with retreating. These counterattacks are much the same as simple attacks, except that the fencer usually goes backward instead of lunging or flèching. The student's attitude must be that he is going to try a stop cut, but that his investment and risk should be minimal—he must get out of the dangerous situation as quickly as possible after making the least necessary motion. His arm should extend fully and immediately pull to a parry. You should follow through with the indicated attack in order to instill the habit of parry-ing/retreating.

Time thrusts and time cuts sometimes happen unintentionally among begin-ners, but their calculated use had best be reserved for advanced fencers. For your information, time strokes are one-count (one-tempo) actions that block or deflect the opposing blade and simultaneously extend. They are occasionally described as "parry and riposte both in one move."

REMISING, ETC.

I've suggested that you practice double and triple cuts. The purpose at that stage was to develop lightness in finger action. Advanced sabreurs continue such drills, and their coaches include multiple cuts in lessons. For example, two stop cuts before parrying in a stop-parry-riposte sequence. The ability to cut twice or three times very rapidly is often useful in remising or redoubling.

The remise is defined as a second cut (or thrust) at the same target area without recovering from the attack. (In the redoublement the second cut is shifted to another target area.) To succeed you must have an opponent who freezes on his parry, opens up after parrying, makes a composite riposte (e.g., by one-two, instead of simple ones), or delays his riposte very much or makes it in a roundabout manner.

If he tends to hesitate on his riposte, making an extra movement that opens the target before he shoots, a remise may get you a touch. Example: Your attack to flank is blocked in Tierce, but your opponent lifts his hand to chop at your head; an instantaneous remise as you recover may hit his outside cuff—you would, of course, parry-riposte as usual. Another example: Your attack to head is blocked in Quinte, but your opponent swings his arm back and around in a large movement to cut your chest or belly, which leaves him open to a second cut on his mask. You should have time to parry Quarte also.

Remising often sets your opponent up for redoubling. If he has a tendency to freeze on the parry anyway, being hit by remises is likely to confirm his habit. He will hesitate to riposte. In that case, you can choose a secondary target. For instance, when you attack to the head he may successfully block but hold the Quinte parry. This exposes his arm to an immediate second cut, and even if he blocks this when he starts to riposte, you should have time to parry also. A some-what more difficult way is to redouble by cutting over (*coupé*) to the head when your opponent freezes in Tierce after your original flank cut. Not many do this, but the drill is worthwhile.

Instructor: The easiest footwork pattern is lunging (after gaining ground), remis-ing or redoubling (arm staying extended), recovering/parrying, and riposting/re-treating. However, students should not depend on actions of this type or any other complex sequence because the risk is enormously increased. The funda-mental strategy would still be the predominant use of simple attacks, parry-ripostes, and stop hits with evasion. The motto is, "Fight and run away," and the sabreur must not assume that any particular action will succeed. Thus, he will not stop or let down until he has recovered and removed himself out of range.

Remise-type actions have been included in this chapter on simple attacks be-cause they are, theoretically, separate attacks. By parrying or evading, your oppo-nent doesn't get the right-of-way, he merely takes yours from you, temporarily.

Right-of-way is obtained by an action that will hit—a cut or thrust. By definition, a remise is another simple attack following an original attack without recovering.

SUMMARY OF SIMPLE ATTACKS

The form of every attack (simple or composite) is: get ground, try to hit, recover (or escape). Getting ground includes making use of your opponent's movements as well as your own. Whenever the range becomes (or *is becoming*) favorable to you, you should try to attack. The broad alternatives are to lure your opponent to come closer or for you to catch up with him. You must be loose and balanced in order to be able to attack the very instant an opportunity appears. With experience you should learn to anticipate by a fraction of a second when the chance will occur and which opening will be offered.

SIMPLE DIRECT ATTACKS—SET I

From	Attack	Recovery to	Practice Repetitions
Tierce	Point	Tierce Parry	3
Tierce	Vertical Cut	Tierce Parry	9
Tierce	Chest Cut	Tierce Parry	3
Low	Horizontal Cut	Tierce Parry	3

SIMPLE DIRECT ATTACKS—SET II

(after studying parry-riposting)

From	Attack	Recovery to	Practice Repetitions
Tierce	Point	Quarte Parry	3
Tierce	Vertical Cut	Quinte Parry	6
Tierce	Chest Cut	Quarte Parry	6
Low	Horizontal Cut	Quinte Parry	6

SIMPLE INDIRECT ATTACKS

From	Attack	Recovery to	Practice Repetitions
Low	Point	Quarte Parry	2
Low	Vertical Cut	Quinte Parry	9
Tierce	Horizontal Cut	Quinte Parry	6
Tierce	Point (large counterclockwise spiral)	Quarte Parry	2

The column "Practice Repetitions" indicates the *relative* amount of work to be given to each type of attack (defined by hand action). This amount has to be multiplied by a number of footwork patterns. You should do at least two footwork patterns for each example in the table, and preferably more for the most important (head cut) attacks. Much of this will have to be done fairly slowly in prearranged conditions, such as practice with classmates.

Chapter 19

PARRY-RIPOSTING IN SABRE

ONE WAY OF dealing with attacks is by parry-riposting. *Riposte* means "answer." It is the attack a fencer makes after he blocks or deflects an opponent's attack.

Note that there can be, by definition, no riposte without a parry. Conversely, there should be no parry without a riposte: If you're going to bother to parry at all, you must immediately riposte. Also, ideally, you should *never make two parries in a row.*

We might make a distinction between a parry, which is defined as a move that blocks or deflects an attack, and an *attempted* parry, which fails to do so. These moves would look alike, and ordinarily the same word is used for both. We could add a third category, the change of invitation. The theoretical difference would depend on what the fencer meant to achieve and whether it worked or not. For the moment, let's keep it simple.

I use the term "parry-riposte." You must think of the action as a UNIT. Don't think of "the parry" and "the riposte" as two separate things. Each parry-riposte must be drilled in fairly well before going on to the next, rather than repeating transitions from one so-called parry to another.

This implies that you should, as far as possible, control the situation by *inviting* the attack in the first place. By holding your hand a certain way, you show your opponent where you are open, and by moving (or not moving) your feet, you show him that the distance is favorable. Of course, if the distance were genuinely favorable, he would be able to hit you regardless of your attempt to parry—most often you will have to retreat with your parry.

Also, by implication, you must learn not to try to block your opponent's feints (false threats). You want to make *one* parry-riposte that blocks his attack and hits him. Sometimes you might have to wait for his third, fourth, or tenth move—the one on which he commits himself. While you wait, you move your feet. You also take every opportunity to attack.

The easiest parry is "automatic"—the one your opponent makes for you by cutting against your shell or the forte of your blade, as when you are in Tierce. This happens accidentally through his inaccuracy, or when he miscalculates, thinking you are going to open. You will not have actually moved your hand to parry, but you will certainly want to riposte without hesitation. Teachers commonly instill this reaction by deliberately cutting at the shell, reminding the student frequently that he should extend (point or edge) the instant contact occurs. As a matter of practice, if your opponent does cut at your wrist, you should shoot right away, whether or not he hits you or your guard: The instant after his attack is a time gap—he is recovering and therefore vulnerable to an attack.

Except for two or three original practice repetitions standing still, you should do every parry-riposte with co-ordinated footwork. There might be occasions in combat when you would remain in place, but ordinarily you would give ground as your opponent attacks. Thus, considering the parry-riposte as a two-count action, you should retreat or hop back with the first count—or before it—and extend on the second. For basic training, each parry-riposte will be done two ways: with retreat and with hop back. In every case, your pattern must include recovery: For these basic combinations, recover to Tierce parry.

Beginners often make the great mistake of reaching out to parry. The effective way is to block. That is, you should create a wall at a right angle (approximately) to your opponent's cut, and the wall should be no farther from your threatened area than absolutely necessary. There you RECEIVE the cut. It is like catching a ball. If you reach out stiffly, it will get away from you, but if you softly bring it to you, you will have it.

The three main parries, Tierce, Quarte, and Quinte, are said to form a box with vertical sides on right and left and a horizontal roof above. This box should be no wider than your body and no higher than the top of your mask. Ideally, the sabreur parries "on the final," receiving the attack at its end, not trying to meet it halfway. Reaching out would expose your arm or leave you more open to secondary actions. Reaching out is disastrous when the opponent's action is a fake. Some practice in front of a mirror may be helpful in learning just how small your parries can be—and how wide they *must* be.

Before we decide where we're going, we must know where we are. You have just two invitational positions of the hand, Tierce and low. From the first position you will be able to do three basic parry-ripostes, and from low, two. These actions have features in common, however, so your labor will not be needlessly long and tedious.

PARRYING TIERCE

The most elementary is the action from Tierce invitation to Tierce parry—pulling the hand straight back. Your elbow will graze your ribs. You should already be familiar with this action since it was part of your recovery from simple attacks. A long-range attack to your cuff may be *evaded* altogether by this move (with or without retreating or hopping backward). A flank attack will most probably be blocked, if not entirely evaded.

Since you should already have had some work on a point riposte from Tierce parry as part of your very first blade lesson, we won't count that as one of the basic actions. You should also have had some work on the head-cut riposte from Tierce parry, but this is worth a good deal more practice.

By footwork and slight alterations in your invitation of Tierce, where your elbow is a few inches in front of your ribs, you may actually be able to get your opponent to attack with a flank cut. At any rate, you should be aware of the range at all times and alert to the start and direction of his attack (which might,

96. *Parrying Tierce with evasion by withdrawing hand*

of course, be a fake). When you decide that he really means to cut outside cuff, elbow, or flank, parry-riposte.

Normally, as I've mentioned previously, you would retreat or hop back. On rare occasions, when you are already quite far away, you could spoil your opponent's judgment of the distance-to-be by advancing or hopping forward. That is, if he anticipates that you will back up, and plans his footwork accordingly, the unexpected change will throw his timing off.

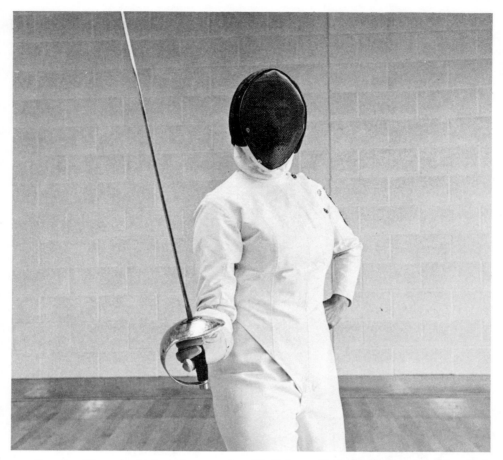

97. Parrying Tierce: wrist bent for complete block (note blade tip farther right than fist)

Tierce to head is the most frequently successful parry-riposte, as shown by the analysis of the 1965 National Finals. Set up practice in couples with a classmate, who will start in low and try to make a flank cut. At long range, when his cut is to the outside cuff, you should lunge with your riposte.

Next, start in low invitation. Your partner may attack by direct point or top-cuff cut from Tierce, or by flank cut from low. Parry to Tierce by a sharp clockwise rotation of your wrist, tucking your elbow back to your ribs, so that your blade whips from horizontal to vertical—*point leading*. Your fingers will grab the sabre handle, rolling it slightly more into your palm. This can effectively block or sweep away the prescribed attacks. Again, co-ordinate with footwork, retreating or hopping back with the parry, extending, extending/advancing, or extending/lunging on the riposte, which will be, of course, to the head.

PARRYING QUARTE (FROM TIERCE)

Suppose when you're inviting Tierce your opponent attacks with point or by some sort of chest or belly cut. You must block to the inside (to the left, for

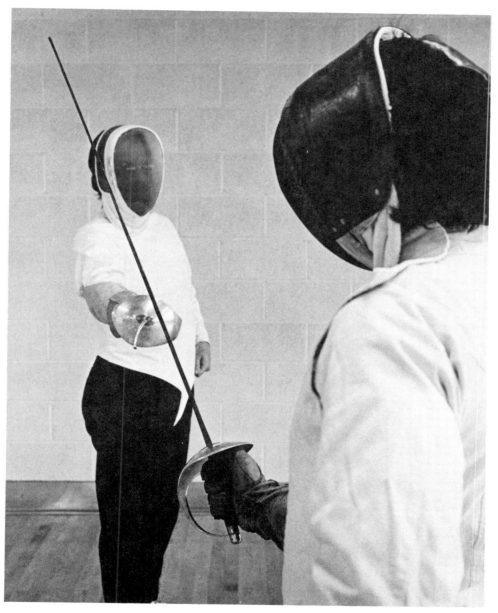

98. Parrying Quarte: note edge against opponent's cut

right-handers). This is an almost instinctive reaction: in its refined form it is called Quarte parry or parrying Quarte (pronounced, French style, *kart*; Italian style, *kwahrt*). Point leading, move your fist across, thumb up, so that when you glance down, you will see your leading knee to the right of your fist, if you're right-handed. Your blade should be nearly vertical, although the point will be farther to the left than the shell and still somewhat forward. You should have pulled your elbow in contact with your body above your hip. Your elbow is a

99. Parrying Quarte: another view

pivot for the sideways swing of your forearm. Your fingers should have curled slightly more, rolling your knuckle bow and main edge against the direction of the cut.

Don't raise your hand in an attempt to make a stronger block of a high chest cut or cheek cut. With the right time and distance, your blade will intercept the cut point first and divert it down the slant toward your shell. If you lift your hand, the cut may loop under and hit your belly or forearm. If you do not lead with your point, a chest or cheek cut will either hit before the parry or force through (inadequate parry). You can always lean your head and body a little to the side, away from the cut.

The best riposte is by head cut. If your opponent has committed himself to an attack to your chest or belly—and you shouldn't have parried otherwise—it is very difficult for him to parry your riposte or escape from it. Again lead with your point, taking the shortest path *forward*. Having swung your hand a little to make the parry, don't make the mistake of swinging in the opposite direction. Concentrate on shooting your fist straight toward the center of his chest. Your cut should be a vertical one, hitting his right temple if you are right-handed. Recover to Tierce. You should have made a thin triangle: across, out, and back.

Instructor: Use a point thrust or chest cut to lead the student to parry Quarte and riposte. After two or three attempts standing still, he should retreat and parry, riposting with feet planted. Next he should hop back and parry-riposte. He should be told to pay attention to the distance, so that he will riposte with an advancement or by lunging if, and only if, extension alone will not reach.

Except for the first few repetitions to get the pattern, the student should not pause on the parry-riposte. Once he begins he should complete the given sequence, no matter whether he parries too soon or too late, whether contact is made or not. If you deceive (e.g., by disengaging under the shell), the parry should be of the same width and the riposte should be followed by a head cut. A time cut may result automatically, given good distance and unhesitating action. In any case, the student should parry-riposte when the stroke is delivered and not when it is merely indicated.

For practice in couples, the dummy should attack only with point, lunging and recovering to Tierce.

PARRYING QUINTE (FROM TIERCE AND LOW)

Now we come to a parry that doesn't work often enough and should be used rarely—Quinte (pronounced, French style, *kant*; Italian style, *kwint*). This is done when your opponent attacks with a vertical cut to the head. The handwork is most complicated and quite different from anything you have done so far with any weapon.

From Tierce again the point leads, traveling to the left and somewhat backward (to be sure of being ahead of your opponent's point). Your fist rises straight up and stops at about the level of your temple. Your palm will be forward, the main edge and knuckle bow of your sabre upward to oppose the cut. Your fingers should be loose.

As soon as you receive the cut, curl your fingers and turn your wrist so your thumb points backward, then throw your fist toward the center of your opponent's chest. By doing this you should cut him on the mask. The whole action is like catching and throwing a ball—especially since when you hit, your hand shouldn't be clutched. The cut is never a downward chop but a forward action with the point arriving first.

Instructor: This could give you a headache unless you (1) wear a leather-hooded mask and (2) very soon make students hit lightly. You may, of course, parry Quinte yourself. In any case, cut horizontally as soon as the student has delivered the riposte, to make sure he recovers to Tierce. For practice in couples, the dummy should lunge with head cut and recover to Tierce in proper form, but at the best speed he can manage; the active partner will have to parry-riposte quickly to keep from being hit and to reach target before it escapes.

You should now try parrying Quinte from low invitation. Starting thus, the blade is already crosswise and merely needs to be raised high enough to block a vertical cut at your head.

Instructor: At about this stage, assuming they have worked well on the simple direct attacks and the three basic parry-ripostes, the students can be allowed to bout for the first time. With lecture discussions on rules and theory, they should be able to conduct themselves with good sense, if not with great skill.

I should emphasize that they must not be allowed to indulge in "free play," but only self-judged bouts of five touches—because the limit or goal of winning will discourage wildness and recklessness (although some of the actions will seem

100. Parrying Quinte: in process, tip moving left, hand rising

101. Parrying Quinte: receiving the cut

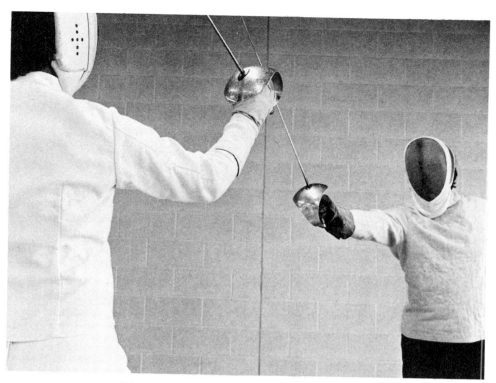

102. Riposting from Quinte: hand turned by finger action

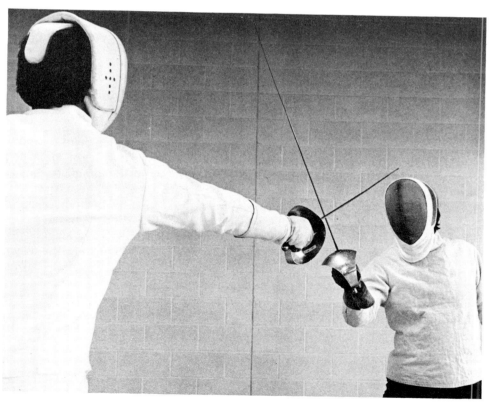

103. Riposting from Quinte: tip about to hit

desperate). Free play without counting touches is good at times for more advanced students, since it is more relaxing and conducive to experimentation. In unsupervised bouting, any hit on which the pair can't agree as to time or right-of-way should be disregarded without a lot of futile argument.

REACTION GAMES

Suppose two fencers face one another, standing on guard at easy lunging range. They agree that one will attack with a head cut, and the other will parry Quinte. The attacker is not allowed to make any faking moves, and the parrier is not allowed to retreat or jump back. This is simply a test of whether the attacker, from a standstill, can do a head cut/lunge before his partner can parry.

If the attacker telegraphs—by hunching his shoulder or lifting his foot before shooting his blade forward—he should lose. If he stands on balance, loose, and extends easily and lets the lunge follow, he should hit just ahead of the parry, even if the parry is correctly done.

At long lunging range, the parrier should succeed. If he is tight or not sufficiently watchful, he will lose, assuming the attacker does not telegraph.

In this kind of reaction test, parrying Quinte can be done either from Tierce or low. The parrier will, of course, riposte whether or not the parry succeeds.

Similarly, the game can be played with the attacker making a point thrust or chest cut, either of which must be met with a Quarte parry. Ordinarily, the attacker should not succeed, even at easy lunging range, because the Quarte parry is so easy to do.

ELABORATED PRACTICE IN COUPLES

Now that you have some idea of parry-riposting, you can work on some new routines with your classmates. At the end of Chapter 18 is a table of "Simple Direct Attacks—Set II," which should be thoroughly practiced.

For example, if fencer A starts in Tierce and lunges with his point, fencer B should make a Quarte-head parry-riposte. In this situation, it's almost impossible for fencer A to block with Quinte unless he was cheating in the first place, but he might just barely brush away the head cut by parrying Quarte as he recovers. He should try to do this, and of course riposte by head cut. Fencer B should make at least one more Quarte-head. Repeat sequence 3 times.

Assuming both partners are loose and light, and fencer A really lunges fully, fencer A should normally lose. The main thing you should learn from this is *not* to attack deep with point in combat—unless you have completely deceived your opponent with footwork.

Next, fencer A starts in Tierce and lunges with a head cut. Fencer B parries Quinte and ripostes by head cut. Fencer A should, therefore, parry Quinte as he recovers and riposte by head cut. Fencer B should make at least one more Quinte-head. Repeat sequence at least 6 times.

As noted in the previous section on reaction games, the attack would succeed at easy lunging range. A little farther away the attack might or might not work, but the riposte should hit. Farther yet, the attacker's recovery to Quinte should block the riposte, and possibly the attacker's counterriposte will hit. This exercise demonstrates the influence of distance on the effectiveness of similar actions.

Next, fencer A will attack from Tierce by chest cut/lunging. Fencer B will parry Quarte and riposte by head cut. Normally, at medium or long range, the parry-riposte should win; the chest cut would get through, however, if fencer B did not start his point across ahead of his fist. Assuming B parry-ripostes correctly, A's best chance is to recover parrying Quarte—as he did after point attacking—in hopes of deflecting the riposte. Again, A would riposte by head cut, and B would parry-riposte by Quarte-head. Repeat 6 times.

The chest cut attack from a standstill would not be expected to work except at easy lunging range. At somewhat longer range, the riposte should hit, and from any greater distance, the person being attacked would probably be better off if he merely retreated a few inches and made a straight head cut/lunge as the original attacker was recovering. You should note that this type of attack would depend for success on preliminary footwork that would put your opponent off-balance or lead him to expect an attack to another target.

Finally, fencer A, starting from low invitation, will attack by a horizontal cut. Fencer B might show a slight opening by shifting his hand to the left, still more or less in Tierce invitation, or he might adopt low invitation instead. Fencer B will parry Tierce and riposte by head cut. Then A should be recovering, parrying Quinte, and riposte by head cut. B should make at least one more parry-riposte, Quinte-head. Repeat at least 6 times.

The simple horizontal cut can hardly be expected to succeed except at long range: That is, the cut should be to outside cuff. At any closer range, the attack would probably not work, and the attacker would almost certainly be hit by the riposte.

These exercises are based on the assumption that the opponent will riposte to head more often than any other way, and therefore you should develop a new habit of protecting your head on recovery. Previously you used a standard recovery to Tierce, which would be effective if the opponent cut to your flank, or possibly if you immediately jumped back *after recovering*, simply because your opponent would fall short. You would do well to repeat the entire series with extra footwork, agreed to in advance by both partners, with the attacker at least advance lunging and the original parrier retreating.

Instructor: For the most part, the class can get through this material by themselves. There are no new actions, merely chains of elements. You can wander about the class and drop a word or two here and there—keep the distance from getting too close, lighten handwork, etc. After each attack and exchange has been repeated the requisite number of times, students should change partners; certainly, a student should have a different opponent after the whole set has been explored.

A similar series of exercises can be done according to the final table at the end of the preceding chapter, after the class has had indirect attacking. Or each type of attack and exchange can be practiced by couples as soon as it has been introduced.

HALF-PARRY

At long range, when your opponent can only possibly reach your wrist, a full parry would be unnecessary and wasteful. Having developed your elementary parry-ripostes, you should now work on a few half-parries. Sometimes these can

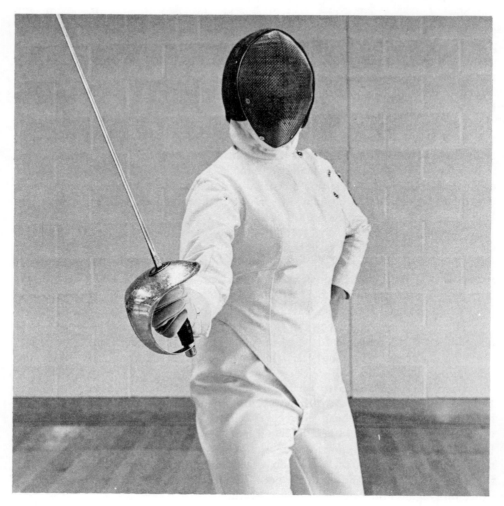

104. Half-parrying Tierce (note knuckle bow turned out)

be done when, at a suitable distance, you have extended your arm without immediately going into an attack; essentially you're offering your wrist for your opponent to cut at. Then the appropriate half-parry can be done with a slight break in
your elbow, possibly accompanied by a retreat.

Half-Tierce from Tierce. The first half-parry is made from Tierce invitation
or extension with blade vertical, when your opponent is inviting low. His attack
is to your outside cuff. With your fingers, roll your sabre handle so that your
knuckle bow meets the cut; your wrist will have to bend so that your palm is
more forward. Make sure your hand is not higher than your waist, or the cut may
get under your shell. Riposte loosely by head cut, straightening your wrist and
rolling your main edge forward. Recover to Quinte.

Half-Tierce from Low. When you're in low invitation at long range, your
opponent may attack with point or by cut to top cuff or outside cuff. Twist your
wrist so your blade whips to the vertical—your fingers and hand should come to

105. Half-parrying Tierce (note vertical blade)

the position described in the example just above. Riposte as before, and recover to Quinte.

Half-Quarte from Tierce. Suppose you are either in Tierce invitation or extended, as in the first example. Your opponent starts from Tierce and makes a top-cuff cut. Roll your sabre handle in your fingers so that your knuckle bow is to the left. If your arm is extended, let your elbow bend a little.

It is possible to parry half-Quinte from Tierce, but hardly worthwhile to do so. At the right distance, any top-cuff cut will be blocked by half-Quarte. A more useful move is to parry half-Quinte from low or from a palm-down extension, but we'll look at this one in the next chapter.

Instructor: In the introductory lessons, you should sometimes use thrusts instead of cuts, to re-emphasize lightness. Even against a cut, the hand need not be tight to resist force—at long range the cut will consist of the tip-most third of the blade striking the guard or forte. Therefore, there is less reason to worry about the cut getting through an inadequate parry.

Also, at long range the riposte from half-parry might just as well be to cuff as to head. Usually, lighter is faster, and the student should at least try a quick riposte to the forearm, which could be done without lunging.

The drawing (Fig. 108) shows that the half-parries, including that of Quinte,

106. Half-parrying Quarte: knuckle bow turned in

form a box like that formed by the basic parries, but considerably smaller. The two boxes, connected together, suggest a wedge or sort of pyramid lying on its side, with the point toward the opponent. Except for the fact that fencing is a dynamic process involving almost infinitely flexible living tissues, we could say that the point of the pyramid was at some source of the opponent's attacking action, such as his shoulder socket. Roughly, the farther the target from the source of the attack, the smaller the parries would have to be, and less time would have to be spent on lateral (or up-and-down) movements.

Instructor: By this time class members should have participated in any extramural tournament available. They could have done so with as little as simple direct attacking and basic parry-riposting. Maybe indirect attacking, counterattacking, and half-parrying would actually be a burden in the first meet—giving the students too many choices to make. The main advice would be to keep moving, stay loose, watch the distance, and try to hit again and again.

Very possibly no other school or club in your neighborhood will have any

107. Half-parrying Quarte: another view

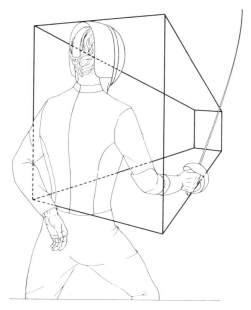

*108. Extended box for half-parrying: the
closer the opponent, the wider the parry*

sabreurs, and team matches (inter-group) might not be convenient. If a long trip is necessary to put your students into competition with strangers, no matter how poor or how great, that trip ought to be made. The nearest AFLA Division should be contacted. Perhaps no more than a half-dozen older, experienced sabreurs will be residing in the area, and your class will outnumber them, so that your students will for the most part be competing among themselves. Nevertheless, they will get the experience of playing with other opponents, under strange officials. Observation of these other fencers, and conversations with them, will broaden the conceptions of your students. Post-tournament "skull sessions" are often very educational.

As far as the subject of parry-riposting is concerned, we are far from having exhausted it. Students can make do, and very well indeed, with the material already presented. We have not discussed Prime or Seconde, and we have not explored ripostes other than to the head. Theoretically, there are several possible ripostes from every parry. This, however, would have given us several more unit actions, each to be done with several footwork patterns, and each of those co-ordinated sequences to be repeated several times for skill development. The whole procedure would be very time consuming, and not very rewarding in relation to the time spent. If the objective is to give students basic training so that they can play the game and have a foundation for further development, we have to stick to the most important elements and almost the minimum of techniques.

TABLE OF BASIC SABRE PARRY-RIPOSTES

Your Invitation	Opponent Cuts	Parry	Riposte to	Recovery to	Practice Repetitions
TIERCE	Flank or Outside Cuff	Tierce	Head	Tierce	3
TIERCE	Chest or Top Cuff (or thrusts)	Quarte	Head	Tierce	6
TIERCE	Head	Quinte	Head	Tierce	9
LOW	Flank, etc.	Tierce by rotation	Head	Tierce	3
LOW	Head	Quinte	Head	Tierce	6

Omitted is any parry-riposte from low against a chest cut. The low invitation is meant as an *occasional* change from Tierce, and you should always be aware that you have no standard blocking action from there. At long range, the sweep to Tierce by rotation might work against a chest cut, and the Quinte parry might be even better; the best answer is to retreat farther, completely out of reach, and strike when the opponent misses. An advanced fencer would probably parry Prime. A *very* advanced fencer could parry Quarte by a kind of counter.

TABLE FOR SABRE EXCHANGING PRACTICE

(Two or more parry-ripostes in succession)

Your Invitation	Opponent Cuts	Parry-Riposte	Opponent Parry-Ripostes	2nd Parry-Riposte	Repetitions
TIERCE	Flank	Tierce-head	Quinte-head	Quinte-head	3
TIERCE	Chest (or Thrusts)	Quarte-head	Quarte-head	Quarte-head (evading)	6
TIERCE	Head	Quinte-head	Quinte-head	Quinte-head	6
LOW	Flank (or Thrusts)	Tierce-(by rotation) head	Quinte-head	Quinte-head	6
LOW	Head	Quinte-head	Quinte-head	Quinte-head	6

After the second parry-riposte (or possibly the third, but no more), the partners should recover to Tierce, relax, and start again. Multiplying out, you will get a lot of practice in parrying Quinte from the two invitations and also after an extension (the first riposte). Multiply again for a couple of footwork patterns (advance to invite, retreat to parry-riposte; advance to invite, hop back to parry, lunge to riposte, for examples), and again for changes of partners. Different people will attack and answer your parry-ripostes in their own styles—you should not become too accustomed to one opponent, even though the same person may change from day to day.

TABLE OF SABRE HALF-PARRY-RIPOSTES

(Arm bent as for invitation or almost extended: no pull)

Your Invitation	Opponent Cuts	Half Parry	Riposte to	Recovery to	Practice Repetitions
TIERCE	Outside Cuff	Tierce	Head	Quinte and continue	6
TIERCE	Top or Inside Cuff	Quarte	Head	Quarte and continue	6
LOW	Outside Cuff (or Thrusts)	Tierce (by rotation)	Head	Quinte and continue	6
LOW	Head	Quinte	Head	Quinte and continue	6

Practice between students prepares them to get the most out of their time with the teacher, which in a class may be a few minutes a day, at the most. So practice carefully to work out the sequences, first move, second move, etc., in proper order.

Chapter 20

SABRE COMBINATIONS

FENCERS USUALLY TALK about composite attacks in terms of handwork. You have already had experience not only with parry-riposting, which is a kind of two-count action (although you must act as if it were a single move), but also with several attack variations. And, from one viewpoint, there can be no simple (one-count) actions in sabre (or any kind of) fencing.

By this I mean that every attack in sabre (and foil and épée) requires one or more steps for adjustment of the range. Your advance, hop, retreat, or whatever by itself may very well cause your opponent to parry, stiffen, counterattack, commit himself to attack, or otherwise react. We must recognize the influence, intentional or not, of the *foot feint*. Be alert to the possibilities.

A seasoned fencer is even more likely to be sensitive to moves of this kind than the novice. At the risk of repeating myself, I'll say that in order to fence like an advanced competitor, you should pay a lot of attention to distance and try to move so the distance is in your favor as much as possible. Although your handwork is simple—one cut or thrust, direct or indirect—you will to some extent have prepared the way for your attack by footwork.

Note that seemingly contradicting the first paragraph of this chapter, we could say that *all* attacks are simple. From this viewpoint, ignoring everything that goes before, we would define the attack as only the single stroke that hits, or would hit if not blocked or evaded. The rest is preparation. Nevertheless, in almost all cases preparation is necessary; the attack would not succeed without it.

Here we shall look into some of the traditional combinations. A few are strictly defined as composite attacks: those with a hand feint followed by a real attack. Others consist of elementary actions linked together: secondary intentions, countertime, stop-parry-riposting.

Combinations depend on actions by your opponent that fit your pattern—if he doesn't do the right thing (for you—wrong for him), your combination will not succeed. Or at least not as you intended. The goal is always a hit, and you should get there regardless.

The more complex a sequence is, the more risk that something will go awry. Hand combinations are to be used sparingly, to vary your game, and should be figured out on the basis of your opponent's reactions to earlier simple attacks. Convince him that you can and will make deep, fast attempts to hit. Normally this doesn't take much time because he, like you, has been trained into certain habits.

SECONDARY INTENTIONS

The idea of secondary intentions is that your original attack is false and you *let* your opponent parry-riposte. You must feed him something he will probably think is a real attack—but one he can block. Don't try (or expect) to hit with your original move, but make it look real: (1) If you're going to lie, tell a good one, and (2) if your lie is to be believed, you have to tell the truth most of the time. Your plan is to parry his riposte and hit with what is called a counter-riposte.*

Success of an "attack in second intention" depends heavily on a good estimate of your opponent's favorite parry-ripostes.

Flank-Quinte-Head. Let's suppose your opponent has been taught, like a great many sabreurs, to make a fast head cut from Tierce the instant any cut hits his shell. You discover this by making a short cutting attack to his outside cuff or flank, recovering and retreating immediately.

The next time, deliberately tap his guard and parry-riposte by half-Quinte head cut. Although this is a rudimentary example, your footwork can be varied a great deal. At least practice (1) advance lunging, parrying half-Quinte without recovering, and (2) attacking originally by advancing only, lunging with your counterriposte. Your false attack can be made directly from low, or indirectly from Tierce.

A useful variation on this theme would be a counterriposte by flank cut. Especially when you have lunged on your original (false) attack, you should be low enough to have a clear opening. If you consistently lunge short and recover backward immediately, your opponent may move forward with his riposte.

In any case, you must customarily parry again, whether you need to or not. A further sequence could be called an "attack in third intention"—you didn't really intend to do it when you started, but certainly you should always be in shape to keep going. Perhaps your opponent will give ground. Then recover forward and strike once more (a reprise, or whole new attack).

Head-Quinte-Head. Having made a simple attack to the head and found that your opponent does parry Quinte pretty well—some don't, and then you would continue to set up more of the same—you can plan to parry his riposte and counterriposte with another head cut.

For your original attack, if he doesn't react too promptly to a direct attack from Tierce, try an approach in low invitation and do an indirect head cut.

We're assuming in these lessons that the answer to your false attack will be a head cut. It is quite common. Once you have the feel of attacking in second intention, you can invent suitable combinations whenever you find an opponent who ripostes some other way. Some normally riposte from Quinte by a roundhouse belly cut (which you'd better block for your own comfort), and others make a simple direct cut to the flank. Not so many will do a different one each

---

* The word "counter" is used several ways in fencing, which is confusing. Here it indicates a riposte after parrying a riposte. That is, when fencer A attacks, fencer B parries that attack and ripostes, and then A parries B's riposte and ripostes, then A's last move is called a counter-riposte.

109. Secondary intentions: false attack to flank with lunge

110. Secondary intentions: half-parrying Quinte

111. Secondary intentions: riposting by head cut

112. Secondary intentions: riposting by flank cut

time, provided the attack is surprising. Secondary intentions are designed to work against the opponent's favorite actions.

You will also have noted, by starting from quite far away and being reserved on the original as well as by using half-parries, that your sequence will speed up. Each move should be quicker than the one before. That doesn't mean that you work harder to be faster—you can only do it by making lighter, smaller movements.

Each move should be quicker than the one before. This is the normal rhythm: (comparatively) slow, faster, fastest. It's possible to create patterns that go quick-slow-quick, or quick-quick-slow, etc., but you will hardly ever succeed with one in which all the parts are of the same length, no matter how fast you move.

Chest-Quarte-Head. The final example gives you a chance to flèche, assuming you have practiced this move a lot and your coach has given permission. Threaten a chest cut, co-ordinating with a rapid advance or advance check. The opponent's most likely response will be a Quarte-head parry-riposte. Since a head cut is difficult to block cleanly with a Quarte parry, you should sway your head to the right, parrying, and flèche with head cut. Dodging will thus aid the risky parry.

This maneuver should be prepared for by a chest cut, lunging short, with a fast, immediate recovery backward and retreat out of range, or a standard Quarte-head parry-riposte on the recovery. If your opponent succeeds in hitting you, that makes it more likely that he will repeat his action the next time. If he parries well but doesn't reach, he will probably react more promptly in the future. And surely, if you do hit him with a chest cut, he will begin to worry about covering that side. In any case, you will have a better chance for a secondary-intention attack because he will not (we hope) begin thinking about some other kind of response.

The pattern should, of course, be practiced with other footwork, as for the previous examples. Depending on the opponent's reach, speed, etc., you need to be able to fit your handwork together with management of the distance.

Instructor: A foundation has been laid by the exchanging practice described in Chapter 19. You might choose to work on only one of the above examples, or two, or make up one of your own.

Give the student a few repetitions of each model sequence with footwork variations. These will be sufficient to illustrate the idea of secondary intentions. Students should then be able to devise variations of compound attacks of this type for themselves, and learn, by experimentation in bouting, which of them will work against different classmates.

Otherwise there should be no routine practice in couples. A fencer who knows about secondary-intention attacking should work it out in more realistic situations. One who has been hit with such a combination ought to be able to recognize it and change his reactions accordingly. There's no need for new technique. By shifting distance, by changing the timing of parry-ripostes, or by counterattacking into what is essentially a preparation, he should be able to spoil his opponent's pattern.

Often enough students will come to you with complaints that actions don't work—simple ones as well as combinations—or that opponents won't react in any of the ways studied as prototypes. It would be strange indeed if nothing worked, but these problems can never be solved by talking about them in the ab-

113. Secondary intentions: false head cut, advancing

114. Secondary intentions: half-parrying Quinte

115. Secondary intentions: riposting to head, lunging

116. Secondary intentions: false chest cut, opponent parrying Quarte

117. *Secondary intentions: half-parrying Quarte against head-cut riposte, with evasion by leaning to right*

118. *Secondary intentions: head cut (or chest cut) with flèche*

119. *Countertime: extension in Tierce*

stract. There should be frequent sessions of bouting with a full jury. Whether you act as president or stand aside to criticize that officiating function as well as the fencing, you should be able to catch the live moment to explain why an action failed. In early sessions of this kind you would probably bear down on very basic faults such as incorrect distance, poor balance, telegraphing, and heavy-handedness, for which you would prescribe mobility drills and routine practice as corrective measures.

Sometimes students with good technique will be very stubborn about trying to make a certain attack work when it should be obvious that they are playing into their opponents' strong areas. This is a strategic fault. Such a student is capable of doing something else that will succeed, and the best advice is for him to quit being pig-headed and change his game. Perhaps after attacking another way, and then still a third way, and then luring the opponent to attack into a good parry-riposte, this student would be able to make the original combination work. It is best to find these things out in class bouting sessions, or else the student will lose too many touches in outside tournament or team match bouts and be unable to recoup.

A bout has to be developed. Initially, perhaps, the fencer should come out from the word "Go!" with a simple all-out attack, driving forward with two or three advances and a lunge or flèche. Then the "ifs" apply: if successful, repeat; if not, start the same way but stop short; if successful the second time, change pattern anyway. Time should be spent trying two or three different attacks and trying to get the opponent to attack or, with an aggressive opponent, trying to beat him to the attack, or succeed with a counterattack or parry-riposte. The first phase of the bout, in which perhaps three touches are scored (with no more than

120. *Countertime: half-parrying Quarte against top-cuff stop cut*

two against our man, we hope), is a period of checking out the opponent. Although aggression is shown, there should be a considerable amount of reserve until more is known about the opponent's reactions. After this there is often a period of greater commitment, in which the fencer acts upon the conclusions of the earlier fact-finding phase. Here it may be discovered that the opponent was also keeping a lot in reserve and had given a number of false impressions.

As an alternative, the fencer might begin by adopting a teasing, inviting scheme, drawing the opponent out. A fencer who is quick on his feet and good with parry-ripostes and stop cuts with evasion (retreating) can profit greatly, gaining points, frustrating the opponent, and wearing him down. Then our man might shift over to an aggressive policy.

When two fencers are well-matched physically and technically, the issue may seem in doubt when the score is 3-all. But if one is a better strategist, the touches he has had scored against him, as well as the ones he has scored, will enter into his calculations about how to play the rest of the bout. He may very well be able to finish it off easily by turning his opponent's habitual reactions against him.

COUNTERTIME

An "attack in countertime" occurs when one fencer makes a preparation of some sort, the other counterattacks on the preparation, and the first, having so planned it, blocks (or evades) the counterattack and attacks.

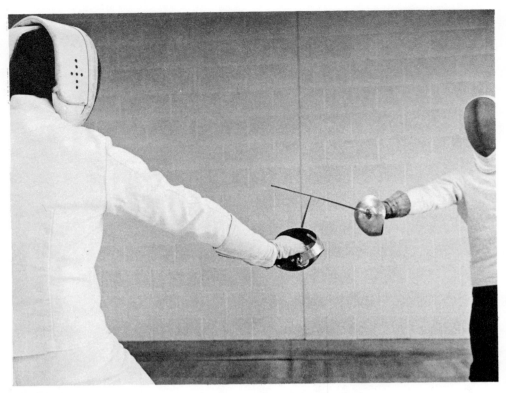

121. *Countertime: extension in low invitation*

122. *Countertime: half-parrying Tierce by rotation against top-cuff stop cut*

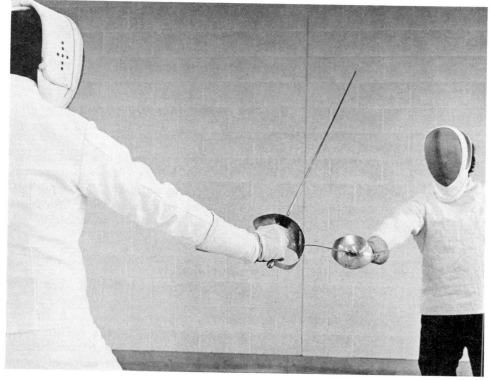

123. Countertime: half-parrying Tierce against outside-cuff stop cut from low

You've probably already done something like this. For example, if you have a classmate who habitually stop cuts as soon as you advance into range, the situation for a countertime attack exists: You advance offering your arm, block the anticipated stop, and lunge or flèche.

Tierce-Quarte-Head. The first sequence you should practice is as follows: In Tierce invitation (or more than half-extended), close the distance suddenly. The stop stroke is most frequently made to your top cuff when the opponent is in Tierce. Meet the cut by parrying half-Quarte, just rolling your knuckle bow to the inside, and attack directly by head cut.

Recover and parry Quarte (your opponent will most likely make another vertical cut), unless you have flèched.

The sequence is somewhat similar to that of secondary intentions, except that you don't cut or thrust to get the opponent to parry, you offer your wrist for him to shoot at. In both instances, though, his blade comes out where you can meet it.

It's possible to achieve the same effect—that is, get the opponent to come out of his closely held long-range attitude—by offering your wrist and pulling your hand backward so his stop cut misses. Of course there is a risk in putting out bait, whether you block or evade: Your opponent may cut more quickly than you anticipate, may counterfake in a number of ways, or may simply come blasting at your head. That's the kind of thing that makes the game fascinating. You can't afford to wait to find out, but should carry through the pattern without hesitation once you have begun.

Pulling back too often might discourage your opponent, and he might give up trying stop cuts when he doesn't even hit your guard, which might make him hope he could reach your forearm next time. Alternatively, he might be stimulated to follow up with a deeper attack. You should probably only do one countertime attack per bout, or two at the most if your opponent seems to do a lot of stop strokes. These fancy patterns must be mixed in with many simple actions and a few other combinations.

Another variation would be to finish with a chest cut instead of a head cut.

Low-Tierce-Head. When you extend from low invitation and your opponent is in Tierce, the stop cut will again probably be made vertically. You could **half-parry** Tierce by rotation (but without bending your arm more than a little) **and** lunge or flèche to the head. You can deal with a stop thrust (counterattack with point) in a similar manner.

You could, alternatively, parry half-Quinte and finish your attack with a flank cut, lunging (flèching isn't so effective in this case).

When your opponent himself is in low, the stop cut will most likely be a horizontal cut to your outside cuff, and the twisting half-parry to Tierce would still be effective provided, as always, you have the distance and timing. In this example, your opponent has a fair chance of covering himself with a Quinte parry, and you must be prepared to continue with at least one more parry-riposte, Quinte-head, as you recover backward from your lunge. If you have chosen to flèche, get past him and away at the greatest possible speed.

Tierce-Tierce-Flank. When your opponent is in low invitation and you extend in Tierce, his probable stop will be an outside cuff cut. You should make a half parry of Tierce, rolling your knuckle bow outward. You might have to drop your hand a centimeter or so to make sure his blade doesn't get under your guard —the point might then be aimed at you.

Since your opponent has a good possibility of parrying Quinte very easily from a horizontal cut, and may have been trained to do so instantly, you might practice cutting indirectly to flank with a lunge. Then you also would do a Quinte-head parry-riposte on your recovery.

Instructor: Time allowing, work over these examples. If time is short, select one, with at least a couple of different footwork patterns, to get across the idea of deliberately inviting a stop in order to take the blade (although in one variation the stop is avoided, which is good to think about) and attack. Advanced students should certainly do more complex foot patterns such as advance balestra, advance-check-lunge, advance-appel-lunge, or even advance-hop-back-lunge. The last-named would be useful against an opponent who attacks in depth instead of merely stopping, and students should be aware that invitations do, often, lead to full attacks.

It should be understood that the prescribed footwork for the attack combination as such always comes out of earlier footwork. Nobody in modern sabre play starts a combination from a standstill. Work should be done on mobility drills, and you can make appropriate comments when supervising practice bouts. All in all, the actual final motion of an attack might, on the average, be preceded by at least 5 steps.

Likewise, students should be aware of the possibilities of confusing the opponent by making meaningless hand movements. At a distance at which the opponent absolutely can't reach, a fencer can pretend to parry Quarte or Quinte or Seconde, or he can swing his blade around as if countering Tierce or Quarte

124. *Stop cut to top cuff, from Tierce, retreating*

(*clockwise and counterclockwise circles*). *These moves would serve to keep his hand and arm loose. As the distance becomes feasible for the start of an attack pattern—about equivalent to a couple of advances and a lunge—he should go into Tierce or low invitation.*

Students who have been pretty well trained to parry-riposte with a lunge after retreating from an attack may already have developed combinations very like secondary intentions and countertime. The notion of faking to get an opponent to react is a natural one. The teacher's job here, as elsewhere, is to save the student the time required to work out all the possibilities, some of which are not as fruitful as others, and to stress basics such as balance, lightness of hand and foot, distance, timing, recovering in order to continue, etc.

STOP-PARRY-RIPOSTING

Now that you have realized very clearly that *any time you're* NOT *attacking you're inviting* as soon as you begin to come into range (no matter who approaches whom), you can perhaps anticipate your opponent's attack by a small fraction of a second.

The extra time could be used just to make a good parry. But by now you should be light-handed enough, and therefore fast enough, to try to stop cut *before* you parry. Certainly if you succeed with reasonable frequency, your opponents will have to quit doing fancy complicated attacks, especially attacks that

125. After stop cutting, starting to parry Quarte against head cut, while retreating (note tip moving up, leading hand)

break in the middle. Any opponent who swings wide, raises his hand to chop, etc., should lose very quickly.

At any rate, trying two actions—the stop cut and the parry-riposte—when your opponent starts to move will help you speed up, so if you meet a faster person, you'll at least have a chance of doing a parry-riposte. Even when your opponent makes a simple attack, your stop cut will count provided your parry succeeds (but riposte anyway—it should be a habit.) Some opponents may hesitate, breaking what should have been a simple attack, when they feel the stop, and thus lose right-of-way.

These combinations, as you might have imagined already, could be considered as a type of answer to the possibility of a countertime attack against you. The opponent who expects a stop, blocks it, and finishes his attack, could be caught with a parry-riposte. Looked at another way, the stop-parry-riposte combination is a kind of secondary intention in reverse.

Vertical-Quarte-Head. Suppose as you invite in Tierce your opponent attacks by head cut from Tierce. The speediest stop cut you can make is to top cuff. But you can never get to Quinte to parry the attack. You must parry half-Quarte—under the circumstances it is the only feasible parry. Generally, you should be retreating as you stop cut, but at the same instant, tilt your head away to the right. Co-ordinating this with footwork, you should strike as your rear foot reaches back and parry on the movement of your front foot. You should be going away, and a

126. *Stop cut to outside cuff, retreating. Opponent cutting cheek from low*

good idea is to retreat more than once, parry-riposting again. The opponent's attack may fall short. Remember, you must never get any closer than necessary, and your basic protection is distance.

By edging sideways to the right, you also have the possibility of a riposte by chest cut. Your opponent would normally parry Quarte, but you might be able to get around enough so his parry is inadequate. If he flèches, pivot and keep cutting, because you are entitled to one more stroke as he passes you or goes off the side of the strip.

Horizontal-Tierce-Head. As you invite low against an opponent also inviting low, he may attack directly by a horizontal cut which, depending on distance, aims at your elbow, shoulder, or cheek. Try an outside cuff cut the moment you think he is going to start. Retreat simultaneously. Parry with the sweep to Tierce and riposte to the mask.

Since your hand should have been well back in the first place, your opponent should choose higher and deeper targets. At the longer distances, the combination should also be effective against a head cut. His head cut should not reach if you're moving back, and actually the combination might be regarded as an attack upon the opponent's recovery, by taking his blade and cutting—a lunge with the riposte might be needed.

Horizontal-Quinte-Head. When your opponent approaches in Tierce and you're in low, he could attack by point thrust or head cut. Again the stop cut should be the shortest one, to his outside cuff. Immediately parry half-Quinte and riposte to head. Your parry should deflect the point or block the cut, but need not be large or strong if you're retreating with it.

Another good possibility is to riposte to flank—that is, by another horizontal cut, which might hit his wrist or elbow from the outside—plus another Quinte parry and riposte.

One problem here is that the opponent may seem to be starting a head cut from Tierce, but actually may divert his blade for a horizontal cut, which might

127. *Half-parrying Tierce by rotation (note head kept back)*

hit your forearm. You shouldn't worry too much about such possibilities: Remember, you wouldn't try the combination unless you had seen that your opponent often raised his hand to make a chopping head cut. You could dance back out of reach, parry-riposte, or simply attack into his attack, and by using a different response each time, you could confuse him.

Instructor: Other stop-parry-riposte combinations are possible, of course—many of them. Those given seem to be more reliable in real play, and are worth a number of repetitions with each footwork pattern, at different speeds and in different rhythms.

STOP-PARRY-RIPOSTING

Opponent's Attack	From Your	Stop Cut	Parry-Riposte	Continue
From Tierce, Head or Chest Cut or with Point	Tierce	Top Cuff	Half-Quarte, Head or Chest Cut	Quarte, etc.
From Low, Flank Cut	Low	Outside Cuff	Half-Tierce by Rotation, Head Cut	Quinte, etc.
From Tierce, Head Cut or with Point	Low	Outside Cuff	Half-Quinte, Head or Flank Cut	Quinte, etc.

After introductory practice, continue for one more step so the student must parry-riposte again, retreating. Occasionally call for a lunge on the riposte.

128. Low invitation, offering head

When sabre play gets to this stage (everybody knows about and has some skill at combinations), then you are likely to return to the daring and difficult game of simple hand actions on a foundation of extremely rapid and variable footwork. Somewhat related to this is the common fact that intermediate competitors have the most trouble with two kinds of opponents: the beginners and the advanced. Beginners, with some training, still do not recognize small openings and subtle threats and therefore do not respond as required for secondary intentions and countertime. Their reactions are often erratic and, consequently, unpredictable—they may very well attack vigorously and accurately when they shouldn't. The intermediate may then flinch or hesitate, thereby losing time.

129. Stop cut to outside cuff as opponent starts gross head cut

The advanced opponent, of course, *deliberately* changes his timing, distance, and patterns; reacts earlier or later than expected; and makes a great many swift and powerful attacks. Against this sort of skill the intermediate will have to learn to do the same, seizing the initiative if possible, moving rapidly forward to strike, or running backward at top speed while parry-riposting. The intermediate should try to adopt an attacking game, even though he loses with it at first.

COMPOSITE ATTACKING

At the beginning of this chapter the foot feint was mentioned. This is not necessarily a special kind of foot movement or pattern. The mere fact that the distance has shortened so that an attack might reach may be enough to cause the opponent to parry. More often than not, this occurs when the opponent is already retreating and is being overtaken, but sometimes when he has just begun to advance and you unexpectedly go to meet him.

The defensive reaction is based on experience: Sabreurs become quite sensitive to the possibility that a simple attack might come blasting in when the distance is right, and if the opponent at that moment is not set on his feet to do his own attack, he is apt to move his hand to block. It is an error because he should not leave his invitational position until a real threat is shown.

Suppose you are in Tierce and manage to close the distance, either by advancing one step quickly when your opponent might expect you to retreat, or by

130. *Half-parrying Quinte, having retreated*

131. *Riposing by flank cut. Opponent's remise is out of time*

increasing the speed of your forward movement as already established. If your opponent is also in Tierce, he may parry Quarte against an anticipated chest cut or Quinte against an anticipated head cut. Either response will expose him to an indirect attack, a flank cut that may actually hit his arm. Your blade in Tierce *was* a potential threat, even though you didn't extend your arm. Now as you do extend, turn your hand and lunge or flèche, squeezing your fingers to cut him somewhere between his upper arm and cheek if he has gone to Quarte, or on his forearm or high flank if he has gone to Quinte. Your recovery to Quinte and continuation with a head cut should be automatic.

When you are in low invitation and suddenly close the distance, your opponent may go to Tierce parry in reaction to the foot feint. Your attack would be an indirect one, by rotating your wrist, to head or chest.

How are these examples any different from the simple indirect attacks described in Chapter 18? In the standard definition of a feint, such as you might find in the rule book, the attacker's arm is supposed to be extending, in which case the opponent must parry (or evade) because just a little more forward motion will result in a hit. This is the rational view of composite attacking.

Practically, the feint is in the opponent's *mind*. A feint is whatever he will react to by parrying. It may be the unexpected decrease in the range, even though your arm remains bent, or it may be a tilt of your head or a twitch of your elbow. Maybe he is reacting unconsciously to some movement of yours that you habitually make just before attacking, which we would otherwise call telegraphing. The only things that matter are that he parries and that you attack where he is opening rather than where he is closing. In each of the examples below, your feint should be just enough to convince him. Using a big, strong feint when it is unnecessary will slow down your attack.

Feint Head, Cut Flank. This is very much like the previous example of foot feinting, with the addition of an arm extension. Advancing in Tierce, extend your arm as if for a head cut, then divert your blade and cut flank. Don't ever lock your elbow on the extension—probably you will still have a very slightly bent arm when you make the real cut. You shouldn't lock your elbow on the cut, either, but loosely fling your arm forward with the finger squeeze at the limit of the lunge. Your arm should feel rubbery and bounce right back to a Quinte parry.

Feint Flank, Cut Head (or Chest). In the same manner in which you might have carried out a foot feint, you can start in low invitation, extending as if for a flank cut, together with an advance. Of course, you might have changed invitations from Tierce to low just an instant before. Your opponent is expected to parry Tierce, and your real attack should be diverted to head or chest.

Instructor: These are two examples of straight feints with coupés to the openings. Each can be co-ordinated with one or more footwork patterns. Initially, the student should make the arm feint with the advance, exactly with the sharp movement of the rear foot, and the real cut with the lunge or flèche, but all very lightly and quickly and without pause. Certainly by this time you shouldn't need to break the whole sequence down into five counts—front foot, back foot, arm, hand turn, lunge—but should be able to start with three—front foot, back foot and arm, lunge-with-hand turn. This can still be fairly slow at first.

At a later stage, the feint and coupé should be done with the lunge or flèche. That is, the lunge or flèche should begin at the same instant as the extension, the coupé being done while the front foot is in the air in the lunge or while the rear foot is crossing in the flèche.

There are distinct advantages to using an extension on the feint. The most important one is that the extension establishes right-of-way: You are correct even if you extend with the first movement of your front foot on the advance, provided you do not hesitate in the slightest in bringing up your rear foot and lunging. The second advantage is that, having reached out with your arm in the beginning, your real cut can be delivered in less time. The rhythm is (relatively) long-short. Using only a foot feint, your real attack must be longer, and your opponent may be able to make another parry—successfully.

The disadvantage in extending is that your arm is exposed to your opponent's stop cut. If you hesitate, he gains the right-of-way. Even if you don't hesitate, he may stop cut with evasion, retreating or dodging sideways, and if your attack doesn't hit, you lose a touch. Keep these possibilities in mind as you practice. In combat, don't just do a feint attack any old time. Set up for it. When you do it, do it completely. Follow up with an automatic parry-riposte, Quinte-head.

Possibly you've already thought of doing a feint attack as a secondary-intention combination. Sure you can. Your practice should always include a recovery, even considering the runoff after flèching as a recovery, with a parry-riposte. The only difference will be in managing the distance and timing so that the original composite attack would not quite reach.

In preparing for this, you would first do a direct attack to convince your opponent that he ought to make that first parry. Next do a feint-deceiving attack with intent to reach, and finally the same kind of feint coupé to lead to a secondary intention. You might as well stick with the most likely succession: From Tierce, attack quickly and fiercely with head cut, perhaps more than once; when your opponent gets the idea that he'd better parry Quinte, or something to prevent that attack, feint to head and cut whatever is available on the side; when he covers against that, parrying Tierce or never leaving it, do the same attack as a secondary intention, parrying Quinte and finishing off with a head cut.

One-two. The term "one-two" is commonly applied to two indirect actions. That is, if you start from Tierce invitation, feint a flank cut and then cut head, or if you start from low invitation, feint a head cut and then cut flank. These should be done with your arm extending on the feint, so that you will have the long-short timing; by gaining a good deal of reach with your arm extension and advance, you won't have so far to go on the second movement of the pattern. Remember, in this type of attack especially, that you should only feint *enough to get a response* from your opponent. A gross feint loses too much time. In fact, you can't afford to wait to find out whether he responds—once started, you must go through with it as fast as you can.

AND SIMPLIFY AGAIN

A good deal of material has been presented in this chapter. You could survey it in perhaps a semester at two or three hours a week, in a small class with an expert coach, but five years or more might be consumed in achieving a high level of ability.

Mention has been made of remising and redoubling, the feinting effect of foot action, and other ways of creating longer sequences from comparatively elementary movements. A vast number of variations can be made just with simple (even simple-direct) attacks, the five parry-ripostes, and footwork. The variations are inherent in footwork, the size and speed of steps (with instants of immobility) by both fencers making all the differences in distance and timing.

Add to this the fact that nobody EVER does the "same" movement in exactly the same way twice in a lifetime, and you have a factor of randomness that certainly keeps the game interesting. You can't be absolutely sure that a chosen action will succeed—or fail—against any opponent.

What you can't do is win by standing still. In order to score touches, you must try to make them. More opportunities occur than you can possibly take advantage of. The initial opportunity appears the moment the range is feasible for one or both of the fencers. After that, one of the best policies is just to keep on striking. As long as you've gone to the trouble of getting yourself started, you might as well make a minimum of three—and up to six or seven—attempts to hit in one burst, before the president even has time to say "Halt!"

Too many beginners don't think ahead beyond a planned attack of two moves, or invitation-parry-riposte. Some don't plan that much: They are always caught reacting to the opponent's initiative. On the other hand, some think too much—the time to plan is when the distance is too long for anyone to reach.

It is very common for energy to be knotted up in one defensive move or in what the fencer thinks is his final. He says to himself, "This is *it!*" and if that move doesn't work, he freezes. The best way out of this is to consistently send yourself into sequences that won't stop until five or six moves have been carried out. You can start practicing on a target or in thin air. At first it will probably be muddled in real bouting—any action could be smothered when the distance closes unexpectedly—but at least you won't bear down too hard on the original or second action.

Strangely enough, this going on is easier than stopping. Assuming that you do ninety-seven moves in a row, you won't bear down on any particular one of them. The chances are that your actions don't have to be as hard as you're making them.

Chapter 21

TEACHING SABRE

WHEN YOU GO into teaching, you may have had a good deal of background in study and competition, or you may have had comparatively little. I expect that few readers will have been through a full training course in teaching, and even they, I hope, will find something of value here if they are facing their first classes of beginning sabreurs.

I'd very much like to see more amateurs try teaching. There aren't enough highly trained coaches or masters in the United States to take care of the students who would turn out and do turn out whenever fencing is publicized. Many potential fencers are lost simply because no instruction is available. The existing professionals spend a lot of their time teaching beginners, who could be taught almost as well (or maybe better, in some respects) by teams of amateurs.

What would the qualifications of an amateur coach be? First, desire or willingness to teach—based on a feeling that fencing is enjoyable, healthful, etc., and that more people ought to do it. You should have had a minimum of about twenty-four hours in class, during which you would have observed some of the teaching techniques of your coach. You should have competed, and you should have judged. If you have competed twice or more, and have tried presiding, so much the better. Some experience as an assistant to your coach, helping demonstrate and leading students through the lessons, would ease you into teaching on your own or with a companion of about the same level. This might be sufficient for an amateur teacher of an introductory course.

The rest is on-the-job training. If your master can come around and see what you're doing once in a while, he'll probably have a few helpful words of advice, but otherwise, you just have to experiment. Keep it simple. Get your students into bouting as soon as you can—better too soon than too late. Continue your own studies, tournament bouting, officiating, and so forth. By the time your class has learned the first series of essential techniques that you've mapped out for them, you should be ready to lead them on.

Some teaching experience would probably do every fencer a bit of good. You must look carefully at students to see what they're doing wrong, and you'll develop the ability of keen observation. You must think about how to explain and demonstrate correct technique, thereby clarifying your own understanding. Showing people over and over how to do footwork patterns will improve your own footwork. You will naturally get a tremendous amount of hand exercise, while conducting bouting, judging, and presiding sessions will increase your mastery of application of the rules, etc.

However, teaching isn't for everyone—not all fencers find it attractive or enjoyable. Should you quit after leading one class for two or three months, you will already have done a lot for the sport—but your final responsibility is to arrange for another coach to carry on with those students who wish to continue.

Some people think that teaching will spoil your own competitive ability. I've already mentioned several ways in which the experience will help you improve. Assuming you continue to take lessons, compete, and bout with equal or better fencers, there should be no deterioration, but rather the reverse. If you were to devote yourself entirely to teaching for several months or a year or two, you might not do so well on your return to competitive play, but I fully believe that in a few weeks you would be better than ever. If you study, compete, and teach concurrently, you will simply have more to bring to your students.

The novice needs accuracy, mobility, and some variability. In order to achieve these qualities, co-ordinations of hand- and footwork, even though rated as "simple," must be repeated over and over. Speed and good timing take still more practice. If you were to try to cover all the possibilities of movement with the sabre, the process would take years. Besides, the student would not necessarily be better prepared for competition, and keeping him away from competition too long is discouraging and stultifying.

Variability, which we think is needed to confuse and surprise the opponent, is possible with comparatively few distinctly different movements. By advancing or retreating with more or less speed, by pausing for greater or lesser intervals, etc., the fencer can create broken rhythms. He may choose to parry or to retire out of range—choosing irregularly to spoil his opponent's expectations. He may choose to attack or invite, and he may vary his attacking quite a bit even though he only knows, speaking of handwork, three ways: point thrust, vertical cut, and "horizontal" cut.

The teacher who is pressed for time, having only one semester assigned for the course, or having a large class (more than a dozen), needs to select the most essential actions and combine them with a few useful, not-too-complicated, not-too-difficult footwork patterns. The objective is to get students into play.

For this purpose, they must have two or three simple attacks, at least the first three parry-ripostes from Tierce, to form the "box," and a knowledge of the rules. If this is all you can accomplish, it is far better to do these few things *well* than to try to do many things. Anyone who could perform these actions *excellently*—assuming he used several footwork combinations to vary range and timing—would not really need any more, up to quite a high level of competition. (Observe how many good fencers have, seemingly, a limited repertoire.) A few refinements, such as stop cutting, extra ways of riposting, composite attacks, etc., have been suggested for the small class that has an ample schedule, but these refinements come after the basics and after students have actually gotten into bouting, preferably in formal meet conditions.

Regardless of how good you may be, a class of twenty meeting one hour a week, or even twice, can't be led beyond the absolutely necessary actions, and progress will be slow. You can give each student about *two minutes* a day. A lot of the introductory sessions must be devoted to conditioning and drills, then the pace of the lessons picks up because students have command of underlying balance and fundamental co-ordinations. Meeting twice a week is, as you might imagine, much more than twice as good as once a week. Working with a class that has already had some basic training in a foil course is a good deal easier than teaching a group that is totally ignorant. But you still don't want to spend a lot of time on fancy stuff when simple maneuvers will do.

One great help in teaching is an assistant—an advanced student. Sometimes amateur instructors, trying to promote the sport in a Y or recreation center, can form teaching teams of two or three with very good results when the course is planned thoughtfully. Demonstration of a particular bit of technique is much easier: New students can see somebody doing what they're about to do, rather than having to figure it out from verbal directions. Students also have the advantage of reviewing actions with more than one teacher—each teacher naturally having his or her personal style compounded of reach, strength, quickness, timing, etc.

Sabre classes should be attractive since this form of fencing resembles what people have seen in films or on TV. It appears easier, because all the fencer has to do is flip his blade around to hit torso, head, or arm, instead of thrusting carefully. And it is a lot of fun. Yet, at this stage in history, there are not as many classes, nor as many opportunities. You may have to pioneer in a high school, college, or city recreation program.

If the requirements are that students should have had a foil course and that they must buy their own weapons (schools, etc., will not want to invest at first), your pilot class may not be very large. Good. We hope that it will be large enough to justify the use of gym space, but a small class can progress faster, even allowing time for working out all the problems that turn up in a new situation.

Another difficulty is that there may not be many other sabre fencers around for your students to compete against. Your novices may just have to go out and enter against much higher-class opponents right away. This may be an advantage. Where there is a great deal of lower-class competition, it is often seen that students get locked into a "high-school style" that they have a lot of trouble outgrowing. For lack of proper training and experience, many become disappointed and drop out as soon as they graduate. It is hard for a teen-age "star" to take the losses when he goes into adult competition, but is is easy for a beginner to accept that he is outclassed. The novice will try, lose, watch, listen, and learn.

THE LEFT-HANDER

There seem to be fewer left-handers in sabre than in the other branches of the sport. This may be because the southpaw discovers that he can be more successful in foil or épée, while in sabre he receives many hits on the outside of his arm. Or perhaps my impression of the scarcity of left-handed sabreurs is mistaken. There have been, certainly, a number of outstanding lefties in the game, such as Mike Dasaro, 1963 Pan-American Games winner for the United States, and Calarese of Italy, bronze medallist in the 1960 Olympics and again in the 1963 World Championship.

When two fencers use opposite hands, the horizontal cut becomes a chest cut or belly cut rather than a flank cut. This can be made directly from low or indirectly from Tierce. The standard answer is a Quarte-head parry-riposte, about the strongest action in anybody's repertoire. However, the original attacker also has an easy Quinte-head or Quinte-chest parry-counterriposte, and the situation doesn't seem to promise any brilliant interaction.

At longer range, the man being attacked can make a narrower parry and riposte to top cuff or, in the same manner as making a chest cut against an opponent of the same hand, a cut to the outside of the arm. If you were the one starting with the chest cut in this instance, and you had this result, you would be wise to leave that attack out of the game from then on, unless you could somehow very definitely fake your opponent into a big Tierce or Quinte parry beforehand.

Point attacks are not very useful. Perhaps a student with foil and épée background could use them occasionally to snag the arm, but in most cases point attacks cannot be direct, and since they approach the chest at a smaller angle, they are not as likely to catch. They can be deflected fairly easily with a half-parry of Quarte. Unintentionally, though, the attacker may score with a point continuation when his cut from the outside has been blocked. That is, if you were to attack in the same manner as a chest cut against an opponent of the same handedness, and if the opposite-handed opponent blocks with a Tierce parry, your blade might whip over and your point might catch on his arm. Unless his riposte is immediate, your remise with point should be allowed.

The left-hander against a right-hander (and vice versa) must be careful to cover the elbow of his fighting arm. He carries his hand a bit more to the outside in Tierce invitation, and usually parries Tierce a bit wider. He may, therefore, expose himself somewhat to horizontal cuff cuts on the inside of his wrist, but he should rather quickly learn to block these with half-Quarte (riposting) and to stop cut to top cuff with evasion, two rather easy alternatives.

Sometimes when a left-hander suddenly advances in low invitation, his opponent mistakenly guards/invites Quarte (a practice I have NOT recommended). The left-hander's attack would then be made to the head by preference, or to the exposed elbow with a little more turn of the hand, depending on the distance. The person thus attacked could parry Quinte or Tierce respectively, but the left-hander should have a good deal more practice with right-handers than the other way around, and his attack has a good chance of succeeding. A better answer for his opponent would be to accept the original low invitation, cutting top cuff or head from Tierce and instantly recovering to half-Quarte. The attack into the invitation would most likely force the lefty to parry half-Quinte or Quinte (an attempt to stop cut against a simple "untelegraphed" attack would be out of time).

When two men of different handedness come to middle distance in Tierce, there is liable to be an engagement (contact of blades) of some sort. Each would prefer to have the other outside. Beginners often go through a tedious muddle of countering Tierce alternately, with no gain. A similar motion used as an attack—to the other's chest or inside cheek—might score, for the fencer who continued to counter-Tierce would pull the cut into himself.

Another experiment, frequently seen, is the attempt to beat or press the opposing blade from the outside, to uncover targets such as the arm, shoulder, and head.

None of this would happen if the sabreurs stayed out of range and kept their blades nearly vertical. It would be to the interest of both parties to avoid the closer distances and to avoid engagement. Any fencer, particularly the beginner, who becomes preoccupied with seeking engagement overlooks the object of the

132. *Left-hander cutting chest*

133. *Left-hander recovering, parrying Quinte*

134. Left-hander cutting forearm of opponent who is parrying Quinte

game, *to hit the target*. He distracts himself by trying to hit the blade when it isn't threatening him.

The head is still a fine target for the lefty or on him. The simple direct attack from Tierce and the simple indirect from low, with proper footwork (management of the distance), are just as likely to succeed as when both men are right-handed or both left-handed. The left-hander, being more accustomed to facing right-handers than the other way around, may not be as reluctant to parry Quinte, but both should be aware that this parry exposes the forearm, either to the real motion of a feint attack or to a remise. Preference should be for keeping the head back out of reach. The Quarte parry may be adapted to deflect head cuts.

The left-hander against the right-hander can often score with strong cuts to cheek or shoulder from the outside (this is the chest cut when opponents use the same hand). Such actions force through the Tierce invitation or parry. If the receiver of such attacks then raises his hand to achieve a more solid block, he may expose his elbow or flank, and he certainly sets himself up for feint attacks which now end on the inside.

You (the instructor) should give students one or two review lessons on attacking a left-hander, and one or two on parry-riposting against a left-hander.

135. Left-hander inviting low, opponent mistakenly covering Quarte

136. Left-hander cutting inside elbow from low

137. *Left-hander flèching with head cut, to pass behind opponent*

138. *Left-hander running behind, right-hander pivoting with Tierce parry against re-mise cut*

139. Left-hander beating from outside to open cuff and elbow targets

Most probably you are a righty, and students will have an easy time of working through your slow left-handed actions. But there is usually one left-handed student in each class, and he should be very popular as a practice partner.

As long as a student is not completely inexperienced when he meets his first left-hander in competition, he should do well enough. Just this much classwork will prepare him to *learn* from tournament bouts, whether he wins or loses.

The left-handed student should train himself very carefully. His initial advantage of looking strange to his right-handed opponents can be completely thrown away if he allows himself to get into sloppy habits. Right-handers eventually accumulate experience and will be able to beat a left-hander with ease, if he has poor technique.

Lesson Plans

The courses outlined below could be adapted to fit approximately twelve class hours. You might choose a different order of presentation for the later courses. The indicated units might take as little as one class period or be extended over several, depending on the time allotted (minutes per day and sessions per week) and on how the group is progressing.

INTRODUCTORY

1. Conditioning calisthenics, footwork drills without weapons.

2. Point attacking with lunge, recovery to Tierce parry, point riposte, recovery to Tierce parry. Construct the chain link by link, then repeat entire sequence a few times with two or three footwork variations. Even this early, students should become used to making several moves in a row before resting.

3. From Tierce, direct head-cut attack with lunge, recovery to Tierce parry, riposte by head cut, recovery to Tierce parry. Slight variation, substituting chest cut. These establish the consistent minimum pattern of cut-parry-cut-parry. Footwork variations.

4. Advance to invite in Tierce, retreat to parry-riposte by Tierce-head cut, repeat parry-riposte, and rest in Tierce. From Tierce invitation, retreat to parry-riposte by Quarte-head cut, repeat parry-riposte by Quarte-head cut, and rest in Tierce. These establish the consistent pattern of invite, parry-cut-parry-cut-recover. Retreat with parries, sometimes lunge with ripostes.

5. Advance to invite in Tierce, retreat to parry-riposte by Quinte-head cut, repeat parry-riposte, and rest in Tierce. Chain can be lengthened by one or two more parry-ripostes: Tierce-head-Tierce; or Tierce-head-Quinte-head-Tierce.

6. Review against left-hander: from Tierce, simple direct attacking (point thrust, head cut, chest cut), and parry-riposting.

7. Bouting and judging.

INTERMEDIATE

1. From low invitation, direct attack by flank cut, recovery to parry-riposte by Quinte-head cut, recovery to Tierce.

2. From low invitation, indirect attack by head cut (later variation by chest cut), recovery to parry-riposte by Quinte-head cut, and rest in Tierce.

3. From low invitation, advance to invite, retreat to parry-riposte by Quinte-head cut, repeat parry-riposte and rest in Tierce. Chain can be lengthened by one or two more links.

4. From low invitation, advance to invite, retreat to parry-riposte by rotation to Tierce-head cut, followed by Quinte-head cut, and rest in Tierce.

5. Variations on indirect attacking: from Tierce to flank cut; from Tierce, as if to flank cut, disengaging under guard to point thrust; from low, disengaging under guard to point thrust.

6. Review against left-hander.

This finishes the introduction to simple (direct and indirect) attacking and the five basic parry-ripostes. Students should be able to practice in couples. Students should enter any available competitions and continue bouting and judging in class, approximating tournament conditions.

ADVANCED

1. Review of simple direct attacking: from Tierce by point thrust and head cut; from low by flank cut.

2. Review of simple indirect attacking: from Tierce by flank cut and by coupé-disengage point thrust; from low by head cut and by disengage point thrust.

3. Review of parry-riposting. Students practice exchanging with each other.

4. Secondary intentions. One example: from Tierce, feint of flank cut (striking opponent's guard), Quinte parry, attack to head. Two or three footwork variations, perhaps one finishing with a flèche.

5. Countertime. One example: offer Tierce extension, block stop cut with half-parry (or evade by withdrawing arm), attack by head cut. Two or three footwork variations, perhaps one finishing with a flèche.

6. Composite attacking with foot feint: from Tierce, indirect attack to flank; from low, indirect attack by head cut (or chest cut). Various footwork, both preliminary and finishing.

7. Composite attacking with hand feint, similar to above: feint head cut, attack by flank cut; feint flank cut, attack by head cut. Various footwork.

This completes the introductory phase. If time allows, stop parry-riposting can be worked in, but it is a variation on the cut-parry-cut-parry theme. Students should have the ideas of simple attacking, parry-riposting, secondary intentions, countertime, and composite attacking, all of which can be resurveyed again and again at higher levels of refinement.

Practically all class members should have had at least one outside competition, and preferably three or more. Certainly an intramural meet should be arranged, especially if there are two or more sections taking the course.

After the program has begun cycling, intermediate students can assist with introductory classes, and advanced students with intermediate classes. Advanced students should try presiding. Club or team members, who put extra time into fencing, should prepare to serve as jury presidents. You, as advisor to the club or coach of the team, will have to see to this. There can be special weekend clinics on officiating and teaching.

EQUIPMENT

The protective uniform has been described elsewhere. As the coach, you should make sure that your students wear all of it and take care of it. Torn or worn items should be repaired or replaced immediately. The inner plastron should definitely be required for class bouting as well as for tournament participation. Padded gloves and elbow guards must be worn.

Sabres should have these features: a strong duralumin guard of the "international"—wide Hungarian—shape; a stout blade, but with a Y cross-section. I happen to like a handle covered in ribbed rubber; others like smooth rubber over a plastic core, or cord-wrapped or leather-wrapped handles. The trouble with the old favorite checkered-wood handle is that it is liable to split fairly soon.

Remember that the shells (guards) are shaped differently for right- and left-handers. The tang of the sabre blade can be bent slightly in the same manner as that of the French foil blade (Fig. 60). Likewise, the blade should be curved slightly to the left for a right-handed fencer and to the right for a left-handed fencer.

Appendices

Appendix A

SELECTED READINGS

HISTORICAL

KNOWING THE HISTORY of fencing probably won't help your performance, but it is fascinating. The trouble is that various sources disagree on a number of points; a French writer is likely to claim that all the important advances in technique were invented by Frenchmen, while an Italian writer will make the same claim for Italians. Aside from encyclopedia articles, you might enjoy looking at:

Angelo, Henry. *The School of Fencing.* New York: Land's End Press, 1971. A photo facsimile of a textbook written in the late eighteenth century, with numerous engravings showing the origins of foil and sabre technique in small-sword and cavalry-sabre practice.

Barbasetti, Luigi. *The Art of the Foil.* New York: E. P. Dutton, 1932. One of the most admirable books ever produced on foil technique and bouting—thorough, intelligent, and helpful, even for the contemporary fencer; not just a series of mechanical descriptions—but long out of print. If you're lucky, you'll find it in a library or through a rare-book dealer. There is a historical section, with reproductions of woodcuts and engravings from early times.

Castle, Egerton. *Schools and Masters of Fence from the Middle Ages to the Eighteenth Century.* York, Pa.: Shumway, 1969. A famous text by a scholarly Briton, recently reissued in facsimile. This kind of book required a great deal of research, because medieval chroniclers took fighting techniques and teachers pretty much for granted.

Jackson, James L., ed. *Three Elizabethan Fencing Manuals.* Delmar, N.Y.: Scholar's Facsimiles, 1972. Reproductions of some of the earliest texts in English: Giacomo Di Grassi's *True Arte of Defence* (1594), Vincentio Saviolo's *His Practise* (1595), and George Silver's *Paradoxes of Defence* (1599). These give you an insight into real swordplay at a time when the rapier was coming into fashion. Silver's spirited arguments against the Italian methods are shrewd and amusing. Intriguingly, the experts of nearly four hundred years ago discuss fencing in terms of timing, distance, and other theoretical factors.

FOIL

Lukovich, István. *Electric Foil Fencing*. Budapest, Hungary: Corvina Press, 1971. A very fine instructional text, provided you have several years of background—excellent for the *advanced* competitor and coach.

ÉPÉE

Crosnier, Roger. *Fencing with the Épée*. New York: A. S. Barnes, no date. This extensive discussion of épée technique was written by a French master, formerly National Coach of Great Britain, in the early 1950s. It is the only separate text on épée play. Outlines of class practice in couples is included.

SABRE

Beke, Z. and Polgár, J. *The Methodology of Sabre Fencing*. Budapest, Hungary: Corvina Press, 1963. This is by far the most thorough presentation of the Hungarian system available in English, and the Hungarians were the developers of modern sabre fencing after the original formulation by Italo Santelli. The training program described is so detailed that you might be stunned and discouraged. The book is for advanced competitors and coaches. Unfortunately, there are *no* illustrations!

Palffy-Alpar, Julius. *Sword and Masque*. Philadelphia: F. A. Davis, 1967. The author, a Hungarian master, covers foil, épée, sabre, and theatrical fencing in one volume, which makes each section rather brief. Good for comparison with all the above-mentioned manuals on the sport.

The competitive student and the instructor should, of course, have (and study) the latest *Fencing Rules*, 1974, which may be obtained from the Amateur Fencers League of America, c/o Eleanor Turney, 601 Curtis St., Albany, CA 94706.

NUTRITION, PSYCHOLOGY, ETC.

A number of sideline topics have been mentioned in this book. If you want to study these matters further, you can start with the following:

Benson, Herbert, M.D. (with Miriam Z. Klipper). *The Relaxation Response*. New York: William Morrow and Co., Inc. 1976. "Meditation" without mystery—this book tells you in objective terms how to achieve the special kind of relaxation that is supposedly a "secret" of yogis or Oriental meditators. The benefits are said to be lower blood pressure, improvement of physical and emotional health, relief of inner tensions, more effective dealing with stress situations, etc. This may be a good way for a fencer to rest in the recesses of a long tournament.

Davis, Adele. *Let's Eat Right to Keep Fit*. New York: New American Library (paperback), 1972. An example of a well-researched and well-documented study of nutrition by probably the most famous author in the field. How to get more health and energy out of your food.

Hayakawa, S. I. *Language in Thought and Action*. New York: New American Library (paperback), 1974. A mind-expander, changing your ways of thinking through analysis of your everyday language. Since fencing is not a verbal activity, you must be careful when reading, listening, or talking about it. After working through Hayakawa's guide, you should get a lot more out of fencing texts, matching them with your own experience.

Kohler, Wolfgang, *Gestalt Psychology*. New York: New American Library (paperback), 1974. A reissue of a "classic" text. Another way to reorient your thinking. Good scientific writing, not difficult to read.

McDonald, John. *Strategy in Poker, Business and War*. New York: W. W. Norton, 1950. A popular explanation of "games theory." The cartoons by Osborn are worth the price all by themselves: instant understanding of deception, planning your actions within the current situation, considering many factors and the past actions of your opponent and yourself.

Miyamoto, Musashi. *A Book of Five Rings*. Woodstock, N.Y.: Overlook Press, 1974. A guide to fighting strategy by a famous Japanese *samurai*, possibly the greatest swordsman of all time. The translation by Victor Harris is probably faithful to the original, but the language is poetic or allusive for the most part, rather than specific and detailed. Try to get the feel of hand-to-hand combat from this.

Watts, Alan. *The Way of Zen*. New York: Random, 1957. Another approach, which may be compared to Hayakawa's and Kohler's "philosophy in action."

TECHNOLOGY

Volkmann, Rudy. *Electrical Fencing Equipment*. Arvee Press, 1975. This is a practical beginning technician's manual on the foil-épée judging apparatus, including the personal gear (weapons, body cords, etc.), explaining how it works, what goes wrong, and how to repair it.

The Rules Book, a copy of which every electrical competitor should have, gives the exact functional specifications for the judging apparatus. Technically minded and skilled students might be able to build a machine that would do what is expected, for a lot less money than a commercially manufactured device costs—however, the "homemade" machine would not be acceptable for official competitions, but it's still useful for practice.

Appendix B

EQUIPMENT SUPPLIERS

ALL SUPPLIERS WILL send catalogues and price lists on request, and will give discounts for school and club orders. Weapons and weapon parts are pretty well standardized in quality. Occasionally the supplier will be short in stock (if you order twenty jackets at once, shipment may not be complete immediately). Anticipate your needs. Best of all, if you can get to the shop, you can choose exactly what you like.

American Fencers Supply, 2116 Fillmore Street, San Francisco, Cal. 94115. Convenient for the western United States, with fairly quick delivery of about one week, on stock items, in that area. Prices on weapons often lower than elsewhere. One warning: if you don't like soft foil blades, order STIFF.

Castello Fencing Equipment Co. Inc., 30 East 10th Street, New York, N.Y. 10003. The firm prefers mass orders from schools and clubs, but also serves the individual. One of their masks, which seems to be heavily chrome-plated, is the strongest available and thus the best for épée.

George Santelli, Inc., 412 Sixth Avenue, New York, N.Y. 10011. Very good mask and jacket designs, made in the United States—at better prices than foreign items, on which duty has to be paid. The men's practice jacket is the best bargain of its kind on the market.

Other suppliers advertise in *American Fencing*, the official magazine of the Amateur Fencers League of America. Those listed here are the largest, but you ought to shop around.

Appendix C

GLOSSARY

ADVANCING. A short step forward with the front foot, immediately followed by a step of the same length (or shorter) with the rear foot.

ATTACKING. Threatening the target at such a range that an immediate hit is possible, usually accomplished by extending/lunging or extending/flèching. Preliminary movements, such as advancing into lunging range, taking the blade, etc., are considered as preparations.

The rule book definition for foil and sabre reads: "The *attack* is the initial offensive action executed by extending the arm and continuously threatening the opponent's valid surface [target]." But this boils down to, "The attack is the first attacking action . . . continuously attacking . . ." Several questions arise, and are not answered by the rule book: What does "initial" apply to—does it mean the first threatening move made by one fencer, out of several that he makes, or the first move made by a fencer as compared to his opponent? Does the arm have to be fully extended for an attack to be established? What does "continuously" mean, and why is it used at all?

This is one of those cases in which "everybody knows," but everybody has a hard time saying exactly what he means. Working backward, if a hit occurs, then, obviously, some kind of an attack was made. Also, if a hit *would* have occurred, except for a parrying or evading movement by the opponent (overlooking the possibility of inaccuracy by the attacker), the action that would have hit was an attack. However, that "would have" is an opinion of the president or director, and it is his or her opinion about when the threat began that is decisive. Completely insignificant for electrical épée competition.

APPEL. A slap of the ball of the front foot on the floor, usually done while lunging (so that the front foot strikes twice—toe and then heel).

ARRÊT. French term (pronounced *array*) for stop stroking (*coup d'arrêt*).

BALESTRA. Italian term for hopping forward, usually followed by lunging. Also the combination, hop lunging.

BARRAGE. Play-off bout or bouts between tied fencers for promotion to a higher round in a tournament or to determine first place in a final round. The tie would be in number of bouts won and lost in the round.

BEATING. A preparation. Sharply tapping the opponent's blade to remove a blade in line to clear the way for an attack (most often a riposte), or a blade not in line to get a reaction.

BINDING. A preparation. A method of removing a threatening blade, usually thought of as carrying the blade from low to high or vice versa, by making a half-circular movement of the weapon tip when the blades are already in contact.

CLASS. Competitive category of the AFLA. Class A is at the top, including possibly 50 fencers in each weapon. Each year "ranked fencers" are also named, approximately the top 10. Class B is comprised of perhaps the next 100–150 fencers. Class C may contain 300–500 competitors for each weapon. The lowest category, the Unclassified, encompasses all other AFLA members except professionals. You can become a Class C by winning an official Unclassified meet of specified strength (10 or 12 or more contestants), or a Class C meet in which Class C fencers may be entered. It is much more difficult to become a Class B, because you must win a meet in which more than one Class B are entered. To become a Class A, you must be a finalist in the National Championships or win another meet in which more than one Class A are entered.

COMPOSITE ATTACKING. Attacking with two or more movements of the blade, all but the last being feints (false threats) meant to cause the opponent to parry. The attacker expects to touch with a continuously progressing sequence, deceiving all parries.

   If these movements are done too slowly, or with even the slightest of pauses between, the opponent has the right to stop stroke before the final. Hence, my contention that *the* attack (see ATTACKING) is the final action that hits or would hit, and the feints are preparations. To leave no gap for a stop stroke, the feints practically have to be done *during* the lunge or flèche.

CORPS à CORPS. French term (pronounced *cor-ah-cor*) for body contact that jostles one or both fencers or prevents fencing (i.e., clinch). The fencer responsible, if either, is warned for the first offense and penalized for each repetition (one touch against).

COUNTERATTACKING. The French term, *coup* (pronounced *coo*), means stroke or blow, an attempt to hit. Thus, counterattacking includes the *coup d'arrêt* (stop stroke) and the *coup de temps* (time stroke): in foil and épée, stop thrusting and time thrusting, and in sabre, these plus stop cutting and time cutting. Counterattacks are meant to strike while an opponent attacks. (See STOP STROKE and TIME STROKE.)

COUNTERPARRY. A movement in which the weapon tip describes a complete oval or circle without moving toward the opponent, intended to deflect or block the attacking blade. For example, countering Sixte or Octave without extending at the same time.

COUNTERRIPOSTE. A riposte made after parrying the opponent's riposte, as in secondary intentions or unplanned exchanges.

COUNTERTIME. A sequence in which the opponent is lured to counterattack, upon which the initiator (who made a false preparation) attacks with removal or blocking of the counterattacking blade.

COUPÉ. French term (pronounced *coo-pay*) for cutting over, lifting the weapon tip over the opponent's blade, to attack. Many indirect sabre cuts may be called coupés.

DECEIVING. The action of avoiding an opponent's parry or other attempt to take the blade. Used in attacking or counterattacking (e.g., stop thrusting with deception).

DEROBEMENT. French term (pronounced *day-rub-mon*) applied to deception of an attempt to take, when the deceiving blade was already in line and the deceiver does not move forward. The opponent who tries to attack with a preparation of taking the blade may run onto the point.

DEVELOPMENT. An alternative term, found in British books, for lunging.

DIRECT. By the shortest path. Attacking, riposting, etc., without disengaging or deceiving.

DISENGAGING. By the widest interpretation, any break of contact between blades. Since most modern fencers play disengaged, "open," or with "absence of steel," the term commonly means avoidance of an attempted contact by the opponent or, very often, merely direction of the weapon to another part of the target, regardless of the opponent's action (or lack of action). (See DECEIVING.) Although a coupé is a type of disengagement, being used to avoid contact, etc., disengaging is usually considered to be maneuvering of the tip *under* the opponent's guard to attack.

DOUBLE. Deception of a counterparry by a circular movement of the point, usually after feinting into an open line.

DOUBLE TOUCH. When both fencers are hit at the same time, it is referred to as a double hit. If one has the right-of-way (in foil or sabre), the touch is scored against the other. If neither has right-of-way ("simultaneous action" or *tempo commune*), no touch is awarded. In épée, both fencers have a touch scored against them.

ENGAGEMENT. Contact of blades. In the early age of the sport, most of the action began from engagement, both fencers being in Sixte, for example, with blades crossed.

ENVELOPMENT. A taking in which an extended blade that is already deflected (e.g., blocked out in Sixte) is carried in a complete circle (e.g., in the same manner as parrying by countering Sixte).

EXTENDING (or EXTENSION). Straightening the fighting arm toward the target.

FEINTING. Threatening, intended to cause the opponent to parry, with the expectation of deceiving that parry. Usually the threat is made with an arm extension, thrusting or cutting. However, sometimes an opponent will react to a foot feint, or other movement of body or head, especially in sabre play, in which the fighting arm is kept back as much as possible to avoid stop cuts. Almost always, the hand feint is accompanied or closely followed by advancing. It can also be done while lunging or flèching.

FLÈCHING. The French term ("arrow") for a method of driving the weapon to target by, more or less, diving forward. The attacking weapon is *not* carried to target by running; rather, having thrown himself off-balance, the attacker must run to keep from falling on his face (which he often does anyway). If done incorrectly, and that means at the wrong time/distance as well as clumsily, it (1) leaves the attacker vulnerable to counterattack or parry-riposte, and (2) may result in the attacker being penalized for (a) colliding with his opponent, (b) dangerous style of play, or (c) going off the strip. Flèching is much used in sabre, but requires a lot of practice.

FOIBLE. Another term for the so-called weak part of the blade, the outer third.

FORTE. Another term for the so-called strong part of the blade, the third nearest the hand.

FROISSEMENT. A forceful taking, more or less by slicing forward and across the opponent's blade.

GLIDING. A gentle forward action in contact with the opponent's blade.

GUARD. The piece of metal on the weapon, which protects the hand and sometimes deflects or blocks the opponent's blade. Foil and épée guards are also called "bells," and the sabre guard is also called the "shell."

GUARDING/INVITING. A fencer is always active, even when he appears to be standing still. Therefore guarding/inviting, which may be called a position or posture, is truly an action preventing the opponent from attacking in one line, or from one direction, but leaving other lines open. The alternatives are to leave all lines open (pure inviting) or to threaten—unless the opponent has already begun an attack, in which case the alternatives are to counterattack, parry-riposte, or evade.

HIGH LINE. Applied mostly to fencing with the point weapons, this term refers to targets from about mid-chest up. The traditional high-line parries are Quarte, counter-Quarte, Sixte, counter-Sixte, Tierce, counter-Tierce, Prime and counter-Prime, variously meant to deflect the attacking blade so that it points past the upper back (outside) or past the chest (inside). In épée, Sixte and counter-Sixte are the high-line deflections used almost exclusively, and these most often are done as time thrusts (extending and deflecting simultaneously).

H I T . In foil, the penetrating contact of the foil tip with the opponent, judged either by eye or electric apparatus. In épée the criterion of a hit is that a light on the electric apparatus turns on. In sabre, a hit may be made by a cut or thrust, ending in contact of blade with the opponent's body. If a cut, it must make a popping sound. Also, in foil and sabre, decisions must be made as to whether the hit was valid or invalid (foul), and whether it had right-of-way (time) or not.

H O P P I N G . A footwork action, either forward or backward, in which the balls of both feet strike the floor at the same time: bouncing.

I N D I R E C T . Attacking (including riposting or counterattacking) by disengaging or cutting over to an open (or opening) target.

I N S I D E . For a right-hander, the left. For a left-hander, the right. Term used to describe the direction in which the attacking blade might be deflected, past the chest or belly, or the direction from which a cut might come.

J U D G E . An official whose duty is to see hits in foil or sabre and signal the president immediately when he has seen one. For electrically judged fencing, "floor judges" are sometimes employed to see when the foil or épée tips hit the floor (which would register on the apparatus), unless the floor is covered with copper screening which is neutralized.

L A B E L L E . French term ("the beautiful one") for the final touch when fencers are tied at 4–4 in a normal bout. "Sudden death." This touch should be quite clear in foil or sabre, with no doubt about right-of-way or validity.

L O W I N V I T A T I O N . A stance in which the hand is too low to prevent any attempted attack, usually with the arm hanging loose from the shoulder, which is good for resting when out of distance.

L O W L I N E . From the lower ribs down. The traditional low-line parries are Seconde, Septime, Octave, and their counters, mostly used in the point weapons. In sabre, Septime and Octave are not used, and Seconde is used very rarely today. In épée, Septime is a very poor parry, and others that carry the attacking blade to the inside are not recommended. Also in épée the deflections are almost always done while extending.

L U N G I N G . The most common and basic method of carrying the weapon to target. An action led by extending the arm (although the arm does not have to be fully straightened before the rest of it occurs), in which the rear leg straightens, propelling the body, while the front foot takes a long step forward. The rear foot remains in place or slides flat. For practice, the student should invariably recover to a guarding/inviting stance and not develop a bad habit of slumping after the effort of lunging.

N O V I C E . Usually one who has not won a prize by placing first, second, or third in an extramural individual competition. This is an unofficial sub-section of the AFLA Unclassified category.

OCTAVE. Functionally, toward the low outside, with palm upward. A parry or time thrust of Octave deflects the opponent's blade to point past the lower back. Not used in sabre.

"ON GUARD!" A command which, if given by the president or director, means "Be alert!" or "Get ready!" No special posture is then required, but if the teacher says it in class the students are expected to guard/invite in some fashion.

ONE-TWO. An attack by disengaging twice, deceiving two parries or attempted takings.

OPPOSITION. Resistance to pressure. A "parry in opposition" keeps contact with the other blade until the riposte begins, and the riposte itself may be made in opposition—in contact with the opponent's blade all the way in. Attacks in opposition are also made by contacting the opponent's blade and gliding along it.

OUTSIDE. For a right-hander, the right. Term used to describe the direction in which an attacking blade might be deflected, or the direction from which a cut might come.

PARRY. A movement that deflects or blocks an attacking blade so that it does not hit immediately. Note that the action is made *from* some other attitude—inviting, guarding/inviting, or extending—which influences the "feel" of the parry or how it is done, according to the relationships of blades.

By definition, if a movement is made that does *not* prevent an attack from hitting, it is not a parry. We should properly call it an attempted parry: it may be too late, or too small ("inadequate" or "*malparé*"), or it may have been deceived. Even when successful, a parry is a wasted move unless the parrier immediately ripostes.

PHRASE. Short for the French, *phrase d'armes*. A sequence of meaningful actions in foil or sabre as interpreted by the jury president or director. A phrase can be as short as one move (a simple attack that hits) or may involve a volley of several moves by both fencers. The director must be able to keep up with the sequence in order to establish which fencer, if either, had the right-of-way at the instant a hit (fair or foul) was made. Sometimes a phrase ends without a hit, as when one fencer goes out of bounds, body contact occurs, or an exchange becomes so confused (rapidly repeated jabbing or cutting at close range) that the director cannot analyze it.

PISTE. French term ("path") for the fencing strip.

POMMEL. A nut that holds the weapon together by screwing onto the threaded end of the blade shank. It may be recessed in a molded aluminum foil or épée handle of the pistol-grip type.

PREP. Beginner. Usually a fencer within his or her first year of training, or one who has never completed extramurally. This is an unofficial sub-section of the AFLA Unclassified category, lower than Novice. Some kind of local definition is convenient for offering easy steps of advancement to new fencers, who might be justifiably timid about entering meets loaded with much more experienced opponents. For young people there is a program with age grades: under 14, 14–16, and 16–20.

PREPARATION. Any action made prior to attacking, such as an adjustment of distance, a taking of the opponent's blade, a feint (if there is any time lapse before the final real attack), or a combination of these.

PRESIDENT. The official in charge of a bout, who starts and stops the action, decides right-of-way, etc. For épée and electric foil, called the director.

PRESSING. A taking of the blade, pushing it to one side or another, as a preparation to attack or to get a reaction (e.g., to invite an attack).

PRISE DE FER. French term (pronounced *preez-duh-fair*) for taking the blade.

PRONATION. Palm-down attitude of the hand.

QUARTE. Functionally, toward the inside (for a right-hander, left) high. A beat or parry of Quarte deflects or blocks the opponent's blade so it points past the chest or stomach. In sabre, a parry from guarding/inviting Tierce or thumb-up extension, to block a cut to the chest or belly (and, in certain situations, to the head), to deflect a point attack to the inside, and sometimes to deflect a vertical cut. In abbreviated form (half-parry), it may block a cut at the wrist from the inside.

QUINTE. Fifth parry. In sabre, a blocking of a vertical cut, by placing the blade horizontally in the path of the cut.

RECOVERING. Returning to guarding/inviting after lunging or extending.

REDOUBLING (or REDOUBLEMENT). Immediately attacking again by disengagement or cutting over, without recovering, when the opponent has parried without riposting. Similar to remising, this is considered to be a continuation of the original attack.

REMISING. Immediately attacking again, often called "continuation" or "insistence," when the opponent makes an inadequate parry, reopens the line (without riposting) after parrying, or delays in riposting. Remising is considered to be direct, while redoublement is indirect. Sometimes remising is done by angling around the opponent's blocking action.

REPLACEMENT. Often used as an alternative term for a remise or redoublement, but usually to describe "digging in" with the point when the initial attack was flat, or withdrawing and jabbing when the initial attack went past the target.

REPRISE. French term ("retaking") for an immediate second attack when the first has fallen short, accompanied by recovering forward from lunging or otherwise pursuing the opponent.

S A L L E . French term ("room" or "chamber") for the classroom, gym, or practice building.

S E C O N D A R Y   I N T E N T I O N S . Maneuvers in which the original attack is false, leading the opponent to parry-riposte, the true attack being a parry-riposte or time stroke against the opponent's riposte. In "third intention," the original attack and the counterriposte would both be false, the true attack being a parry-riposte or time stroke against the opponent's second (counter-counter) riposte.

S E C O N D E . Functionally, toward the low outside. In practice, a method of beating with the foil or épée to deflect the opponent's blade past the lower back. The Seconde parry in sabre is rarely seen now, but is done by placing the hand palm down to block a flank cut with guard and blade.

S I M P L E . In one move or count. The term is applied to attacks or ripostes, whether direct or indirect. Also refers to those parries that are not counters or half-counters.

S I X T E . Functionally, toward the high outside. A taking in Sixte deflects the opponent's blade past the upper back. Formally, the hand is palm upward. In sabre, Tierce-parry is used for the same effect. Tierce is seldom used in foil and épée, and Sixte is never used in sabre.

S T O P   S T R O K I N G . Counterattacking without taking the blade. (See A T T A C K I N G , C O U N T E R A T T A C K I N G , and P R E P A R A T I O N .)
     The three weapons must be considered separately. No discussion is necessary in regard to épée, since officially the time is determined by the electric apparatus. For the conventional weapons, however, decisions must be made about right-of-way ("time")
     The foil rule reads: "In composite attacks . . . the stop must precede the conclusion of the attack by a period of fencing time, i.e., the stop must touch before the attacker has commenced the last movement of the conclusion of the attack." Literally interpreted, this would mean that the stop thrust in foil is utterly *impossible* to do successfully (unless the stop-thruster's arm is at least two feet longer than that of the attacker) because the stop cannot *touch* before the beginning of a lunge.
     And yet, even leaving aside the possibility of evasion, the stop is frequently called right. The way that recognized and certified high-class directors consistently call it is this: The attacker prepares (by advancing, feinting, attempting to take the blade, etc.), the receiver of the attack extends (or starts extending) before the lunge, and both fencers are actually touched *at the same time*; the stop thrust was clearly started before the attack or the final movement of a composite attack.
     If necessary, we can refer to Article 233 (a) 1: "If the attack starts when the opponent is 'in line' (i.e., 'with the arm extended and the point threatening a valid surface'), the attacker must first deflect his adversary's weapon," and it follows logically that if the attacker fails to deflect the blade in line and runs onto the point, the touch is against him. The time difference here can be a small fraction of a second (perhaps $\frac{1}{10}$th) for good fencers—that is, in the execution of their moves. With electric apparatus, the opposing lights turn on simultaneously

as the attacker's lunge hits but also brings his own body in contact with the stopper's point.

The possibilities are slightly better in sabre, although the rule reads nearly the same. Usually the stop stroke is a cut to the attacker's wrist, a nearer target, while the attack is aimed at the head or torso. There is also a somewhat better chance of evasion. Again, a stop *thrust* may be extended before the lunge or flèche begins, so that the attacker runs onto a point in line.

There can be no question when one fencer hits and the other misses, the hit has absolute priority. In such cases, the one who misses might make a remise or other continuation, but any action of that sort would obviously be later. Sometimes both the attack and the stop are faulty (too slow or hesitating), and the result is a true double hit with neither fencer having right-of-way: If both hit, no score is awarded.

STRIP. The playing area, 2 meters by 14 meters.

SUPINATION. Palm-up attitude of the hand.

"TAKING." Blade-vs.-blade action such as beating, binding, pressing, enveloping, croisé, froissement, gliding, etc. Often used as parries to deflect attacks, otherwise to deflect blades in line or to excite reactions (response beating, response pressure, etc.), which may be deceived.

THRUSTING. Extending the arm and threatening the target with the weapon tip, which may result in a point hit.

TIERCE. As an invitation in sabre, a thumb-up attitude of the hand, with the main edge of the blade toward the opponent and the elbow of the fighting arm a few inches forward of the ribs. As a parry, the main edge is turned outward and the elbow is pulled against the ribs.

In foil and épée, guarding/inviting Tierce may be used as a substitute for Sixte: the hand is held in pronation, the weapon tip slightly higher than the guard. The attitude is not used much today; nor are the parries of Tierce or counter-Tierce.

TIME. For foil and sabre, the rule book defines: "Fencing time [or: period of fencing time; 'Temps d'escrime'] is the time required to perform one simple fencing action." Further, "The action is simple when it is executed in a single movement; either direct (in the same line) or indirect (in another line)."

Here again there could be arguments because the definitions don't define; they lead us around in a circle. A unit of fencing time is the time needed to do a simple action ("action" meaning "attack"), and a simple action takes one movement, and one movement marks off a period of fencing time. Arguments rarely occur, because "everybody knows" what a simple or single movement is: You can *see* (if trained to do so) whether a fencer makes one move or more. Besides, and conclusively, the time is whatever the president or director says it is; that is one of the "facts" on which you CANNOT make an appeal.

However, a simple move can be very short (a jab during infighting) or quite long (a full lunge, even done rather slowly, from the instant the arm starts to extend). Therefore, we find that a "period of fencing time" is a variable! You can't define it in terms of real time, but it may be something between ½₀th of a second and a little over a second—or thereabouts. This is important in cases of stop stroking, remising as compared to the riposte, etc. When you find that a president or director has to have a fairly large piece of real time before he will recognize a stop or remise, you must fence accordingly.

Also called a *tempo*.

TIME STROKING. Lately the term "stop with opposition" has been substituted for the time-honored *"coup de temps,"* "time thrust," or "time cut." This is an improvement over "time hit," since the French *coup* does not really mean a hit but an attempt to do so. The time stroke, or stop with opposition, resembles a stop except in that the attack is blocked or deflected with the same move that threatens the attacker. Several examples are given in the text. The advantage of time stroking (most often, time thrusting in foil and épée) over stop stroking is that, successfully done, the attacker does not hit, or hits later, and as we have seen, a later hit has zero significance.

TROMPEMENT. French term ("betraying" or "fooling") for deceiving.

UNCLASSIFIED. The lowest official category of AFLA competitors. Novice and Prep are unofficial sub-sections of the Unclassified group, and may be defined differently in different locations.

YIELDING (or CEDING). A type of movement, classified as a parry, that slips off an attack made by binding the blade. This is done essentially by not resisting when resistance is expected by the attacker. It is quite an advanced technique, not described in the text.

Index